CONCEPTS AND CASES IN

NURSING ETHICS

CONCEPTS AND CASES IN

NURSING
ETHICS

SECOND EDITION

EDITED BY

MICHAEL YEO AND ANNE MOORHOUSE

broadview press

Canadian Cataloguing in Publication Data

Main entry under title:

Concepts and cases in nursing ethics, 2nd edition
Includes bibliographical references.

ISBN 1-55111-082-2

1. Nursing ethics. I. Yeo, Michael Terrence. II. Moorhouse, Anne.

RT85.Y46 1996   174'.2   C96-931628-3.

Broadview Press Ltd., is an independent, international publishing house, incorporated in 1985.

North America:
P.O. Box 1243, Peterborough, Ontario, Canada k9j 7h5
3576 California Road, Orchard Park, ny 14127
TEL: (705) 743-8990; FAX: (705) 743-8353;
E-MAIL: 75322.44@compuserve.com

United Kingdom:
Turpin Distribution Services Ltd.,
Blackhorse Rd., Letchworth, Hertfordshire sg6 1hn
TEL: (1462) 672555; FAX (1462) 480947; E-MAIL: turpin@rsc.org

Australia:
St. Clair Press, P.O. Box 287, Rozelle, nsw 2039
TEL: (02) 818-1942; FAX: (02) 418-1923

www.broadviewpress.com

Broadview Press gratefully acknowledges the support of the Ontario Arts Council, and the Ministry of Canadian Heritage. We acknowledge the financial support of the Government of Canada through the Book Publishing Industry Development Program for our publishing activities.

Text design and composition by George Kirkpatrick

PRINTED IN CANADA

Contents

Truthfulness (Michael Yeo and Sandra Mitchell)   139

Confidentiality (Michael Yeo, Anne Moorhouse and Irene Krahn)   173

PREFACE TO THE SECOND EDITION

Health care in Canada has changed dramatically in the five years that have passed since the first edition of this book. Well-publicized cases such as that of Nancy B., Sue Rodriguez, and Tracy Latimer have brought issues of refusal of life-sustaining treatment, euthanasia and assisted suicide into greater prominence. The new reproductive technologies have been scrutinized by a Royal Commission and the federal government has introduced legislation to regulate practices in this area. Public confidence in the blood system has been seriously shaken. Regionalization of health care has been embraced in many parts of the country. Institutions providing health care have merged, down-sized, or otherwise restructured. Beds, and in some cases hospitals, have been closed, and many nurses have been laid off as a consequence. The viability of the *Canada Health Act* and its founding principles has become questionable in light of continuing economic imperatives and new financial arrangements for transfer payments from the federal government to the provinces.

In the name of health reform, change in the organization and delivery of health is proceeding across the country at a rapid pace. In principle at least, nurses have reason to support the main goals of health reform. Historically, the profession has staunchly advocated for such worthy goals as client-centred care, care in the community, self-reliance and independent living in the home, and disease prevention and health promotion. However, nurses worry that in practice health reform may be driven less by these lofty goals than by the economic bottom line. There is much apprehension about how changes justified in the name of health reform will impact on the quality of care for clients and the quality of working life for nurses.

This edition has been updated to address the new reality of health care in Canada as we approach the end of this century. The analysis in each chapter has been amended or expanded in light of new developments. Cases have been modified. In addition, a new chapter on ethical theory has been added.

We would like to thank those people who read or used the first edition of this book and responded to a request for feedback with suggestions about how it could be improved. We have tried to incorporate these suggestions as best we could. We would also like to thank our colleagues who reviewed draft material for this new edition, and in particular Robert Butcher, Dennis Hudecki, and Anthony Kerby. Finally, we would like to thank the various authors who applied themselves with diligence to the task of revision.

Michael Yeo
Research Directorate
Canadian Medical Association

Anne Moorhouse
Faculty of Nursing
University of Toronto

INTRODUCTION

The unexamined life is not worth living.

—SOCRATES

Overview of the Book

The profession of nursing, like the health care system, is undergoing rapid development. New and diverse roles are emerging, and old roles are being redefined. Nurses are becoming more and more reflective about the meaning of nursing. What is nursing, and what ought nursing to be? Increasingly, it is recognized that such questioning is intricately bound up with ethics.

The aim of this book is to present a unified perspective on the ethical dimension of contemporary nursing. Its objective is to furnish nurses with a clearer understanding of the key terms and arguments in which ethical issues in nursing are interpreted, discussed, and analyzed. Such understanding will better equip nurses to face the challenges of their profession and to practise responsibly in their chosen fields and specialties.

The book is divided into seven main chapters. The first chapter is a brief primer on ethics to familiarize the reader with the main lines of thought in ethical theory.

Chapters two through seven are devoted to the elucidation of six fundamental ethical concepts: beneficence, autonomy, truthfulness, confidentiality, justice, and integrity. Each of these concepts denotes a value, principle, or virtue highly prized in health care. Almost any ethical issue in nursing involves reference to one or more of them. Each of these chapters includes cases for discussion.* Cases derived from actual incidents have been modified to preserve confidentiality. Each case is preceded by an introductory preamble, which puts the issue raised by the case in context, and is followed by a critical commentary in which ethical analysis is brought to bear.

The book is designed to be read from beginning to end but each chapter is self-contained and stands on its own. An introduction at the beginning of each chapter elucidates the main problems and issues associated with the concept to which that chapter is devoted. Other related terms and concepts are introduced and analyzed whenever they help to clarify the matter under discussion. Where applicable, quotations are given from various codes of ethics in nursing. Several of these codes are appended at the end of the book. At the end of each chapter, a list of study questions is provided to stimulate further reflection and discussion. Those who wish to do further reading or research on selected topics will find the extensive footnotes and references a good starting point.

This introduction provides a general overview of nursing ethics and establishes a framework within which to understand the various issues discussed throughout the book.

What is Nursing Ethics?

In order to avoid confusion, it is helpful to identify and distinguish various meanings that may be assigned to the term "nursing ethics." Used in one sense, nursing ethics refers to the express ethical norms of the nursing profession: the values, virtues, and principles that are supposed to govern and guide nurses in everyday practice. These are typically phrased as moral injunctions of the sort "be truthful with clients" or

---

* Beneficence Case 1, Autonomy Case 2, and Integrity Case 2 are adapted from cases given in *Guidelines for Ethical Behaviour in Nursing* (College of Nurses of Ontario, 1988). (This document has since been updated — see College of Nurses of Ontario, 1995.)

"respect client confidentiality." They may also be expressed as exhortations to adopt and practise particular virtues, such as caring or fairness. As publicly expressed by the profession in codes of ethics, these norms serve not only to guide nurses in their practice and character formation but also to inform the public about what they can expect from professional practitioners.

Ethical norms thus expressed state the profession's ethical ideal: how nurses *ought* to conduct themselves. However, for a variety of reasons, nurses may or may not in fact so conduct themselves. The working environment in some institutions or settings may be less conducive to the realization of professional nursing values than in others. Ethical sensitivity and conscientiousness will vary somewhat from nurse to nurse and institution to institution. A sociologist or a psychologist studying moral behaviour among a group of nurses might form a very different picture of ethics in nursing than the one presented in a professional code of ethics. The phrase "nursing ethics," accordingly, can also be used descriptively to refer to the norms that do in fact guide the moral behaviour of nurses.

In yet another context, "nursing ethics" refers to the growing body of writing in books and professional journals that deals with the moral dimension of nursing wherein various ethical issues are analyzed, discussed, and debated. Used in this sense, nursing ethics is not a set of norms, actual or ideal, but a field or discipline in which such norms are explored and analyzed.

These three meanings are interrelated. Ideal ethical norms as stated in professional nursing codes shape the actual behaviour of practitioners. The nursing ethics literature builds from and modifies both the actual and ideal norms of the profession. To understand contemporary nursing ethics, in each of the three senses indicated, it is helpful to situate it in the broader context in which it has evolved and continues to evolve.

Nursing Ethics and Bioethics

Nursing ethics has developed alongside the much broader phenomenon of bioethics. Bioethics may be defined as reasoned enquiry about the ethical dimension of interventions in the lives of human beings directed to or bearing on their health good, individually or collectively. Health care is an obvious example of such an intervention, and in this regard bioethics is sometimes used synonymously with "health care ethics." Issues of research and experimentation also come under the field of bioethics.

Several factors bear on the emergence of contemporary bioethics and have also influenced present-day nursing ethics. The three described below are especially noteworthy.

1. Technological Developments

Rapid scientific and technological developments have presented health professionals with new powers, and with these, countless ethical issues. The respirator is a good example. It enables the prolongation of life (or dying) but with this power difficult ethical questions arise. Under what conditions ought someone to be put on or removed from a respirator? Whose decisions are these to make? There has been considerable uncertainty and disagreement about what is morally (and even legally) right in these matters, as was learned from the landmark case of Karen Quinlan (Pence, 1990). In Canada, the issue of withdrawal of life-sustaining treatment was brought to a head in 1992 by the Nancy B. case (Roy, Williams, & Dickens, 1994).

The respirator is but one example of how "progress" in modern science and medicine generates difficult moral issues. Equally poignant examples can be drawn from reproductive technology, transplantation, and genetics, to name only some of the more topical ones. Contemporary health care, thanks in large part to technological developments that have outpaced the ethical consensus in our society, presents us with more and more confusing grey areas. Those engaged in bioethics, drawing upon moral philosophy, attempt to think critically and systematically about these difficult grey areas.

2. Research and Experimentation

The negative publicity about gross abuses in research involving human subjects that took place in Nazi Germany and of questionable research practices in North America generated considerable discussion about ethics in research (Beecher, 1959; 1966). Should some categories of people — for example, children, captive populations, mentally incompetent persons — be excluded from research? What measures and controls will best ensure the voluntariness of research subjects? How do we decide acceptable ratios of benefit to harm, and who should decide on these ratios? Many of the main concepts and principles of bioethics such as informed consent, autonomy, and beneficence have been defined and redefined against this background.

3. Authority, Consumerism, and Patients' Rights

Throughout the 1960s, the idea of consumer education and protection took hold in North America, and the rhetoric of rights became more and more prominent in discussions about matters ethical (Fleming, 1983). In this climate, increased scrutiny was directed toward the health care system as a locus of considerable power. "Patients" increasingly came to view themselves as "consumers." An important landmark occurred in 1973 when the American Hospital Association introduced a twelve-point "Patients' Bill of Rights," which was subsequently translated into policy in numerous American and Canadian institutions (Storch, 1982).

The rise of the patients' rights movement occurred concurrently with rising public distrust of the authority vested in religion, government, scientists, and professionals. Increased scrutiny was brought to bear on the practice of health professionals, and with this came higher standards of public accountability. Many ethical matters once trusted to the discretion of professional authorities came to be designated as public questions. A new ethic emerged and took shape around the watchword "autonomy." This was in part shaped by a growing cultural and political pluralism in which the values of individual rights and liberties ruled the day. The paternalism long entrenched in the health professions came to be widely criticized. Patients demanded to be more involved in decision-making regarding their health care. Broad legislative changes both reflected and shaped new public expectations about patient involvement in health care planning, the doctrine of informed consent being a prime example of this trend. What public consensus existed on health care ethics was strained as new ethical issues came to the fore and old ones took on a new complexion and urgency.

Social developments along these lines opened up the space of questioning within which contemporary bioethics developed. Professional philosophers and theologians brought their traditions and skills to bear on the many ethical questions and issues that were emerging, and health professionals became increasingly interested in moral philosophy and moral reasoning.

To date, the greatest amount of work in bioethics has been in the specific area of *medical ethics*. The relationship between nursing ethics, medical ethics, and more generally bioethics is a matter of some controversy (Fry, 1989; Twomey, 1989). To what extent is nursing ethics distinct from medical ethics? Certainly there are interconnections and lines of influence, but there are differences as well. Whatever distinctness contemporary nursing ethics has emerges out of the situation of contemporary nursing.

Nursing Ethics and Nursing

Several features of nursing have helped to shape contemporary nursing ethics. To begin with the most obvious, nursing has been predominately a woman's profession and remains so today. Some authors, building from the premise that women (whether by nature, culture, or both) value such things as nurturing and caring more than men, argue that an "ethic of care" may be especially appropriate for nursing (Huggins & Scalzi, 1988; Crowley, 1989). This point of view, and the assumptions that inform it, is a matter of debate, as we shall see when we discuss the matter in greater detail in the next chapter. Regardless, there is evidence that nursing, by contrast with the "medical model," for example, has been more oriented around "caring" than "curing" (Watson, 1979; Gadow, 1985; Benner & Wrubel, 1989; MacPherson, 1989). Moreover, nursing has tended to work with a broader understanding of health than have most other health professions. This has implications for the kinds of ethical issues that arise and the way in which they are framed.

Gender is also significant as concerns the value society and other health professionals have attached to the work of nursing and it bears on such important matters as the drive for professionalism in nursing (Delamothe, 1988). Historically — and this is not unrelated to sexual difference — nursing has been in a position of subordination in the health care system. In this regard, it is instructive to recall the motto of the Mack Training School for Nurses, the first of its kind in Canada: "I see and am silent" (Coburn, 1987).

The experience of powerlessness — and this experience is by no means a thing of the past — has especially sensitized nursing to issues of power in health care (Rodney, 1988, 1989; Rodney & Starzomski, 1993; Tunna & Conner, 1993). Yarling and McElmurry (1986) go so far as to claim that, under existing legal and institutional arrangements, many nurses do not have the freedom or power to practise ethically. Although this thesis is open to debate (see Bishop & Scudder, 1987), there can be no doubt that the situation of nursing *vis-à-vis* the distribution of power in the health care system informs and shapes many of the ethical issues nurses face in their daily practice. Potentially, current reform trends towards restructuring and re-organizing in health care may be empowering for nurses. However, if driven by the economic bottom line, health reform could exacerbate the problem of powerlessness.

Related to the distribution of power is the fact that many ethical issues arise because nurses often find themselves in institutional situations wherein they have multiple obligations (Storch, 1988). In the classic scenario, there may be a conflict between the nurse's commitment to the client, on the one hand, and the "orders" of the physician, on the other. Although today the profession proclaims that the primary loyalty is to the client, nursing still must struggle against the legacy of Florence Nightingale, who pledged the primary loyalty of the nurse to the physician (Storch, 1982). Notwithstanding the trend toward team care based on shared decision-making, the legal and institutional horizon of nursing is such that nurses sometimes must contend and live with the effects of decisions into which they may have had little or no input, and with which they may disagree. This reality is reflected in the nursing ethics literature, in which themes such as conscience and integrity figure prominently.

Another feature of nursing constitutive of present-day nursing ethics is what Storch calls "being there" (1988, p. 212). Nursing care is often less episodic than that provided by other health professionals. In a hospital setting, for example, physicians may come and go but nursing is there for the client around the clock. Other health professionals tend to get unconnected snapshots of the client whereas the nurse gets a full-length movie version. The contact between the nurse and the client is such that many dimensions of the client's being are disclosed in the relationship. As Gadow (1980) puts it, "the nurse attends the patient as a whole, not just as a single problem or system" (p. 81).

The duration and nature of his or her contact with the client makes it possible for the nurse to know the client somewhat more intimately than do other health professionals. This puts the nurse "in the ideal position among health-care providers to experience the patient as a unique human being with individual strengths and complexities" (Gadow, 1980, p. 81). This experience bears on a number of ethical matters. For example, it is one thing to be less than fully truthful with someone one knows only superficially and another to be so with someone with whom one has established a closer relationship.

Models of the Nurse-Client Relationship

The ethical landscape of nursing appears differently depending on how the relationship between nurse and client is viewed. Smith (1980) distinguishes three typical roles nurses adopt in relation to clients: surrogate mother, technician, and contracted clinician. Curtin (1979) adds several other roles to this list: champion of the sick, health educator, physician's assistant, healer, and patient's advocate. Some of these are manifestly less acceptable than others, but all have some basis in the reality of nursing. The ethical question concerns the roles nurses ought self-consciously and deliberately to adopt. Those that are most favoured in the nursing ethics literature are based on the contractual and advocacy model of the nurse-client relationship, as described below.

1. The Contractual Model

Following the contractual or covenantal model, the nurse and the client negotiate the moral parameters of the relationship and through dialogue make explicit what each expects from the other. Does the nurse or the client have any special values likely to come into play in the course of the relationship? How involved does the client want to be in the decision-making process? What family members or friends are to be consulted should the occasion arise? In the course of discussion, either the nurse or the client may find that the other has unacceptable expectations or demands. If so, it is best that this be known in advance of any issues that might arise.

The contract or understanding thus negotiated subsequently comes to serve as a guide and reference point for whatever ethical decision-making might be required in the course of the relationship. It builds trust in the relationship because each person knows what to expect from the other (Cooper, 1988). It also empowers the client by creating a sense of control at a time when he or she may be disoriented by illness and by being in a foreign environment (Ziemann & Dracup, 1989). The preference many nurses have for the word "client" in place of "patient" is in keeping with the empowering spirit of the contractual model, emphasizing as it does the agency of the client/patient and the voluntary element of the relationship.

2. The Client's Advocate Model

The role of patient or client's advocate has been adopted and endorsed by nursing to a far greater extent than by other health professions. One reason for this may be that nurses, because of their own experience, are better able to identify and empathize with the vulnerability and power-lessness of the client.

Although widely embraced, the notion of client advocacy is often vaguely understood. The term "advocate" itself is imported into health care from law. It came into vogue with the emergence of consumerism and the patients' rights movement in health care. To advocate in the context of health care is often taken to mean advocating on behalf of the patient's rights (Annas, 1974), and in particular his or her right to be informed about and involved in treatment decisions.

Conceived in terms of clients' rights, advocacy is often presented as a kind of foil or corrective to a perceived tendency in the health care system to deny the client his or her rights. Kosik (1972) expresses this view of advocacy very clearly: "Patient advocacy is seeing that the patient knows what to expect and what is his right to have, and then displaying the willingness and courage to see that the system does not prevent his getting it" (p. 84).

The rights-based model of advocacy has been criticized on a number of counts. Many nurses conceive the scope of advocacy as defined by the client's interests or good more broadly conceived (Curtin, 1979; 1983). Gadow (1980, p. 84), critical of viewing the client abstractly as a bearer of rights, speaks of "existential advocacy" directed to the client as a whole being. Existential advocacy steers a middle course between paternalism (unilaterally imposing upon the client one's belief about what is good) and what she calls "consumer protection" (the nurse becoming an instrument in the service of what the client wishes).

To Gadow's cogent critique of the rights-based, consumer-protec-tion model of advocacy, an historical footnote can be added. The rights-based idea of advocacy developed as a corrective to widespread paternalism in the health care system. Although paternalism still exists in contemporary health care, it is less common and much less acceptable, thanks in part to the contribution of nursing. Therefore a rights-based model of advocacy may not be as appropriate today as it was at the birth of the patients' rights movement in the 1960s.

A Knowledge Base in Ethics for Nursing

Having described the context in which contemporary nursing ethics has developed, what does all this mean to the individual practising nurse? A helpful way of focusing this question is to ask what knowledge base in ethics is appropriate for today's nurse. There is room for debate around this question, but the nursing ethics literature reflects consensus around at least three main areas of knowledge and reflection: (1) moral beliefs and values; (2) relevant codes, policies, laws; and (3) fundamental concepts of moral philosophy.

1. Moral Beliefs and Values

The Socratic injunction "know thyself" names the task at the entrance to the moral life. Through our upbringing and acculturation — the influence of family, peers, and so on — we acquire numerous beliefs about right and wrong and good and bad. Beliefs thus acquired are deeply constitutive of who we are as adults, and may manifest themselves in our actions without our ever having reflected upon them. We may not realize how these beliefs express themselves in our lives until challenged by others. The choice of the ethical life as expressed in the injunction "know thyself" commits one to bringing such unreflected beliefs to light and, having clarified them, to explicitly and responsibly embrace, reject, or modify them. As proclaims another famous Socratic dictum: "The unexamined life is not worth living."

The task of acquiring self-knowledge may also be expressed with reference to "values" rather than to "moral beliefs," and indeed this is the preferred language in nursing. Values clarification has been a major theme in the nursing ethics literature, and various techniques for education in values clarification have been developed (Steele & Harmon, 1979). In its essentials, values clarification is a process of becoming more aware and reflective about the values that have been inculcated in us through various influences. This enables us to decide in a self-conscious way what values we ought to prize and promote, and to assess how various practices stand in relation to these values. Flaherty (1985) states the challenge clearly: "The examined life is lived today by those nurses who are willing to question the prevailing customs and taboos of the situations in which they find themselves, including their own behaviour, to identify whether what they see is consonant with the standards of practice for which they stand accountable" (p. 104). Such an examination should also include consideration of how either personal or professional values may come into play in relation to the values of clients.

Intervention in the lives of others with respect to matters about which they care and value deeply carries tremendous responsibility. In nursing, such intervention is mandated and legitimized in the name of health and health care. Therefore, health is the most obvious value that matters in the health care context. However, beneficent concern for the health of the client may come into conflict with several other, sometimes competing values, such as autonomy, truthfulness, confidentiality, and justice.

Where values are concerned — where things about which people care deeply are at stake — one whose professional promise is to benefit and respect the client must acquire a certain facility in moving within the dimension of values. This means, first of all, becoming sensitive to the values dimension of nursing. At every step in the nursing process questions of value should be raised, if only the question "Are there any questions of value to be considered here?" This is not to say that every nursing intervention, however routine, will raise an explicit ethical issue requiring an explicitly ethical decision. Indeed, few do. But every nursing act, as an intervention in the lives of others, has at least the possibility of promoting or transgressing some good or value. The best prophylaxis against such transgression is a vigilant sensitivity and attentiveness to questions of value.

The values dimension of nursing, then, is very complex. It encompasses full-blown ethical dilemmas — situations involving two or more conflicting values or principles such that one can be satisfied or realized only at the expense of not satisfying the other — but much more besides. Many situations raise or present ethical concerns but are not necessarily crises or dilemma situations. Whatever the situation, knowing what one values and being sensitive to the values of others is an essential condition of responsible and ethical practice

2. Relevant Codes, Policies, and Laws

A knowledge base in ethics for nursing should also include codified ethics — codes, policies, and laws — as they relate to nursing practice. These include codes of ethics promulgated by professional associations in which one is a member or even a stakeholder. At the international level, there is the *Code for Nurses: Ethical Concepts Applied to Nursing* (International Council of Nurses, [1973] 1982). At the national level, there is the Canadian Nurses Association (CNA, 1991) *Code of Ethics for Nursing* and the American Nurses' Association (ANA, [1976] 1985) *Code for Nurses with Interpretive Statements*. At the provincial or state level, there are such documents as the *Guidelines for Professional Behaviour* (College of Nurses of Ontario, 1995). Various professional organizations also publish helpful policy statements related to particular issues or addressed to nurses working in a specific context or area. For example, nurses actively engaged in research could be expected to be familiar with *Ethical Guidelines for Nurses in Research Involving Human Participants* (CNA, 1994). Nurses working in a variety of institutional contexts can find guidance in the document Joint Statement on Resuscitative Interventions (CMA, 1995), which was developed in collaboration with and approved by the Canadian Nurses Association.

The nurse would also be well-advised to be familiar with any relevant policies issued by the institution in which he or she works and to measure these against personal and professional values. Indeed, it is wise to familiarize oneself with such policies before entering an employment contract, especially if one has intense convictions about issues likely to arise in the institution. At the broader level of society, morally responsible nursing requires the nurse to be familiar with whatever social norms and laws bear on his or her practice.

As important as they are, codes, policies, or laws cannot take the place of or eliminate the need for ethical decision-making. For one thing, they are bound to be vague or silent about many ethical issues that arise for nurses. Even when they are explicit, the answer that one was simply doing what was mandated by a code, policy, or law is never enough to satisfy the demands of ethical accountability when the moral appropriateness of a particular action is called into question. Ethics is largely about being able to give reasons in defense of what one decides, and this includes even the decision to abide by (or to reject) the injunctions of a given code, policy, or law.

Moreover, codified ethics are not absolute or infallible. To take the case of law, an action may be legal, yet unethical from one standpoint or other. Many people believe that this is so as concerns abortion in Canada and the United States at the present time. Similarly, something that is illegal may be ethically permissible or even required in some values systems.

Although ethical codes, policies, and laws do not settle an ethical issue in absolute terms, they do furnish a good starting point for reflecting on a given issue at hand. They embody the collective wisdom of our profession, institution, or community. Although those who bring ethical analysis to bear on an issue may arrive at contrary conclusions, it would be arrogant to do so without having at least considered the codified ethics, policies, and laws on these matters. Moreover, given the authority that stands behind them, the consequences of ignoring or transgressing such official edicts can be very grave, and ought to be weighed in the deliberations of a prudent person. On the positive side, codes of ethics, policies, or laws, in addition to providing guidance, can give powerful support and backing for someone working in a setting in which other people are inclined to ignore ethical concerns.

3. Fundamental Concepts of Moral Philosophy

A knowledge base in ethics for nursing should also include some knowledge of moral philosophy. Moral philosophy is a highly specialized discipline, and there is disagreement about how much competence a nurse ought to have in this knowledge base. What ought the nurse to know by way of ethical theory? How well-versed should he or she be in the methods of moral reasoning? Should he or she know something about metaethics?

If ethical theory is not an essential component of nursing knowledge, it is certainly desirable at least for nurses to have some grounding in this subject. For this reason, this text includes a primer on ethical theory to provide the reader with some rudimentary knowledge of the main lines of theoretical enquiry.

Whatever might be obligatory as concerns knowledge of ethical theory, we believe that at the very least nurses should have facility in the use of fundamental concepts by means of which to identify, describe, and analyze ethical issues. The six concepts that form the skeletal framework of this book — beneficence, autonomy, truthfulness, confidentiality, justice, and integrity — have been chosen because they are foundational in nursing ethics. Fortunately, most of these concepts are already part of the ordinary language of nursing, and so education in this area is largely a matter of building on or deepening what one already knows. Ethics, after all, applies to everyone, and everyone has the basic equipment necessary for the conduct of a moral life.

However, the common sense usage of moral concepts has many inadequacies. In the first place, these concepts are frequently assigned vague and even contradictory meanings. In moral disagreements people often talk at cross purposes because they interpret terms and concepts differently. Secondly, moral analysis often comes quickly to a point where two or more positions, each of which expresses a competing value, are at odds. To take treatment refusal as an example, one person, appealing to autonomy, might insist on the client's right to refuse whereas another, guided by beneficence, might insist on the duty to do what will benefit the client. A more philosophical understanding of the fundamental concepts used in moral analysis and the tensions between them can help to sort out confusions, clarify disagreements, and promote creative problem-solving. This is desirable both with respect to the nurse's ongoing commitment to self-examination and his or her desire to do what is right.

Such an understanding can be pursued at different levels. The literature in nursing ethics and bioethics, for example, provides analyses that clarifies these concepts considerably beyond their often imprecise and confused usage in everyday language and contains helpful discussions of the basic ethical issues that nurses face. At a more philosophical level, which may exceed what the nurse needs to know, moral theorists situate these concepts somewhat more systematically in the context of moral theories.

The three subject areas described above (moral beliefs and values; relevant codes, policies, and laws; and fundamental concepts of moral philosophy) constitute a reasonable knowledge base for ethics in nursing. However, it is important to realize the limits of becoming more reflective about this knowledge base. Acquiring knowledge is not the same thing as becoming virtuous, except insofar as acquiring knowledge can itself be said to be a virtue. That people are good at the process of values clarification; well-versed in relevant ethical codes, policies, and laws; and well-read in the nursing ethics literature and in moral philosophy does not mean that they will be good in the sense of acting with virtue. Someone can be well-informed about ethics but insensitive or even cruel. Conversely, someone may be very kind but ill-informed about ethical concepts and moral reasoning. Even so, becoming more reflective may at least complement the cultivation of the virtues thought to be desirable for nursing. At the very least, it can help nurses to become clearer about what virtues are desirable and why.

More directly, reflecting on the knowledge base for ethics in nursing will help the nurse to develop certain skills. Such reflection will help the nurse to:

- become more sensitive to the ethical dimension of nursing;

- become more conversant in the moral values and principles that are at issue or at stake in the scope of his or her nursing practice;

- recognize and identify ethical issues when they arise;

- analyze ethical issues more thoroughly (e.g., describe the main arguments that can be deployed on either side of a given issue, bring relevant concepts and principles to bear on options, and so on).

The moral life presents itself to us as a task and a challenge, and the task will vary somewhat depending on one's life situation. This book is specifically designed for people whose life situation is nursing and who face the special kinds of ethical issues nurses tend to face. A good part of the moral task for nursing is to gain a better understanding of its ethical dimension. In this regard, this book will be both useful and informative.

The moral task for nurses, however, is not simply a matter of knowing but also of doing or even becoming, and whether good comes of this knowledge depends on the activity of the reader who at this very moment is finishing this sentence. Writes Levine (1977): "Ethical behaviour is not the display of one's moral rectitude in times of crisis. It is the day-by-day expression of one's commitment to other persons and the ways in which human beings relate to one another in their daily interactions" (p. 846).

Ethical Analysis and the Nursing Process

In a field of human interaction where values are as pervasive as in health care, it is virtually inevitable that conflicts of value will arise in a nurse's practice. In any given situation, the beliefs and values of the nurse, of the profession, of the client, of the client's family or friends, of other health professionals, and of society in general, may come into play. Sometimes the values of all concerned will not be congruent, and the nurse will be faced with an ethical conflict or issue.

The nature of ethics is such that there can be no mechanical formula for resolving issues when they arise. However, familiarity with the values dimension of the situation, any codified statements that may bear on it, and the main concepts of ethics and the ability to bring them to bear on a given issue can be of considerable help. In this regard, a first point to emphasize about ethical analysis — although hardly much of a help to someone in the throes of an ethical issue — is that big problems usually start off as small problems, and can be prevented, arrested, or at least minimized by thoughtful intervention at an early stage. Thus, it is important to become vigilant about proactively raising questions of value in one's daily practice.

Whatever the nature of the ethical problem, three interrelated components of ethical analysis can be brought to bear: descriptive analysis, conceptual analysis, and normative analysis (Martin & Schinzinger, 1989). *Descriptive analysis* is directed toward ascertaining the truth and acquiring knowledge. What is going on in the situation? What are the relevant facts of the matter? What do we know for sure, and what do we need to know in order to make an informed decision? The task here is to gather whatever data might bear on ethical choice and practice. Such data may include facts about the health status and medical condition of clients, the perspectives of the main agents involved, information about relevant policies and laws, and a wide range of other topics.

Conceptual analysis has to do with clarifying the meaning of key concepts involved in the analysis of a case or issue. In addition to the fundamental concepts around which this book is organized, numerous other concepts may also come into play. Sometimes these concepts are vague or ambiguous, such as "quality of life," "health," and "harm." Often, concepts are laden with values which skew the analysis of the issue towards one side or the other. In a discussion about abortion, for instance, the concept of "personhood" may load the dice in such a way as to prejudice the outcome. In an examination of euthanasia the concept of "killing" may function in a similar way. The task of conceptual analysis is to sort out the various meanings of key concepts and to unpack terms loaded with values and questionable assumptions.

Normative analysis is directed toward deciding what ought to be done. It involves sorting out the various moral values, duties, or principles that may bear on the choice at hand. What values or duties are in conflict, and on the basis of which criteria or arguments should they be weighed? Who among those involved in the case ought to participate in making decisions? What options are available, and, ethically speaking, what counts for and against the various options?

All of the above aspects of ethical analysis may be relevant to the solution of an ethical problem at hand and can be integrated into the nursing process. In addition, the nursing process itself can be adapted to furnish a useful framework for ethical analysis, as described below.

1. Assessment

When faced with an ethical issue, the first step is to work out a reasonable assessment or interpretation of the issue at hand. The emphasis here is on the word "reasonable," for it is quite likely that one already has a preconceived interpretation to begin with. That the situation presents itself as an "ethical issue" indicates at least some minimal interpretation.

One's initial interpretation of the ethical situation may be vague, incomplete, or even false. Interpretation in matters of value may be extremely complicated and subtle. Certain questions should be asked by way of testing and deepening one's initial interpretation of the issue. What exactly is the issue? Is it properly an ethical issue? What kind of ethical issue? What ethical concepts does it bring into play? What is the context in which it has arisen? In part this context may be defined by the mission statement of the institution, relevant policy statements, one's professional code of ethics, legalities, and so on. What bearing if any do they have on the issue? What are the relevant facts and how clearly are they understood? What values are at stake? Whose values? Who are the significant people involved? In what terms do they interpret the issue? Are you certain that you know how they view things? Do they understand your point of view? What are the main arguments on the different sides of the issue?

Such questions must be raised in order to work out a responsible assessment or interpretation. The most reasonable way to answer them is likely to involve talking with others and putting questions to them. The nursing literature on ethics may also be helpful. In the course of working toward an interpretation, one will often find that the issue is based on a misunderstanding or lack of communication.

By way of interpreting the issue, it is also extremely important that the nurse be as clear as possible about his or her values. In some instances, the nurse may learn that he or she is ambivalent about an issue that has arisen. Of course, it is always better for the nurse to have thought about and decided upon his or her values prior to being thrown into an issue. In part, the purpose of this book is to facilitate such an enquiry into one's values in a moment of quiet reflection. Even so, sometimes we only discover what our values really are (or perhaps discover that we are not as sure about things as we previously believed we were) when challenged with a real life issue.

2. Planning

Having arrived at a reasonable interpretation of the situation (or even in the course of doing so), a second step is to identify and plan options. What are the alternatives? Who supports which option and why? What are the main arguments for and against each? What bearing, if any, do law, institutional mission statements and policies, and professional codes have on the options? Have all of the relevant people been taken into consideration? How much input ought each of those involved to have? Who ought to be involved? Do they understand the options?

Having sorted out the options, the task then is to weigh them and choose the one that, all things considered, is morally best. Some options will be more promotive of certain values than others. Sometimes the scale will be loaded heavily on the side of one particular option, in which case the decision will be relatively easy. Other times two or more options evaluated in terms of conflicting values may approach being equal in weight, and the judgement between them will be difficult.

3. Implementation

Having decided on an option, or in order to decide, questions arise about how best to implement the option in a sensitive and effective way. Do relevant others understand why this particular option was chosen? Who should be involved in its implementation? What effects is it likely to have? To what extent can these consequences be managed and negative outcomes anticipated and warded off? Some adjustment of one's planned course of action may be necessary as one gets feedback from the implementation process (e.g., when unexpected complications arise).

4. Evaluation

Having implemented an option, in the interests of learning from experience and ensuring effective care, one is obliged to review the situation. How are things working out? To what extent are they working out as anticipated? How do those involved (and especially the client) feel about how things turned out? Does the issue have any broader dimensions (e.g., implications for institutional policy) that should be addressed in light of what happened? Is there anything that can be done to prevent such issues from arising in the future? Questions about process should also be raised. Is the process by which the decision was made a good one? Could better procedural mechanisms be established to facilitate future decision-making?

Incorporating ethics into the nursing process is a good way of ensuring ethical practice, and using the nursing process as a framework for analysis is a good way of working through an ethical issue that has arisen. Other frameworks for moral reasoning and decision-making for nurses are available (e.g., Curtin, 1982, p. 61; Thompson & Thompson, 1985, p. 99), but not surprisingly they tend to agree in essentials. One such framework developed by the author is presented in Appendix F.

Frameworks or models of this sort can indeed be useful, but a word of caution is in order. They are intended to aid decision-making and not to replace it. Decision-making requires judgement, and judgement guides the use of any framework as much as it may be guided by it. Hence, one should not be too rigid in following the direction of a given model. A good chef knows the importance of recipes, but knows as well how to add, subtract, and substitute ingredients as necessary.

Strategies for Case-Based Teaching and Learning

The intended audience of this book includes not only practising nurses but also nurse educators and students. The case method adopted in this book has proven itself a useful and effective way to teach ethics. Cases help students to see how the tools and concepts of ethical analysis apply in concrete ways. Moreover, whereas ethics in the abstract can be somewhat dry, cases engage the interest of students and make for lively discussion.

The ways in which cases may be used in educational contexts are limited only by the imagination of the nurse educator, but two main strategies are particularly worth mentioning. One such strategy is role-playing. This involves having students assume the roles of the various characters in the case. Students enact the case and flesh out the limited information given with imagined dialogue. This brings the characters to life and helps students to gain a better appreciation of the complexities and of the different points of view. In this regard, it can be very eye-opening for a student to assume the role of a character with whom he or she is unsympathetic.

A second strategy is the classical debate format. This involves having students defend and argue for different sides of the issue. This may be especially appropriate when the issue is a genuine dilemma, and one about which the class itself is divided. Another variation on this strategy is for the instructor or one of the students to assume the role of "devil's advocate," defending the position that appears weaker or less popular.

In addition to these general strategies, a number of techniques can be used to facilitate discussion. Sometimes it is instructive to vary the facts of the case (e.g., change the setting from a hospital to a client's home; modify details about the client's medical condition; reverse sexes; and so on). Such variations may throw new light on the issue and help to clarify the values and concepts involved in the analysis.

Another technique is to invite students to imagine other cases that are similar, or other situations in which the same issue arises with a perhaps slightly different twist. This helps students to develop flexibility in applying the concepts and values under discussion.

It is also useful to invite students to relate the case, or the issue raised by the case, to their personal experiences. Ethical analysis, after all, is little more than a game if students do not integrate what they have learned into their own lives. Relating the cases and issues to personal experiences will help students to shape their lives and practices in light of what they are learning.

References

American Nurses' Association. ([1976] 1985) *Code of ethics for nurses with interpretive statements.* Kansas City: Author.

Annas, G.J. (1974). The patient rights advocate: Can nurses effectively fill the role? *Supervisor Nurse, 5* (7), 20-25.

Beecher, H.K. (1959). *Experimentation in man.* Springfield, IL: Charles C. Thomas.

Beecher, H.K. (1966). Ethics and clinical research. *The New England Journal of Medicine, 274* (24), 1354-1360.

Benner, P., & Wrubel, J. (1989). *The primacy of caring: Stress and coping in health and illness.* Menlo Park, CA: Addison-Wesley.

Bishop, A.H., & Scudder, J.R. Jr. (1987). Nursing ethics in an age of controversy. *Advances in Nursing Science, 9* (3), 34-43.

Canadian Nurses Association. (1994). *Ethical guidelines for nurses in research involving human participants.* 2nd revised edition. Ottawa: Author.

Canadian Nurses Association. (1991). *Code of ethics for nursing.* Ottawa: Author.

Canadian Medical Association. (1995). Joint statement on resuscitative interventions. Ottawa: Author.

Coburn, J. (1987). "I see and am silent": A short history of nursing in Ontario, 1850-1930. In D. Coburn, C. D'Arcy, G.M. Torrance, & P. New (Eds.), *Health and Canadian society: Sociological perspectives* (2nd ed., pp. 441-462). Markham, ON: Fitzhenry & Whiteside.

College of Nurses of Ontario. (1988). *Guidelines for ethical behaviour in nursing.* Toronto: Author.

College of Nurses of Ontario. (1995). *Guidelines for professional behaviour.* Toronto: Author.

Cooper, M.C. (1988). Covenantal relationships: Grounding for the nursing ethic. *Advances in Nursing Science, 10* (4), 48-59.

Crowley, M.A. (1989). Feminist pedagogy: Nurturing the ethical ideal. *Advances in Nursing Science, 11* (3), 53-61.

Curtin, L.L. (1979). The nurse as advocate: A philosophical foundation for nursing. *Advances in Nursing Science, 1* (3), 1-10.

Curtin, L.L. (1982). No rush to judgment. In L.L. Curtin & M.J. Flaherty (Eds.), *Nursing ethics: Theories and pragmatics* (pp. 57-63). Bowie, MD: Robert J. Brady.

Curtin, L.L. (1983). The nurse as advocate: A cantankerous critique. *Nursing Management, 14* (5), 9-10.

Delamothe, T. (1988). Nursing grievances V: Women's work. *British Medical Association Journal, 296* (30), 345-347.

Flaherty, M.J. (1985). Ethical issues. In M. Stewart, J. Innes, S. Searl, & C. Smillie (Eds.), *Community health nursing in Canada* (pp. 97-113). Toronto: Gage.

Fleming, J.W. (1983). Consumerism and the nursing profession. In N.L. Chaska (Ed.), *The nursing profession: A time to speak* (pp. 471-478). New York: McGraw-Hill.

Fry, S.T. (1989). Toward a theory of nursing ethics. *Advances in Nursing Science, 11* (4), 9-22.

Gadow, S.A. (1980). Existential advocacy: Philosophical foundations of nursing. In S.F. Spicker & S.A. Gadow (Eds.), *Nursing: Images and ideals* (pp. 79-101). New York: Springer.

Gadow, S.A. (1985). Nurse and patient: The caring relationship. In A.H. Bishop & J.R. Scudder Jr. (Eds.), *Caring, curing, coping: Nurse, physician, patient relationships* (pp. 31-43). Birmingham, AL: University of Alabama Press.

Huggins E.A., & Scalzi C.C. (1988). Limitations and alternatives: Ethical practice theory in nursing. *Advances in Nursing Science, 10* (4), 43-47.

International Council of Nurses. ([1973] 1982). *Code for nurses: Ethical concepts applied to nursing*. Geneva: Author.

Kosik, S.H. (1972). Patient advocacy or fighting the system. *American Journal of Nursing, 72* (4), 694-698.

Levine, M.E. (1977). Nursing ethics and the ethical nurse. *American Journal of Nursing, 77* (5), 845-849.

MacPherson, K.I. (1989). A new perspective on nursing and caring in a corporate context. *Advances in Nursing Science, 11* (4), 32-39.

Martin, M.W., & Schinzinger R. (1989). *Ethics in engineering* (2nd ed.). New York: McGraw-Hill.

Pence, G.E. (1990). *Classic cases in medical ethics: Accounts of cases that have shaped medical ethics, with philosophical, legal, and historical backgrounds*. New York: McGraw-Hill.

Rodney, P. (1988). Moral distress in critical care nursing. *Can Critical Care Nursing Journal*. 5(2), 9-11.

Rodney, P. (1989). Towards ethical decision-making in nursing practice. *Can Journal of Nursing Administration*. 2(2), 11-13.

Rodney, P., & Starzomski, R. (1993). Constraints on the moral agency of nurses. *Canadian Nurse* 89(9), 23-26.

Roy, D.J., Williams, J.R. & Dickens, B.M. (1994). *Bioethics in Canada*. Scarborough, ON.: Prentice-Hall.

Smith, S. (1980). Three models of the nurse-patient relationship. In S.F. Spicker & S.A. Gadow (Eds.), *Nursing: Images and ideals* (pp. 176-188). New York: Springer.

Steele, S.M., & Harmon, V.M. (1979). *Values clarification in nursing*. New York: Appleton-Century-Crofts.

Storch, J.L. (1982). *Patients' rights: Ethical and legal issues in health care and nursing*. Toronto: McGraw-Hill Ryerson.

Storch, J.L. (1988). Ethics in nursing practice. In A.J. Baumgart & J. Larsen (Eds.), *Canadian nursing faces the future: Development and change* (pp. 211-221). St. Louis: C.V. Mosby.

Thompson, J.E., & Thompson, H.O. (1985). *Bioethical decision-making for nurses*. Norwalk, CT: Appleton-Century-Crofts.

Tunna, K., & Conner, M. (1993). You are your ethics. *The Canadian Nurse*. 89(5), 25-6.

Twomey, J.G. Jr. (1989). Analysis of the claim to distinct nursing ethics: Normative and non-normative approaches. *Advances in Nursing Science, 11* (3), 25-32.

Watson, J. (1979). *Nursing: The philosophy and science of caring*. Boston: Little, Brown, and Company.

Yarling, R.R., & McElmurry B.J. (1986). The moral foundation of nursing. *Advances in Nursing Science, 8* (2), 63-73.

Ziemann, K.M., & Dracup K. (1989). How well do CCU patient-nurse contracts work? *American Journal of Nursing, 89* (5), 691-693.

A PRIMER IN ETHICAL THEORY

It is the mark of an educated mind to expect that amount of exactness in each kind which the nature of the particular subject admits.

— ARISTOTLE

Morality and the Sense of "Oughtness"

Morality is rooted in our sense of *oughtness*. When we judge that some action, decision, or policy is right or wrong, or good or bad, we do so from the point of view of what ought and ought not to be.

Consider the following sorts of moral judgments a nurse might make:

Mr. A. has a *right* to be involved in deciding his plan of care.

Nurse B. *needs to be* more caring in the way she talks with patients.

It's our *duty* to provide care to Ms. C. without bias, even though she did incur her injury in a bank robbery in which she killed two innocent bystanders.

If you have reason to believe that Nurse D. is being abusive with patients, you *must* do something to correct the situation, even if it means jeopardizing your friendship with him.

Each of these judgements has to do with how someone *ought* to act, although some of them do not express this directly. For example, the assertion that Mr. A. has a right to be involved in deciding his plan of care means that his caregivers *ought* to involve him. To say that Nurse B. needs to be more caring means that she *ought* to be so.

The *moral* ought expressed in the above statements is different from other senses of the term "ought." Sometimes we use ought in a non-moral sense, as in the sentence "You ought to get to bed early *if* you want to be alert for the exam tomorrow." In this case, what you ought to do is conditional upon some end or goal that you may wish to achieve. "*If* you want to be alert, *then* you ought to go to bed early." Ought in this sense has to do with the means to an assumed end.

By contrast, the moral ought does not have any "ifs" attached to it. It is not that you ought to respect the client's wishes *if* you wish to be liked by him or her, or *if* you wish to avoid getting into trouble, or anything of the sort. Those may be good reasons for doing so, but they are not moral reasons. The moral ought enjoins you to respect the client's wishes simply because you have a responsibility, obligation or duty to do so. Oughtness in the moral sense is not optional or conditional upon non-moral ends or goals.

This sense of oughtness is common to all moral experience. The language in which we articulate and codify it includes such terms as rights, duties, responsibilities, values, obligations, and virtues — all of which are rooted in our sense of what ought and ought not to be.

Whatever the terms we use to express them, moral judgements and evaluations ultimately amount to claims about how someone *ought* to act. They embody *moral ideals*. These ideals are the basic elements of morality and govern moral life in two main ways. Firstly, they *guide* us in our conduct and decision-making. They give us something to aim for, targets to strive toward. Secondly, we use them to *evaluate* conduct and decision-making, whether our own or that of someone else. For example, to say that a nurse who deceives a patient about a prognosis has acted wrongly is to evaluate his or her conduct negatively in light of some such ideal as "Nurses ought to be truthful with their patients."

Ethical Analysis

Morality is pervasive in our lives. If you think back on any given day of your life, chances are that you will have made several moral judgements or moral choices during that day, whether at work, at home, or even at play on the golf course.

Most of the time, we get by without making the moral dimension of what we do explicit. Sometimes we do not even recognize that a situation in which we are actors has a moral dimension. Moreover, in many situations we do recognize as morally charged, what is morally required is relatively obvious.

However, in many instances, especially in health care, moral issues arise very explicitly and are not easily resolved. Several factors contribute to moral complexity.

One factor is that people sometimes disagree about moral ideals. For example, not everyone would endorse the ideal that the public ought to be actively involved in deliberations about options for health reform. Some believe that the public is not sufficiently knowledgeable about the subject to make wise decisions, or is prone to choosing with its heart rather than its head. According to this point of view, it is better that public involvement be kept to a minimum — managed for public relations purposes perhaps — and that experts make the decisions.

A second complicating factor is that, even among those who agree about a particular ideal, there may be disagreement about how it should be applied in a given situation. For example, some would argue that the ideal of public participation means that the public ought to be involved in details regarding the amalgamation of several health services, whereas others would argue it is enough that the amalgamation proceed consistently with public values broadly construed.

A third complicating factor is that moral ideals sometimes conflict with one another. In some situations it may be difficult or impossible to satisfy all relevant principles at the same time. Suppose, for example, that a health agency is committed both to the ideal of public participation and to the ideal that resources should be allocated in such a way as to yield maximum benefit for every dollar expenditure. If the public preferred an allocation option deemed to be inefficient or not maximally promotive of achieving benefits, these two ideals would be in conflict.

Problems of the sort identified above indicate the need for careful reflection and analysis about moral matters. This is the province of ethics. If *morality* can be conceived as a set of principles or ought statements — a list of do and don'ts — *ethics*, by contrast, is reflective analysis about or using those ideals or principles.

Ethics — careful and systemic reflection and analysis about moral ideals and how they bear on practical issues — is important and useful for a number of reasons:

- Moral ideals or principles as we live them day to day are sometimes vague, or even confused. Ethics helps us to identify, articulate, and clarify them and sensitizes us to the pervasiveness of moral issues in our lives. It helps us to be explicit about our moral choices.

- People often endorse moral ideals or principles without justification for them. Ethics helps us to deepen our understanding of moral ideals and principles and the reasons that can be given against and in support of them and their application in a given case.

- In some situations, moral ideals or principles conflict with one another. Ethics helps us to understand the basis of such conflict and what is at stake in a given issue.

- Working through a process of ethical analysis helps ensure that all relevant considerations are entertained prior to making a decision, and that the decision subsequently reached will be a *morally principled and rationally defensible decision.*

Accountability and Morally Principled Decisions

One of the defining features of the health professions is the trust on which relationships with clients is based. This trust increases the burden of responsibility for health professionals and makes it all that much more important for them to be explicit about their moral choices and the principles and values informing those choices.

When we act in trust, we act on behalf of someone or some group and are accountable to them for what we do. Power, knowledge, and vulnerability are not evenly balanced in the client-professional relationship. People acting in positions of trust have considerable power to cause harm or good.

Morality, especially in a pluralistic society such as ours, is something about which reasonable people may disagree. Almost always people will agree that some decisions are clearly "wrong." In many cases, however, it is not clear which, from among several live options, is the "right" decision.

However, if the plurality of points of view in our society means that not every decision has a morally right answer, this does not mean that anything goes. Being morally accountable does not mean that one will always make what others, and in particular those to whom one is accountable, believe is the "right" decision. But it does mean being able to defend and justify whatever decision one makes.

Thinking about moral decision-making from the standpoint of defending and justifying one's decision to others helps us to focus the task of ethics. Ethics is in the service of being accountable for our choices. When pressed to defend a decision or a policy, answers such as "I didn't really notice that there was a moral issue there at all" or "I just went on my gut feeling" are not good enough. The person to whom we are giving an account for our decision is likely to ask us such questions as "Did you consider and weigh the moral ideal or principles at stake?" and "Did you think about the alternatives and consequences?"

Given the realities of busy schedules and decisions that have to be made immediately, often we do not have the time to be as thorough in ethical analysis as we might otherwise like to be. However, although the real world pressures on decision-making are formidable, they are no excuse for failing to make morally defensible decisions. The person to whom an accounting is owed is unlikely to be satisfied by the answer "I didn't have time to think about that."

Ethical analysis and reflection should not be viewed just as something that one brings into play only in the thick of some crisis or other. The best occasion for ethical analysis and reflection is not in the middle of an issue but in an atmosphere of relative calm. In such moments, one can clarify the moral principles relevant to the role one plays and explore how they bear on the typical sorts of issues one is likely to face in the discharge of one's responsibilities. If one has given sufficient thought to ethics, one will not be starting from ground zero when one finds oneself in the thick of a moral issue. The relevant moral principles will be more readily apparent and their application to options and alternatives will be clearer.

Ethical analysis is no guarantee that we will make the right decision (there may not be one), but it will at least help us to make morally principled decisions, decisions we can justify with reference to the moral ideals and principles at stake and defend if called upon to give an accounting.

Ethical Theory

Ethical analysis is a matter of examining our opinions about right and wrong and probing the moral ideals that bear on moral judgement and evaluation. This typically involves such things as identifying the principles or values relevant to a given issue and evaluating options for action in light of these principles or values.

As described above, ethical analysis is integral to moral life. All of us engage in it at least to some degree. Theorizing about ethics, by contrast, takes ethical analysis to a greater depth. It probes the foundation of morality.

Ethical theory attempts to systematize moral intuitions, values, and principles in a consistent framework or to root them in a common ground. Whereas ethical analysis tends to focus on a particular moral issue of concern, ethical theory operates at a more abstract or general level. Ethical theories purport to say something about how in general or as a rule we *ought* to behave and to furnish reasons why we should act one way rather than another. They systematize our intuitions and unreflective feelings about "oughtness."

The challenges of acquiring facility in ethical theory are considerable. It is a highly specialized and technical area within the general domain of philosophy. Many of the key works are written by and for philosophers and presuppose considerable knowledge about the main ideas and lines of debate in philosophy.

In addition, the field is fraught with controversy. Ethical theorists disagree among themselves about the nature of ethical theory, its practical relevance, the relationship between ethical theory and moral action, which ethical theory is most worthy of our assent, and about a host of other issues (e.g., see Rosenthal & Shehadi, 1988; Clarke & Simpson, 1989; Yeo, 1994).

It would be impossible to do justice to these theoretical debates in a few pages but the summary below will at least acquaint you with the main lines of thought. For those who wish to research the subject further, there are many good survey texts available (e.g., Denise & Peterfreund, 1992; Moore & Stewart, 1994.)

Theories About Morality

Before introducing the main ethical theories of relevance to nursing ethics, it is important to say a few words concerning certain *theories about morality* (as opposed to ethical theories) that raise doubts about the validity of ought judgements and moral ideals. These theories call into question the very possibility of ethical theory, and indeed the possibility of valid moral judgements. Four such theories are briefly outlined below.

i) Egoism

Egoism is the view that the only motive for human behaviour is self-regard or self-interest. It takes this to be a general truth about human nature or human psychology.

Egoism does not say that what people do always is *in fact* in their own best interests. That would obviously be false. People occasionally do things that are manifestly self-destructive. The egoist claims that in such cases the person is nonetheless motivated by self-interest, but mistaken about where his or her interests lie, or unable to subordinate immediate gratification to long-term gains. The bottom line for the egoist is that we are self-interested in everything we do, but not necessarily wise about what our best interests are or disciplined enough to act consistently with them.

The main fact about human behaviour that seems to contradict egoism is that we do sometimes do things that appear to be motivated by selfless moral ideals or concern for others. Sometimes we do something just because we believe it is our duty, perhaps even at considerable personal expense. We make sacrifices to help someone else out. How can egoism be upheld in the face of such examples?

The egoist grants that in some cases it *appears* that people are acting selflessly, but advances that this is really a deception. According to the egoist, someone who acts in a way that is apparently selfless is really acting on the basis of some hidden, self-serving motive, even if only the desire to feel good about seeming to act selflessly.

It is impossible to disprove such a sweeping claim about human psychology and motivation. However, it is also impossible for the egoist to prove it. The egoist's thesis is a postulate that can be neither confirmed nor refuted by experience. As such it does not undermine the "oughtness" that is crucial to the very possibility of morality. In order to establish morality on a solid foundation, it is enough to establish that we do indeed experience a sense of "oughtness" and are able to distinguish experientially between moral motives or reasons and those that are merely in the service of our self-interest.

Moreover, if the demands of morality and the demands of self-interest — duty and inclination — sometimes conflict, they do not always. Although morality requires a willingness to subordinate self-interest to duty, in many and perhaps even most moral situations there is a convergence between our obligations and our interests.

ii) Emotivism

Emotivism is the belief that moral beliefs and ideals are a kind of reflex of our psychological make-up. They merely express personal preferences, likes and dislikes. In this respect, they are akin to judgements of taste: e.g, "I like peas"; "She finds broccoli disgusting." Such expressions of preference tell us something about the likes and dislikes of the person making them, but nothing about the nature of peas or broccoli.

For emotivists, the same is true of moral ideals and judgements. Someone who expresses a moral belief about the rightness or wrongness of some action or practice (e.g., abortion, assisted suicide, etc.) is merely telling us about his or her preferences, and nothing about the objective nature of the action or practice. To say that assisted suicide is wrong is just a confused way of speaking. Just as someone who says that "Peas are good" really means and says nothing more than "I like peas", someone who claims that assisted suicide is wrong really means and says nothing more than "I do not like assisted suicide" or "I feel that it is wrong." In both cases, according to the emotivist, what at first glance appears to be an objective statement is a disguised statement of preference. The belief merely reflects or expresses the subjective preference of the person holding it and contains no information about the objective state of affairs.

In defense of emotivism, it is true that moral judgements vary from person to person and sometimes reflect, in an obvious way, the psychological make-up and conditioning of the one doing the judging. Moreover, such information as they contain is clearly not objective, or at least not in the same way that factual information is. To say that abortion terminates the life of the fetus, or that the procedure involves risks of such and such a kind, is a statement of fact. It tells us something about the act or practice, and what it claims can be proved or disproved by scientific study. To say that abortion is wrong (or right), however, tells us nothing objective, or at least nothing that could be proved or disproved in the manner of a factual claim. However, it does tell us something about the person making the claim, and for the emotivist that is all the information it contains.

The emotivist is certainly right that value judgements sometimes vary from person to person and that they do not have the same status as factual claims. However, this does not warrant the conclusion that value judgements are therefore merely subjective, or nothing more than expressions of preferences.

The critical feature of moral ideals and value judgements that emotivism fails to account for is that they are amenable to rational discussion and persuasion in a way that mere preferences or judgements of taste are not. We expect and even demand that people give reasons to support their moral judgements. We debate and argue about moral ideals. We seek to persuade others about the reasonableness or unreasonable of a particular moral belief. It is true that people do not always come to agreement in the course of such persuasion and argumentation, but they sometimes do. And even when they don't, they do not therefore abandon rationality as the standard by which moral beliefs are to be arbitrated.

iii) Relativism

Relativism holds that moral ideals and beliefs can be reduced to the conditions under which they originate. They are a product of upbringing and conditioning, at best conventions that have developed within a particular society or group. As such, they are not true always and everywhere for everyone but relative to time, place, and person. What is right for one time, culture, or person, may not be right for another.

Cultural relativism is the doctrine that moral beliefs a) are rooted in particular cultures, and vary from one culture to another, and b) have scope or validity only in the culture from which they derive.

The first claim is undoubtedly true. Anthropologists debate whether or to what extent some moral beliefs are invariable or constant across all cultures, but examples that they do vary from one culture to another can be produced at great length. It is also well-known that and how societies inculcate moral ideals and beliefs in their members through various types of conditioning, including education, religion, and media.

The second claim, however, is very questionable and warrants careful analysis. Against the thesis that at least some moral beliefs are true and binding always and everywhere and for everyone, the relativist asserts that moral beliefs have only local validity, to the extent that they have any validity at all. There is no universal standard by means of which to evaluate moral beliefs. Something that is morally permissible in one society may be forbidden in another and there are no grounds upon which one could say that one of these cultures is right and the other is wrong.

One implication of this view is that it is inappropriate to pass moral judgement on or otherwise seek to modify the moral beliefs of someone from another culture. An example currently the subject of controversy may help focus the issue. Female genital mutilation is practised today in certain parts of the world and thought to be morally acceptable there (although many people in these cultures do not agree with the practice). In North American society, on the other hand, the practice is generally thought to be abhorrent.

For the relativist, it makes no sense to ask which point of view is really right or best. There is no standard outside of the plurality of cultures and points of view from which to judge the morality of practices within those cultures. There are no moral absolutes. The relativist would argue that although North Americans may be justified, within their own value system, in condemning female genital mutilation in North American society, there are no grounds upon which to condemn the practice for or in other cultures. Relative to North American moral standards, the relativist would say, the practice is wrong. Relative to the standards of certain other cultures, however, the practice is acceptable. For North Americans to condemn this practice in other cultures, the relativist argues, would be to falsely promote their merely local beliefs to absolute status, and in effect to impose these culturally-specific beliefs on others without justification.

History does indeed record many examples in which one culture arrogantly imposes its will upon another under the pretence that its own beliefs have privileged status. In this regard, relativism may promote a spirit of humility and toleration for others with different points of view, and that is a good thing. Toleration is especially important in nursing, where the commitment to respect the autonomy of clients means respecting (but not necessarily agreeing with) the client's values when those values conflict with one's own.

However, as a general theory about morality, relativism is untenable, and for reasons similar to those pertaining to emotivism. The thesis that an ought statement holds true (to the extent it holds true at all) only for those people who have been brought up or conditioned to accept it is incompatible with the sense that at least some moral judgements have in our ordinary experience, and indeed regardless of our culture and upbringing. For example, when we say that it is wrong to deceive people about their medical condition, we do so in the belief that there are good reasons why it is wrong, and that these reasons ought to be persuasive for everyone and anyone. Whether they actually are is a different matter, but in any event this sense of universal validity is bound up with at least some moral judgements. Moreover, notwithstanding the great diversity among cultures with respect to moral beliefs, there are many principles that virtually all societies endorse. These principles have received their expression in various documents, such as the *Universal Declaration of Human Rights* (United Nations, 1948).

iv) Might makes Right

According to the "might makes right" view, moral norms and rules merely express and serve the will of those in a position of power to make and enforce them. Ultimately, morality reduces to power. As a well-known parody of the Golden Rule puts it, "Those who have the gold make the rules."

This view holds some plausibility as a description of how things often happen in the real world. Most of us can probably recall moral situations in which, at the end of the day, the interests and values of those in a position of power prevailed just because they were able to assert their power. Nurses, who historically have not wielded much power in hospitals, sometimes complain about how much control hospital administrators and physicians have over decision-making, and how this power sometimes expresses itself and prevails when it comes to making moral rules and settling moral conflicts.

However, to acknowledge that "right" is often decided by "might" is not to justify this, or to accept that this is how things *ought* to happen. Indeed, it is our strong belief that right ought not to be decided by might but rather by good reasons that make us feel indignant when right is decided by might, and might alone.

This world is far from perfect, and the institutional arrangements under which nurses practice are often less than ideal. It would be naive to underestimate the reality and force of power and politics, especially in a field as rife with conflict and competing interests as health care. However, it is important to realize that the demand for moral justification can never be satisfied by appeals to power, or to the way things tend to happen.

Moral justification requires reason. Power or might is indeed something to be reckoned with, but it is never by itself a moral justification.

Ethical Theories

Each of the theories about morality sketched above contains some elements of truth. Self-interest is undoubtedly an important factor in motivation. Moral judgements are deeply rooted in our emotional life. There is a great deal of relativity in morals from one culture to another, and even from one person to another. History records many examples in which moral rules reflect and entrench the interests of those who have the power to make the rules.

However, these theories fail to account adequately for what is most fundamental to morality, namely, our experience of "oughtness." In at least some instances, we feel ourselves torn between the pursuit of self-interest, on the one hand, and our sense of duty, on the other. We are sometimes able to distinguish mere emotional response to an issue from what upon reflection we take to be a more properly moral response backed up by good reasons. About some things at least, we reserve the right to criticize the conventions and moral rules deemed authoritative in a given society, whether our own or that of someone else. And notwithstanding that all too frequently it happens that right is decided by might, we nonetheless pass moral judgement on this state of affairs and assert that things ought not to be such.

In the final analysis, our sense of oughtness is incompatible with the view that right and wrong are reducible to self-interest, preferences, cultural differences, or power. To satisfy this sense of oughtness, it is not sufficient simply to assert moral judgements. We expect moral judgements to be justified. We demand *reasons* in support of moral claims.

It is in the search for deep reasons upon which to ground moral claims that ethical theory comes into play. Ethical theory begins from the fact that moral judgements and evaluations have a quality of oughtness, which binds people regardless of their interests, emotional feelings, opinions inculcated by societal conditioning, or power to enforce their will upon others. Ethical theories seek to articulate deep reasons or rationales for judgements about how we ought and ought not to act.

There are many varieties of ethical theories. For our purposes, it will be helpful to group them under four main headings: deontology, consequentialism, virtue ethics, and the ethic of care.

i) Deontology

The word "deontology" derives from the Greek word for duty. Deontologists conceive morality as a system of moral duties, principles, rules, or imperatives. The task of the moral agent is to discern what his or her duties are, and to act consistently with and in the spirit of those duties.

But how do we know what our duties are? Immanuel Kant (1724-1804), the most prominent deontologist, believed that all our duties derive from a fundamental imperative binding on any rational being. He called this the "categorical imperative", which he formulated as follows: "I ought never to act except in such a way *that I can also will that my maxim should become a universal law*" (1785/1964, p. 70).

This is less complex than it sounds at first hearing. Think of the categorical imperative as a kind of test. Faced with a decision, Kant is saying, formulate the rule (in his terms, "the maxim") on the basis of which you are proposing to act. Then ask yourself whether it would be reasonable if anyone and everyone acted on the basis of this same rule. If it would not be reasonable to "universalize" this rule — to apply the same rule to anyone and everyone — it fails the test and is not an appropriate rule for moral action.

An example will help to clarify this. Suppose you are considering telling a lie in order to cover up a mistake you made with a client. The maxim or rule here might be expressed as follows: "It is permissible to lie in order to conceal one's error." If everyone were licensed to lie in order to cover up their mistakes, (if the rule were made universal law), the fundamental trust upon which the health care system is based would be undermined. Such a rule would not pass the test of "universalizability" and therefore would not be morally defensible. The rule that one should tell the truth, on the other hand, does pass the test.

Kant emphasized that the categorical imperative is not imposed upon us from without. No one has to tell us what our duty is, or can rightfully impose a moral duty upon us. In so far as we are beings of reason, each of us is able to apprehend directly what our duty is. To yield to the categorical imperative is not to yield to the will of another but rather to yield to the law of universal human reason, the law of our own reason. This point is of crucial importance for understanding Kant's concept of autonomy.

For Kant, autonomy meant submitting oneself to a law that one gives oneself. The moral law, the categorical imperative, is self-given, since one "discovers" it as the law of one's reason (which is the same for everyone). To be autonomous is to act in accordance with the demands of reason.

When the notion of autonomy is invoked in health care ethics, it usually means the client's right to make his or her own decisions, particularly in the matter of treatment options. This is related to Kant's usage in so far as it is based on the belief that each adult person is responsible for his or her own life, and no one can rightfully usurp this responsibility. However, for Kant autonomy entailed something more than the *right* to make decisions for oneself. It also entailed the *duty* to decide in accordance with the demands of reason.

Thus for Kant autonomy does not mean doing what one desires, or succeeding in having one's will prevail. The person driven by desire is no more autonomous in Kant's sense than is the person under the compulsion of another's will. It is not doing what we desire that makes us autonomous but rather doing what, on the basis of reason, we know to be the right thing.

Desire provides a powerful motivation for human behaviour but it is not a moral motive. The moral question "What is the right thing to do?" is not reducible to the question "What will best satisfy my desires or interests?" The right thing to do — what duty requires of us — is right regardless of whether it happens to coincide with our desires or interests (i.e., it is "categorically" right). What makes something right is its conformity with the categorical imperative, its quality of being morally binding for beings governed by reason.

In some instances at least, what duty requires of us may not match our desires or self-interests. Even when they do coincide, it is still important for Kant that duty, and not desire, be the motive for our action. Accordingly, he distinguished between *acting from duty* (motivated by willingness to do one's duty, just because it is one's duty), and *acting in accordance with duty* (doing the right thing, but not neccessarilly for a moral reason). Our moral worth involves doing the right thing (what duty requires), and for the right reason (just because it is our duty).

Much of what Kant says, although expressed in a terminology that is difficult for the non-philosopher to understand, rings true to our common and philosophically untutored experience of morality. Indeed,

Kant claimed that the categorical imperative expresses in a formal way the moral grounds upon which people act whenever they do act morally. Someone who asks "But what if everyone acted that way?" is expressing the basic logic of the categorical imperative. The same is true when someone asks "What if the roles were reversed and John did to me what I am considering doing to him?"

Kant's categorical imperative can be employed as a test for determining and assigning *moral rights* as well as duties. To determine whether a claimed moral right is indeed morally valid one asks whether the right in question is universalizable. Moral claims expressed in terms of duties can also be translated in terms of moral rights. The statement that Nurse L. has a duty to tell the truth can be otherwise expressed as a claim about what is owed to other people (e.g., Mr. Smith has a *right* to know the truth).

A standard criticism of Kant's theory is that he does not adequately address the problem of moral conflict. The main conflict Kant focuses on is between duty and inclination or self-interest. The most vexing moral conflicts in nursing ethics, however, are not between duty and self-interest but rather between one duty and another, or one right and another. What do we do in a situation when more than one duty comes into play, each of them pulling us in an opposite direction? Kant offers no guidance here because he believed that the categorical imperative furnished a clear and unambiguous test to determine our duty and that, if the test were properly done, there could be no conflict of duties. On this point, Kant's theory appears not to fit well with our moral experience.

In response to this limitation, commentators otherwise sympathetic to Kant have modified his theory to allow for a plurality of duties. This theory is called "pluralistic deontology", in contradistinction with Kant's theory, which reduces all duties to a single source or principle (the categorical imperative).

W.D. Ross is the most famous exponent of this view. Ross (1930) identified seven independent duties (non-maleficence, beneficence, fidelity, reparation, gratitude, self-improvement, and justice), each of which carries some moral weight. Although Kant would no doubt endorse the duties on this list, he would claim that ultimately they can be reduced to a single principle. Ross, on the other hand, believed them to be irreducible. Ross thus allows for the possibility of a genuine conflict between moral duties, which conflict cannot be resolved by reference to any overarching principle such as the categorical imperative.

Another problem critics find with Kant's theory is its rigidity. For Kant, moral rules are binding regardless of the consequences following these rules might have in a given instance. This is captured in the phrase "Do the right thing though the world should perish."

To illustrate this, consider the issue of disclosing potentially harmful information to a client about his or her prognosis. Some might argue that whether telling the truth is the right thing to do will depend upon whether on balance the truth will do the client more harm than good. For Kant, however, the question of rightness in this and other situations is to be decided independently of the projected consequences of the action. And Kant would say that the right thing to do is to tell the truth. His advice, so to speak, would be "Do the right thing, though the patient should perish."

ii) Consequentialism

Whereas for Kant the test or standard of moral rightness is conformity to the law of reason or the categorical imperative, for consequentialists moral rightness depends on the consequences of action. Moral decision-making is a matter of projecting the consequences of various action alternatives and selecting the one that on balance will produce the most good. The moral imperative here is to maximize good consequences and minimize bad ones.

This raises the obvious question of how we measure and assess the goodness of consequences. For utilitarianism, the most prominent consequentialist theory, the highest good is happiness. However, it is not the happiness of the individual decision-maker that should guide decision-making, or at least not his or her happiness alone. Rather it is the happiness of everyone potentially affected by one's decision that counts. Therefore in our actions we should strive to produce the greatest amount of happiness possible for everyone concerned. John Stuart Mill (1806-1863) referred to this as the principle of utility, which he articulated as follows: "The creed which accepts as the foundation of morals, Utility, or the Greatest Happiness Principle, holds that actions are right in proportion as they tend to promote happiness, wrong as they tend to produce the reverse of happiness" (1863/1961, p. 194).

Utilitarianism thus yields a simple formula for making moral decisions. The first step is to project the consequences of each action alternative available to us. The second is to calculate how much happiness, or balance of happiness over unhappiness, will be produced by each action and its projected consequences. The third step is to select that action which, on balance, will produce the greatest amount of happiness for the greatest number of people.

Critics point out several problems with utilitarianism. One problem has to do with the difficulties of accurately predicting the consequences of our actions. A more serious problem has to do with how we determine how these consequences measure up in terms of happiness. How do we measure happiness?

Probably the most serious criticism of utilitarianism is that, in principle at least, it could sanction actions generally thought to be immoral. For example, on utilitarian grounds, it would be acceptable, if not obligatory, to sacrifice the happiness of a few persons in order to maximize overall happiness for the collective. A rather gruesome example will help illustrate this point.

Suppose there are ten candidates waiting for various transplants, and a serious shortage of donors and available body parts. Some of these people are expected to die if they do not get their transplants right away. An enterprising person suggests kidnapping a homeless person to harvest his or her organs and distribute among the ten. This idea sounds morally repulsive to us, since it would violate moral rights and duties thought to be sacrosanct. However, for the utilitarian the fact that such an action would run counter to deep intuitions and fundamental moral principles would not be sufficient to rule it out. Following the greatest happiness principle, he or she would project the consequences of both kidnapping and not kidnapping the homeless person and try to determine how much happiness, on balance, would result from each course of action. If the kidnapping option won this contest, it would be mandated by utilitarianism.

In response to such concerns, philosophers have distinguished between act and rule utilitarianism. Act utilitarianism enjoins us to perform the utilitarian calculation for each action considered separately. Rule utilitarianism, on the other, enjoins us to perform the calculation not for particular actions but rather with reference to general moral rules, such as the rule that one ought not to abduct and kill innocent human beings. If the rule is overall promotive of human happiness, then one should follow the rule, without regard to consequences in particular cases.

Rule utilitarians further argue that the rules of ordinary morality are for the most part promotive of the greatest possible happiness and therefore should be adhered to. Given this qualification, rule utilitarianism is much more compatible with ordinary morality, and indeed with deontological ethics, than is act utilitarianism.

iii) Virtue Ethics

Despite their differences, deontology and consequentialism are alike in their focus on moral rules or decision-making principles. Moral life is conceived as rule or principle-governed behaviour, whether the rule in question be the greatest happiness principle, the categorical imperative, or some collection of irreducible moral principles.

Virtue ethics, on the other hand, views moral life as having less to do with rules or principles for determining right action than with habits and dispositions. The emphasis is on moral character: not on actions or decisions as such, but rather on the kind of person one is and should be.

Aristotle (384-322 B.C.) is the philosophical father of virtue ethics. In the *Nichomachean Ethics* (1934) he roots virtue in a theory of the human good, grounding this in turn in a conception of human nature. What is good for human beings — that towards which we should strive — has its basis in the kind of beings we are by nature. Virtues are those habits and character traits the perfection of which enables us to realize and fulfil our natures.

For Aristotle, what sets us apart as human beings and is definitive of our uniquely human nature is reason. Thus the highest virtues are those having to do with the cultivation and employment of reason. Aristotle also believed that we are by nature social beings. As such we require the society of others to develop and fulfil our natures most perfectly. Accordingly, the virtues proper to us are ones that contribute not only to our own good and excellence, considered individually, but also to the good and excellence of the community. In keeping with this, Aristotle focuses on moral education. The ideal of moral education is to inculcate in the young and impressionable the habits and dispositions — i.e., virtues — that will enable them individually to reach their highest potential and at the same time contribute to the overall good of the community.

Virtue ethics has enjoyed a renaissance in contemporary ethical theory (e.g., Foot, 1978; Dent, 1984). In large part, this is a reaction against the dominant deontological and utilitarian theories. MacIntyre (1984) provides a scathing critique of dominant moral theory in its attempt to ground ethics in universal moral principles and to represent moral life as a matter of following rules. Moral rules or principles thus derived, he argues, are either too general to provide guidance in particular situations, or, if sufficiently particular, too controversial to win the agreement of all persons concerned.

MacIntyre argues that moral life cannot be represented adequately in the absence of a concrete conception of the human good. And this good is not something that can be reduced to an abstract rule or principle, true always and everywhere for everyone. Rather the human good is embodied in moral communities and traditions. Who we are and what we ought to strive for cannot be decided in abstraction from the traditions that have shaped us and the communities in which our possibilities are delimited.

Hauerwas (1977) reasons along similar lines, arguing that attempts to ground the moral life in moral systems designed in accordance with universal principles are bound to fail. Such systems are at best pale imitations of concrete moral life. Living a moral life is less a matter of adhering to the right moral system or following the right moral rules than it is of responding thoughtfully to the myths and stories that have shaped us, and responding to moral situations in light of these stories.

Virtue ethics holds many attractions for contemporary bioethics, and indeed both MacIntyre and Hauerwas have written about bioethics. Bioethicists sympathetic to or working within this approach (e.g., Pellegrino, 1974, 1977; Putman, 1988) remind us that the health professions are moral traditions. As such they embody concrete norms about the good. To enter a health profession is to enter a moral community, the ends and ideals of which are embodied in long-standing traditions. To be a "good" nurse or a "good" doctor is to have the kind of character proper to the ends of nursing or of medicine. In this vein, Pellegrino and Thomasma (1988) champion beneficence, or care for the good of patients, as the paramount virtue proper to those in the helping professions.

Virtue ethics has obvious applications concerning the education of health professionals but its relevance to the myriad of problems in contemporary bioethics is less clear. Should the dying patient's feeding tube be removed? On what grounds should those in line for a transplant be priorized? Should consent always be sought for DNR-orders? About such questions virtue ethics offers little guidance (of course, the same might also be said of competing theories).

The emphasis on particular traditions and communities raises yet other concerns. If everyone were shaped by the same tradition and belonged to the same moral community, a concrete conception of the human good might be workable. But contemporary society is not like that at all. We are a mosaic of people from sometimes very different traditions and communities, with sometimes very different conceptions of the good life. Given this reality, it seems unlikely that we could achieve consensus on a concrete conception of the good life. However, the prospect of consensus on moral rules and principles that would traverse our differences seems much more of a live option.

iv) The Ethic of Care

The ethic of care is like virtue ethics in many respects, and could even be classified as being one kind of virtue ethics. However, given its importance for nursing, and its affinities with other strains in contemporary theorizing about bioethics that cannot be thus classified, it warrants independent consideration.

The ethic of care emerged out of the work of Carol Gilligan (1982), which in turn was responsive to Lawrence Kohlberg's (1981) work on moral development.. Kohlberg posited a stage theory of moral development. At the first and most primitive stage of moral development — the pre-conventional — moral decision-making is guided by the fear of punishment and the desire to satisfy one's own desires. At the next stage — the conventional stage — moral decision-making is guided by the desire to please others, deference to authority, and a slavish obedience to the moral conventions dominant in one's social environment. The pinnacle of moral development — the post-conventional stage — is marked by autonomy and independent thinking. Decision-makers at this level are guided by the independent use of reason, and such moral principles as reason suggests to be universally valid for all people.

Gilligan was troubled by the fact that girls tended to score differently than boys on Kohlberg's moral development scale. If one accepted Kohlberg's hierarchy, one would have to say that they scored lower. Gilligan granted that females do indeed approach moral problems differently than males (although she describes this difference differently than did Kohlberg). However, rather than viewing this difference as a deficiency, she called into question Kohlberg's value assumptions about the importance of autonomy, and posited what is different in female moral reasoning as something positive rather than as a stage to be gotten beyond.

Gilligan elaborated this difference in her own research, in which she "found that girls and women tend to approach ethical dilemmas in a contextualized, narrative way that looks for resolution in particular details of a problem situation; in contrast, boys and men seem inclined to try to apply some general abstract principle without attention to the unique circumstances of the case" (Sherwin, 1989, p. 58). The contextual approach common to girls and women she called the "ethic of care." The principle approach more common to boys and men she called "the ethic of justice."

The justice orientation is very similar to the preoccupation with moral rules and principles shared by deontology and utilitarianism. The care orientation, by contrast, is focused less on rules than on virtues such as kindness and concern. It emphasizes not abstract rules or principles that would apply always and everywhere but rather the particular context in which the moral issue arises and the network of individuals connected by the issue. It values independence or autonomy less than it does relatedness with others, and sensitivity and concern for their needs.

Gilligan's work has generated much interest and controversy in a variety of fields, especially feminism, and has been complemented and developed by others. Noddings (1984), for example, has developed a theory of caring based on receptiveness, responsiveness, and relatedness.

Caring has long been a central element of nursing and has figured prominently in nursing theory (e.g., Watson, 1985; Benner & Wrubel, 1989). This caring focus and the fact that nursing remains today largely a "woman's profession" makes the ethic of care an especially relevant subject matter for nursing ethics (Gadow, 1985; Brody, 1988; Fry, 1989). Gilligan advanced that the care ethic is different from, but not (as Kohlberg's theory would imply) subordinate to, the justice ethic. She celebrated this ethic as the distinct voice of women, which hitherto had been suppressed by the dominant male ethic and relegated to second class status. Huggins and Scalzi (1988) caution that "If an ethical base for nursing practice is built on the ethic of justice, and the nurse's orientation is the ethic of care, there will continue to be a denial of the nurse's own voice" (p. 46). Should nursing ethics embrace the ethic of care?

Many of the concerns expressed about virtue ethics apply also to the ethic of care. In addition, the ethic of care has generated other controversies, within and outside of nursing (e.g., see Sherwin, 1992; Nelson, 1992; Noddings, 1992; Vezeau, 1992; Toronto, 1993). One concern of particular significance for nursing is that the ethic of care reproduces and reinforces clichés about gender roles that have been used to promote and justify occupational segregation. Women (especially mothers and nurses) do the caring, while the men do the "really important" work, like managing, and building, and fixing . . . and curing. Given the way our society values caring compared to the supposedly more masculine traits, buying into the ethic of care could contribute to the undervaluation of nursing in the health care system.

A less strategic and more principled concern about the ethic of care has to do with how this approach is understood *vis-à-vis* other approaches. It makes a great deal of difference whether the ethic of care is championed as competing with or complementing the ethic of justice. It is certainly true that caring has been the central value or virtue in the nursing profession, and few would find reason to quarrel with this focus. However, justice-oriented virtues such as autonomy, fairness and impartiality have also had an important place in nursing and nursing ethics. To the extent that the ethic of care is understood as being in competition with these virtues, and incompatible with a concern for universal moral principles, its suitability for nursing and nursing ethics is very questionable.

Conclusion

This summary account of contemporary ethical theory is necessarily sketchy and incomplete. To do justice to these theories much more would need to be said. A comprehensive account would also include more about other streams in contemporary moral theory, such as narrative ethics, discourse ethics, communitarian ethics, and feminist ethics.

Even so, this sketch of the main lines of thought in contemporary ethical theory should be sufficient for the reader to get a reasonable sense of the range of opinion in the field and of the main ideas and issues. This much should be a good starting point for further reading and reflection.

The final judgement about the strengths and weakness of the various theories discussed rests with the reader, whose task it is to assess them rationally in light of his or her own moral experience. Ultimately, each of us must come to terms in our own way with questions concerning who we are, what we are all about, and what we are committed to. Thinking through the theories described above will help.

References

Aristotle (1934). *Nichomachean Ethics* (2nd ed.), H. Rackham (Trans.). Cambridge: Harvard University Press.

Baier, A.C. (1985). What do women want in a moral theory? *Nous 19*, 53-63.

Benner, P., & Wrubel, J. (1989). *The primacy of caring: Stress and coping in health and illness.* Menlo Park, CA: Addison-Wesley.

Brody, J.K. (1988). Virtue ethics, caring, and nursing. *Scholarly Inquiry for Nursing Practice: An International Journal 2*(2), 87-96.

Clarke, S.G., & Simpson, E. (Eds.) (1989). *Anti-theory in ethics and moral conservatism.* Albany: State University of New York Press.

Denise, T.C., & Peterfreund, D. (1992). *Great traditions in ethics* (7th ed.). Belmont, California: Wadsworth Publishing Company.

Dent, N.J.H. (1984). *The moral psychology of the virtues.* Cambridge: Cambridge University Press.

Foot, P. (1978). *Virtues and vices.* Oxford: Basil Blackwell.

Fry, S. (1989). The role of caring in a theory of nursing ethics. *Hypatia 4*(2), 88-103.

Gilligan, C. (1982). *In a different voice.* Cambridge: Harvard University Press.

Gadow, S. (1985). Nurse and patient: The caring relationship. In A.H. Bishop & J.R. Scudder, Jr. (Eds.), *Caring, curing, coping: Nurse, physician, patient relationships* (pp. 31-43). Birmingham, Ala.: University of Alabama Press.

Hauerwas, S. (with D. Burrell). (1977). From system to story: An alternative pattern for rationality in ethics. In S. Hauerwas, R. Bondi, & D.B. Burrell (Eds.), *Tragedy and Truthfulness* (pp. 15-39). Notre Dame, Ind.: University of Notre Dame Press.

Huggins, E.A., & Scalzi, C.C. (1988). Limitations and alternatives: Ethical practice theory in nursing. *Advances in Nursing Science 10*(4), 43-47.

Kohlberg, L. (1981). *Essays on moral development.* New York: Harper and Row Publishers.

Kant, I. (1785/1964). *Groundwork of the metaphysics of morals*, H.J. Paton (Trans.). New York: Harper and Row Publishers.

MacIntyre, A. (1984). *After virtue* (2nd ed.). Notre Dame, Ind.: University of Notre Dame Press.

Mill, J.S. (1863/1961). *Utilitarianism*. In Max Lerner (Ed.), *Essential works of John Stuart Mill*. New York: Bantam Books.

Moore, N.B., & Stewart, R.M. (Eds.) (1994). *Moral philosophy: A comprehensive introduction*. Toronto: Mayfield Publishing Company.

Nelson, H.L. (1992). Against caring. *The Journal of Clinical Ethics 3*(1), 8-15.

Noddings, N. (1984). *Caring: A feminine approach to ethics and moral education*. Berkeley: University of California Press.

Noddings, N. (1992). In defense of caring. *The Journal of Clinical Ethics 3*(1), 15-18.

Pellegrino, E.D. (1974). Educating the humanist physician: An ancient ideal reconsidered. *Journal of the American Medical Association 22*(11), 1288-1294.

Pellegrino, E.D. (1977). Rationality, the normative and the narrative in the philosophy of morals. In S. Hauerwas, R. Bondi, & D.B. Burrell (Eds.), *Tragedy and Truthfulness* (pp. 153-168). Notre Dame, Ind.: University of Notre Dame Press.

Pellegrino, E.D., & Thomasma, D.C. (1988). *For the patient's good*. New York: Oxford University Press.

Putman, D.A. (1988). Virtue and the practice of modern medicine. *The Journal of Medicine and Philosophy 13*(4), 433-443.

Rosenthal, D.M., & Shehadi, F. (Eds.) (1988). *Applied ethics and ethical theory*. Salt Lake City: University of Utah Press.

Ross, W.D. (1930). *The right and the good*. New York: Oxford University Press.

Sherwin, S. (1989). Feminist ethics and medical ethics: Two different approaches to contextual ethics. *Hypatia 4*(2), 57-72.

Sherwin, S. (1992). *No longer patient: Feminist ethics and health care*. Philadelphia: Temple University Press.

Tronto, J. C. (1993). *Moral boundaries: A political argument for an ethic of care*. New York: Routledge.

United Nations (1948). Universal declaration of human rights. UN General Assembly Resolution 217A(III). Geneva: Author.

Vezeau, T. M. (1992). Caring: From philosophical concerns to practice. *The Journal of Clinical Ethics 3*(1), 18-20.

Watson, J. (1985). *Nursing: Human science and human care*. Norwalk, Conn: Appleton-Century-Crofts.

Yeo, M. (1994). Interpretive bioethics. *Health and Canadian Society* 2(1), 85-108.

BENEFICENCE

The road to Hell is paved with good intentions.

— AN OLD PROVERB

---

*Caring about and for the well-being of others is the mainspring
of nursing. In nursing ethics, this orientation toward the good of
clients is called "beneficence." Beneficence is simple enough in
principle, but it is often very complicated in practice. For example, sometimes it is difficult to know what is best for the client.*
*How ought personal, cultural, and familial perceptions and defi-
nitions of health be assessed, and, in situations of conflict, rec-
onciled? What is an ethical balance between respect for the
client's rights and liberties and the nurse's knowledge or perceptions of what is good for the client? How forceful or coercive
should health professionals be in advancing their views of what
is good for the client? What is required in situations where doing
what is best for the client involves some element of personal
risk or sacrifice on the part of the nurse?*

*Case studies in this chapter discuss the predicament of a
nurse whose client, because of spousal coercion and cultural difference, is reluctant to agree to needed counselling; the difficulty
of resolving a conflict between a nurse and a client about an
appropriate plan of care for the treatment of pressure sores; and
the dilemma faced by a support centre for people with
Alzheimer's disease when a client puts the centre in jeopardy
and threatens its continued existence.*

Beneficence and Benefiting Others

Beneficence (from the Latin *bene* for "well" or "good" and *facio* for "to do") denotes promoting someone else's good or welfare.[1] The same root forms the word "benefit." *Beneficence*, as an ideal or principle of conduct, requires us to act in a way that *benefits* others. Such benefit might take the form of preventing or removing some harm, or more directly acting to produce a good.

The same training, skills, and powers health professionals use to produce benefit can also produce harm. This double edge is captured in the Greek word for drug (*pharmakon*), which can mean either remedy or poison. The same drug that is beneficial in one context may under certain circumstances be a harm. The same can be said of many different interventions.

Because health professionals are in a position to produce harm as well as benefit, it is important to supplement beneficence with *nonmaleficence*, which pertains to the noninfliction of harm (Beauchamp & Childress, 1989, p. 123). Nonmaleficence is the value expressed in the classic dictum *primum non nocere*, that is, "first, do no harm." This injunction exhorts health professionals to exercise due care and caution in going about their business of working to produce benefit for their clients. A medication error, a slip of the hand, or an unguarded disclosure of information may cause a great deal of harm.

Beneficence has always been highly valued in the health professions — the so-called "caring" professions — and certainly in nursing. The first nurses in Canada belonged to religious orders that established hospitals in Quebec City and Montreal in the seventeenth century (Jamiesan, Sewall, & Suhrie, 1966). These Augustinian and Ursuline sisters cared for the settlers as well as the native peoples in much less than ideal circumstances. They often risked their health in their work as they practised the tenets of Christianity — doing good and benefiting others. The religious dimension is much less prominent today, but beneficence remains at the heart of contemporary nursing.

Beneficence is closely linked in meaning with caring. The caring orientation of nursing has been described and analyzed by numerous authors (Watson, 1979; Gadow, 1985; Benner & Wruebel, 1989; MacPherson, 1989) and is sometimes contrasted with the curative orientation of medicine.[2] Nursing's emphasis on caring is evidenced in the various codes of ethics that govern the profession, and is incorporated into various definitions of nursing. For example, the College of Nurses of Ontario (1990) defines nursing as "a preventive, educational, restorative and supportive health related service provided in a *caring* [italics added] manner for the purpose of enhancing a person's quality of life, or when life can no longer be sustained, assisting a person to a peaceful, dignified death" (p. 8).[3] The Canadian Nurses Association (1987) defines nursing practice as "a dynamic, *caring* [italics added], helping relationship in which the nurse assists the client to achieve and maintain optimal health" (p. iii). These statements emphasize the importance of caring to benefit the client.

Veatch and Fry (1987, p. 57) comment that professional statements extolling beneficence tend to be "uncontroversial" and even "platitudinous" (who would speak against the goodness of working to benefit others?) but point out that "we begin to encounter some problems as we probe more deeply" into what beneficence means in the light of difficult cases and examples. In the following discussion, some of these problems are identified and analyzed.

Beneficence, Self-Concern, and Duty

To varying degrees, most of us want to benefit others. For many people, and in particular those working in the "helping professions," caring comes naturally. To the extent that nurses care *about* their clients, caring *for* them may be less a burden than a joyful fulfillment or expression of deep desires and commitments. In many instances, helping others makes us feel good about ourselves. Many nurses report tremendous job satisfaction from making a positive difference in someone's life. Conversely, clients whose condition is such that little can be done to benefit them are among the most trying, partly because practitioners sometimes feel helpless in their presence.

Although caring for and benefiting clients is often in the service of the nurse's immediate desires and interests as well, it is not always so. In some instances, meeting the client's needs may require hard work, personal risk, or sacrifice. Some tasks nurses may be expected to perform for the benefit of the client may be very demanding, or unpleasant. There is some element of risk in taking blood from a person with AIDS. Working overtime to meet client needs in emergency situations or when a unit is short-staffed may be a considerable inconvenience for the nurse. In such cases, caring for others is to some degree at odds with self-concern, or with caring for and about oneself.

Such conflict shows that, although desiring to do what will benefit others is a big part of beneficence, beneficence must be rooted in something else besides, or in addition to, desire. When the nurse finds satisfaction or gratification in caring for the client, beneficence is easy. The situation is different when there is some degree of conflict between the nurse's own desires or self-concern and what is required to benefit the client. Perhaps the nurse would *rather not* attend to the homeless man — dirty, lice-ridden, and reeking of the street — brought into the emergency. Meeting his needs may be very unpleasant. Perhaps the nurse would *prefer not* to take blood from the person with AIDS. Even with precautions, there is some element of personal risk in the procedure, and a mistake could have very grave consequences. Perhaps the nurse really *does not want* to work overtime to cover for colleagues away with flu. There may be other things he or she would rather be doing.

If, in such instances, beneficence enjoins the nurse to attend to the homeless man, or draw the blood sample, or work overtime, it cannot be because this is what the nurse in the first instance desires. Rather, it is because in some sense and to some degree these acts of caring are required as a matter of duty. If, as is often the case, what duty requires is at the same time what the nurse desires, then so much the better. However, beneficence sometimes requires us to do for reasons of duty what otherwise we would prefer not to do. The call of duty may spur us into action when concern for ourselves pulls us in another direction. Leading a moral life — a life responsive to the demands of duty — is a task that involves some measure of self-sacrifice, effort, and striving, even if in many or perhaps most instances what we desire to do and what we ought to do coincide.

How then do we know what our duties are? The grounds upon which our duties may be established are several.[4] In the context of professional ethics, it is often argued that our duties in some sense derive from the phenomenon of promising, as when we speak of "professional promise." According to this view, the duties a professional has emerge from a kind of contract between a profession and society, or between a given professional and a given client.[5] In the case of nursing, society confers certain rights and privileges on nurses, who in return implicitly promise to aim at certain standards of conduct, including those expressed in the profession's codes of ethics. The individual who enters the profession and assumes the role of nurse in our society thereby assumes as well certain duties that go with this role, the duty to act for the benefit of the client being foremost among these. Such a duty is called a "fiduciary duty," meaning that it derives from the trust that professionals will use their skills and powers in the service of their clients. Nurses have been empowered and entrusted to act for the benefit of clients; clients expect them to do so.

By whatever means duty is grounded, it is sometimes difficult to decide precisely what and how much duty requires of us, especially with regard to beneficence.[6] Aside from what we might wish or desire to do, or what we might be inclined to do out of self-concern, what is entailed by a duty to benefit others? To what extent is it enough to avoid causing others harm, and to what extent are we required to produce positive benefits for others? How much sacrifice, effort, and striving does duty require of us? The answers to these questions will depend on the specific context and relationships in which one exists.

Although we admire persons who devote themselves passionately to the service of others even to the point of self-sacrifice, the hero sets an unreasonable standard of duty for nursing. Jameton (1984) points out that "in the name of idealism, nurses have traditionally been called upon to work long hours at low wages," and cautions that "nurses in particular should be wary of self-sacrifice" (p. 215). Yet we also disapprove of the nurse who acts only according to the bare letter of his or her job description or refuses to make any sacrifice for the good of the client. Somewhere between these two extremes a reasonable mean must be found. How much giving does beneficence require of the nurse?

Under ideal circumstances there would be no conflict between concern for others and concern for self: caring for others would coincide with self-development, fulfillment of personal goals, and so on. Unfortunately, the world in which we live is less than ideal. Sometimes the nurse is called upon to do something in the service of the client's good that requires a measure of self-sacrifice or selflessness.

Such a situation might arise when the need for care exceeds the supply of available practitioners. As a result of understaffing, a nurse may feel called upon to work harder or for longer periods of time than would otherwise be reasonable. To be sure, such understaffing may itself be a problem that needs to be addressed. Mindful of the possibility of exploitation, a nurse working in such situations should of course address the problem at the root level. Still, in the interim at least, the nurse is faced with a problem that requires immediate attention. In order to fill the pressing needs of clients, he or she may have to make some sacrifice. How much sacrifice is enough to satisfy the requirements of beneficence?[7]

Another situation in which the requirements of beneficence are unclear is when caring involves an element of personal risk. For instance, nurses may be unsure about the efficacy of the safety precautions instituted by the facility in which they work. Are they obliged to risk their own health or that of their families in order to provide care?[8] Nursing care is sometimes required in situations in which there is risk of physical and verbal abuse from clients. Clients are entitled to good nursing care, but what about when this entitlement comes into conflict with the nurse's own well-being? Acting as an advocate for the client may in certain instances put the nurse at odds with his or her employer or with other health professionals. Does beneficence require the nurse to advocate for the client's good even to the point that this involves a risk to job security?

Every nurse must strike some reasonable balance between the duty or wish to promote the good of clients, on the one hand, and self-concern, on the other. No formula can stipulate in advance what this balance should be. Ultimately, what constitutes a reasonable balance is a matter between the nurse and his or her conscience.

Problems Determining What is Beneficial

Willingness to benefit others is one thing; knowing how and being able to benefit them is something different. *Good intentions* constitute an important aspect of beneficence, but so too does the ability to produce *good outcomes*. These two aspects of beneficence — the motivational or psychological and the consequential — are reflected in the notion of care.

On the one hand, caring can be conceived psychologically, as pertaining to someone's attitudes or dispositions. In this sense, caring applies to persons and the spirit in which they act in relation to others. Thus we praise someone for being concerned about and empathizing with others. We admire caring people for the good wishes or intentions upon which they act, sometimes even when their good intentions lead to bad results. Although caring in this sense may in itself be beneficial to others — just knowing that someone cares can have a therapeutic value — such benefits may be limited. Caring intentions may not be enough.

On the other hand, caring can also be conceived as applying not to persons as such, but rather to skills and abilities. In this sense, caring means *knowing how* to benefit someone and putting one's skills and abilities to work for his or her benefit. In this sense, *nursing care* refers to the kinds of things that the nurse, informed by nursing *knowledge*, might do to benefit the client. A mother might indeed care for her sick child in the psychological sense described above, but, lacking the knowledge of how to benefit, may be unable to care in this second sense. Conversely, someone may know how to care in the sense of being able to secure a good outcome without caring in the sense of being genuinely concerned about the good of the other.[9] Moreover, as Benner and Wrubel (1989) point out, "the same act done in a caring and non-caring way may have quite different consequences" (p. 4).

Ideally, nursing care should combine both these senses of caring. Good nurses both care about their clients and use their nursing knowledge, skills, and abilities to care for them in ways that will produce benefit. "A caring relationship," Benner and Wrubel (1989) advance, "sets up conditions of trust that enable the one cared for to appropriate the help offered and to *feel* cared for" (p. 4). This trust includes both the feeling that the caregiver really does care, and the confidence that he or she has the knowledge and ability necessary to make a positive difference. The caring relationship is diminished if either of these conditions are not met.

In some cases, caring people possessing knowledge and skills to benefit others may be unsure about how best to produce benefit. There may be different or conflicting kinds of benefits to be considered. Benefits may be mixed with burdens or harms, and predicted outcomes may be more or less uncertain or probable. Judgments about how best to benefit the client may be complicated by considerations of risk and burden as weighed against benefit. For example, in many cases it is uncertain whether cardio-pulmonary resuscitation is really in the client's best interests. Often, there is uncertainty, and perhaps disagreement, about the benefit of treatment for clients who are severely damaged. What does beneficence require as concerns treatment decisions for a severely handicapped newborn who, even in the best case scenario, will emerge from surgery profoundly retarded, with limited motility, and unlikely to live beyond early childhood? Considering the burdens, would treatment really be a benefit? What about the burdens for others (e.g., the family, society)?

Treatment decisions in the grey zone where benefit to the patient is uncertain or disputed pose deep and difficult questions about the values, goals and limits of health care. On the one hand, everyone will agree on the importance of *quality of life*, even if they disagree about what precisely it means or how to measure it. One of the reasons we value health care as we do is because it makes a difference in our quality of life.

On the other hand, however, *sanctity of life* is also an important value in health care. This may be interpreted to mean that "human life is precious, needs to be respected, protected, and treated with consideration" (CNO, 1995, p. 10). The respect we owe clients does not vary with their quality of life. The ananecepahlic neonate is as deserving of our respect as is the young mother seeking advice about breast-feeding.

Thus interpreted, both quality of life and sanctity of life are important values in health care. It is important for health professionals to consider the impact of their interventions on the client's quality of life. It is also important for health professionals to demonstrate respect for human life, regardless of its quality. Problems arise, however, insofar as how different individuals interpret, apply, and priorize these values in specific contexts vary. For example, some health professionals interpret sanctity of life to mean that life should be preserved regardless of its quality. Others believe that, in cases where quality of life falls below a certain threshold, it is pointless — and even positively wrong — to preserve life. Such persons may claim that they too value sanctity of life, but argue that respect for human life does not entail that life ought always to be preserved.

The difficulties of determining what is beneficial are compounded by the fact that the scope of beneficence can be understood either in very broad or very narrow terms, depending on how broadly or narrowly benefit to the other is construed. Since the client becomes the nurse's responsibility based on the expectation and trust that he or she will act on behalf of the client's health interests, it seems reasonable to qualify the kind of caring specific to nursing in terms of health. Others may act beneficently toward clients in different ways — an accountant caring for their financial well-being, a priest for their spiritual well-being, and so on — but the nurse's care is primarily oriented toward their health. This, after all, is what nursing experience and knowledge prepares and qualifies nurses to do.

For the moment, let us restrict the scope of beneficence to acting on behalf of the client's good insofar as this good is identified with health (later we will give reasons to question this restriction). Even so, several problems arise. The concept of health, after all, is subject to different interpretations, and definitions of health cover a wide range of meaning. At one extreme are those who hold a narrow conception of health, defining it as the absence of disease or infirmity and restricting it to a biological or medical level. At the other extreme are those who hold a broader conception of health, extending it to include matters of lifestyle and to incorporate psychosocial considerations. The World Health Organization (WHO) definition of health as "a state of complete physical, mental, and social well-being" (Callahan, 1973, p. 77) is the most famous example of a broad conception of health.[10] As a rule, nursing tends to favour broad definitions of health.[11]

Cultural factors may also shape our conceptions of health. The meaning of "health" is to some degree relative to culture. What counts as "normal" body weight? What constitutes a balanced diet? How ought mothers to relate to their newborns? What are the characteristics of a healthy family? To some extent, the answers to such health questions vary from culture to culture. Different people, because of cultural or experiential differences, have varying opinions about what is healthy and what enhances their quality of life, especially when health is interpreted more broadly than physical health. These varying opinions about health and health benefits may cause conflict among health professionals, clients, and their families.

Differences concerning the understanding of health and the means by which it is maintained and restored have a bearing on what it means to act beneficently in the name of someone's health. Consider the controversial example of electroconvulsive therapy; or, shifting to a very different context, consider the debates about "therapeutic" abortion. Both of these "therapies" are legitimized in terms of health; disputes about them underscore the fact that what exactly counts as a health benefit may be far from self-evident.

Matters are further complicated if we question the initial restriction of beneficence to caring about health-related matters. Health, after all, is one good among others, albeit an important one. Many people prize other things above health, such as devotion to a political or religious cause, personal ambition, or the acquisition of wealth. They may even be quite willing to sacrifice their health for such things. How does one assess the value of health relative to other values?

Beneficence *can be* interpreted to incorporate the good of others conceived more broadly than in terms of health. Nurses *also* care about the ability of clients to act in accordance with their own values. They *also* care about the right of clients to be told the truth. However, in the literature and in common usage, the scope of beneficence tends to be restricted to the good of the client as defined in terms of health.[12] Understood in this way, beneficence may come into conflict with other important values, and in particular with autonomy and truthfulness. It is in these terms that the issue of paternalism is usually expressed.

Paternalism

The issue of paternalism comes to the fore when we shift from the question of *what standards* to use in determining the good of another to the question of *whose standards* ought to be accepted as authoritative. In particular, how much weight ought to be given to respecting the client's rights or liberties when doing so is thought to be incompatible with the client's good health? How much ought nurses to value the self-determination of clients to act on their own judgement when this seems contraindicated by nursing knowledge? How forceful or coercive should nurses be in imposing a plan of care in the name of the client's own good? Which is more important, the client's good as conceived in terms of health or the client's autonomy? As do other professional bodies, the College of Nurses of Ontario (1995) proclaims that the nurse has a responsibility to act as a client advocate. How is this possible in situations where the nurse's beliefs and values differ from those of the client? Should nurses advocate only when the client's views and wishes reflect their own or are they expected to advocate even against their own values? Should nurses be expected to carry out treatments with which they are not in complete agreement?

One of the most profound changes in contemporary health care has been a shift in the locus of decision-making from health professionals to clients. Concurrent with this, there has been an increasing emphasis on values such as client autonomy and the right to know the truth. Issues of paternalism may arise whenever one of these values comes into conflict with the beneficent concern to do what is best for the client. Examples are legion. Anticipating that disclosure may not bene-fit the client, or may even be contra-therapeutic, a nurse may be torn about whether to give a client certain information. There may be some uncertainty as to how to proceed with a client who expresses a choice that appears unwise in terms of health benefits (for example, a Jehovah's Witness' refusal of a blood transfusion). The nurse may be ambivalent about helping a client with heart disease who needs assis-tance to smoke.

Such is the classic scenario for paternalism. Paternalism, according to Gerald Dworkin's (1971) well known definition, is the "interference with a person's liberty of action justified by reasons referring exclu-sively to the welfare, good, happiness, needs, interests, or values of the person being coerced" (p. 108). In somewhat more blunt language, Jameton (1980) defines paternalism as "making people do what is good for them" as well as "preventing people from doing what is bad for them" (p. 90). The paternalistic person, acting in the name of benefi-cence, takes steps that he or she believes will promote the good of the other, perhaps even though the other disagrees or protests.

Because of their orientation toward benefiting the client, health pro-fessionals have been inclined to paternalism, often making decisions without their clients' authorization or even consultation in the well-intended belief that they know what is best. Such paternalism used to be much more acceptable in our society than it is today. With the increasing value our society has placed on liberty and individual rights, paternalism has become a derogatory term in the field of health care. Some writers, drawing from the tradition of beneficence in health care, argue that the critique of paternalism has gone too far, that we have been swept away by the rhetoric of autonomy and need to reassess our values (Pellegrino & Thomasma, 1988).

Even those who prize freedom or autonomy very highly grant that paternalism may be justified under certain conditions. The most obvi-ous example is in the parent-child relationship. Indeed, the term pater-nalism derives from this relationship (*pater* being the Latin word for father), and means to relate to someone as a father relates to a child. Paternalistic caring is proper in the case of children because, due to their lack of experience and development in reasoning, children are not mature enough to know what is good for them, and cannot be trusted to make their own decisions in matters of importance.

It is questionable to interfere with the liberty of adults for their own good because adults are sufficiently mature or competent to make their own decisions based on what they value and what they believe to be good. Nevertheless, under certain conditions adults may be sufficiently like children as to warrant paternalistic intervention (e.g., when, because of cognitive impairment or some other deficiency, they are deemed incompetent). If people are incompetent, we generally accept the legitimacy of others making decisions for them. Even so, determining whether someone is incompetent to make certain choices may be very difficult. (These matters will be discussed in greater detail in the following chapter). Moreover, health providers who believe that a prescribed course of treatment is on the whole beneficial may conclude that anyone who would refuse such treatment is therefore irrational or incompetent. In other words, assessments of incompetence may be used to mask paternalism.

The Beneficiary of Beneficence

In the health care traditions, the principal beneficiary of beneficence has generally been the *individual* client. The *Code of Ethics* of the Canadian Medical Association (1990) is quite typical in this regard. The very first principle of ethical behaviour mentioned states that the ethical physician should "consider first the well-being of the patient" (Principle 1). This focus on the individual is deeply rooted in the one-on-one therapeutic relationship. In contemporary society, it gains even greater importance given our current emphasis on the rights of the individual (Shelp, 1982, pp. 204-205).

Although traditionally beneficence in health care has been understood mainly in relation to the individual client, there is no reason in principle to thus restrict its scope. Indeed, the codes of ethics of the various health professions typically express some broader commitment to do good. In nursing, this broader understanding of beneficence is also evidenced by the profession's very strong public health orientation, and its more holistic concern with health in the context of family and community.

However, when we extend the scope of benefit beyond the well-being of the individual, beneficence becomes even more complex. How should the benefit owed to one individual be weighed against possible benefits (and perhaps harms) to others? This question might arise in any number of contexts. For example, the nurse might need to balance the client's good against the good of the client's family, to whom he or she might also have some obligation. How much weight should be given to the possible burdens on the family in a difficult neonatal situation? Such questioning can be further complicated by ambiguity about who precisely is the client on whose behalf the nurse is committed to acting beneficently. On at least some occasions, there is a possibility of conflict between the good of a pregnant woman and the good of her unborn child. In such a situation, are there two patients? Nurses working in the community may speak about the "nursing of families" or of the "family as client." What does this mean when there is conflict between individuals within the family, or individual family members with competing goods?

Increasingly, considerations of justice are coming to the fore in the health care system. How should the nurse proceed when the good of an individual client or group of clients is in competition with that of others? In a busy hospital ward, too much time spent with one client might mean not enough time spent with another. How ought benefits to be distributed in such a situation? How should nurses respond under circumstances in which, as a consequence of institutional restructuring, they lack the time or the resources to provide the level or kind of care their clients require?

Doing good and benefiting others is much more than a matter of having good intentions. Upon careful examination, the apparent simplicity of the concept of beneficence proves to be somewhat deceptive. Each case that follows illuminates a different feature of beneficence and accentuates different issues.

Case 1: Nurse-Client-Family Conflict

Nursing is committed to a holistic approach to health care. This means viewing the individual client as a whole and in the context of his or her environment and biography. A very important part of this context is the family. It is well-known that other family members may have considerable impact on a client's sickness and health, and on prospects for recovery. Sometimes the family is part of the problem, and therefore must also be part of the solution.

Taking the client seriously in the context of his or her family may raise a number of issues. A conflict may arise between the family and the client, the family and the nurse, or the nurse and the client about the family. Such conflicts become even more difficult to manage when cultural differences are involved, as in the following case:

> *Mrs. A., a young mother, was recently admitted to the hospital for investigation of abdominal pain. No physiological reason has been ascertained for the pain, and the physicians are discussing a psychiatric consult. Doreen Dunn, RN, has been caring for Mrs. A. for a few days now and has been able to talk to her about her present condition. Mrs. A. is very guarded about her personal life, but admits to being "depressed." She attributes her depression to confinement at home alone with two very young children. She has tried talking to her husband about her feelings, but he does not understand why she is unhappy. He is a recent immigrant from a country in which the family is rigidly patriarchical and married women are under the authority of their husbands. He expects a wife to be content with being a homemaker and mother. Mrs. A. came from the same place but has been in Canada much longer. Before she met Mr. A. she worked as a teaching assistant at an elementary school and was very happy in this role. When they were married, she did not realize that her husband was as conservative as he later proved to be.*

> *Mr. A. is very much against psychological counselling, and Mrs. A. is reluctant to go against her husband's wishes. Nurse*

Dunn is not convinced that the problem is psychological, or psychological only, but she is sure that Mrs. A. would benefit from some counselling. "It's obvious that Mrs. A. needs counselling and some outside activity," Nurse Dunn says. "How can I help Mrs. A.?"

Commentary

The major ethical issue in this situation arises from the conflict between Doreen Dunn's belief about what will benefit Mrs. A., and the client's husband's beliefs, which may be culturally and even religiously rooted. Mrs. A. is caught in the middle and is reluctant to assert her own feelings.

What should Nurse Dunn do in this situation? How far should she go in promoting her ideas about what is best for Mrs. A.? If indeed it is the case that what is best for Mrs. A. is not best for Mr. A. or for the family, ought Nurse Dunn to balance concern for Mrs. A. against concern for her family? At what point would Nurse Dunn's actions become unjustifiable intrusions?

From the comments ascribed to her, it appears that Nurse Dunn construes the issue mainly in terms of Mrs. A.'s health needs — at least as Nurse Dunn perceives them. Although she feels strongly that some kind of counselling would be best for Mrs. A., she could be wrong about this. The possibility of disrupting the family dynamics is serious. Such disruption could be very harmful to Mrs. A. or her family. Family roles may be very important to her self-esteem. Whatever good counselling might do would have to be weighed against possible harms.

Considerations about what would be most beneficial are by no means the only relevant factors in this case. Concern for Mrs. A.'s good ought not to eclipse another very important value that comes into play in this case — namely, respect for autonomy. Respect for autonomy means valuing client choice, and the client's right "to the information necessary to make choices and to consent to or refuse care (CNO, 1995). The Canadian Nurses Association (1991) *Code of Ethics for Nursing* states that "based upon respect for clients and regard for their right to control their own care, nursing care reflects respect for the right of choice held by clients" (Value II). In this case, there may be some question whether Mrs. A. is sufficiently autonomous to exercise her "right of choice." How serious is her depression? Under the circumstances, is she able to think clearly? There is little evidence given to suggest that she is mentally incompetent, but if she were Nurse Dunn would not be obliged to honour her present wishes. In that event, Nurse Dunn might understand her role as being that of an advocate on behalf of Mrs. A.'s best interests. Further problems could arise because legally the authority for decision-making would then transfer to Mr. A., and it appears that he sees things differently than Nurse Dunn.

Presuming that competence is not at issue — and it does not appear to be — Mrs. A.'s wishes are of paramount importance. Under the circumstances, ascertaining her true wishes may be difficult. She has opened up to Nurse Dunn, but apparently has not expressed her wishes. Indeed, she may herself be confused or ambivalent about what she would like to do.

Moreover, Mrs. A. appears to be in a coercive situation, and may be afraid to express her wishes in deference to her husband. There is also the possibility of coercive influence on Nurse Dunn's part. The desire to secure a good outcome for Mrs. A. is commendable, but what right would Nurse Dunn have to "tell" Mrs. A. what she should do, especially when in doing so she would risk disrupting the family dynamics? The choice to be made in this situation may indeed be between Mrs. A.'s health and the stability of her relationship with her husband, and perhaps even of the family as a whole. Convinced as Nurse Dunn may be that Mrs. A.'s health is the more important of the two, is this not a choice for Mrs. A. to make? Furthermore, even from the perspective of beneficence alone, a good outcome would probably require Mrs. A.'s cooperation. Shelp (1982) submits that "the duty of beneficence is one of cooperation more than coercion or control" (p. 201). How cooperative is Mrs. A. likely to be if she feels pressured or coerced by Nurse Dunn?

Before coming to any decision about what she herself should do, Nurse Dunn needs to do a more thorough assessment and to explore further a number of questions and issues. Does she really have a good grasp of the dynamics of the situation? What is the basis of Mr. A.'s objections to counselling? What does Mrs. A. really want? How do other members of the health team interpret the situation, and what do they think should be done? The physicians seem inclined to label the problem as being psychological, but perhaps further assessment would suggest something different. There may be useful information in the literature about depression in young mothers, or about approaches to cultural differences. Some guidance may be available from community-based nursing organizations, who may be more familiar with this particular culture and may have suggestions about how best to proceed based on experience in similar cases. At the very least, they would be aware of helpful resources in the community, such as a religious group or a community drop-in centre. Might the extended family be of help?

Additional exploration might disclose other options, but based on the information available Nurse Dunn's options are limited. One option, towards which she seems inclined, would be to encourage Mrs. A. to insist on some kind of counselling, psychological or otherwise. This may be compatible with Nurse Dunn's understanding of client advocacy in nursing. In thus "encouraging" Mrs. A., however, Nurse Dunn should be respectful of her autonomy and sensitive to the possibility of pressuring or coercing her. *Telling* her what to do is different than *advising* her, and different again than *helping* her to explore options and work through her own decisions. The most effective way to intervene could be to explore with Mrs. A. the consequences that might follow from the options available to her and ensure that these are considered in the decision-making. What short-term and long-term effects might it have on the family if she decided against her husband's wishes to go for counselling?

Another option would be to approach Mr. A. in order to win his support. Before doing so, it might be helpful to seek advice from someone who understands Mr. A.'s culture and who may therefore be able to mediate the problem. If he is carefully and thoughtfully approached, perhaps Mr. A. could be brought to understand and empathize with his wife's complaint. It could turn out that Mr. A. has some misconceptions about counselling that could easily be corrected. On the other hand, approaching Mr. A. may have negative consequences. Might this alienate Mr. A. and exacerbate tensions between he and his wife? Confidentiality would be an important concern as well if Nurse Dunn decided to approach Mr. A. She is obligated to hold in confidence any information Mrs. A. may have given her in private discussions. Does she have Mrs. A.'s consent to share such information with Mr. A.? If not, how should she proceed?

Yet another option would be for Nurse Dunn to treat only the immediate symptoms and ignore the broader issues. Knowing that Mrs. A. will continue to experience abdominal pain and that the root problem may worsen, this could be construed as a kind of abandonment. Still, Nurse Dunn may feel that her hands are tied. She might rationalize such a decision by telling herself that in her setting she can give physical care only, and that therefore any intervention in the dynamics of the family would be inappropriate. Arguably, this would be incompatible with the holistic view of the client that nursing generally espouses, and incompatible with the advocacy role in nursing.

The issues with which Nurse Dunn must contend are not untypical. A somewhat similar situation might arise in community nursing when a public health nurse visits a home and sees practices that he or she considers unhealthy. The nurse then must decide how forceful to be in "imposing" his or her views about health on the family. Such a decision is made more challenging if it involves considerations about family dynamics and the integrity of cultural practices that may appear less than ideal to the nurse.

The case of Mrs. A. shows that, all things considered, it is sometimes difficult to decide what course of action would be most beneficial, especially when family dynamics and cultural differences bear on the situation. Considerations of autonomy also come into play, but given Mrs. A.'s reluctance to express herself and the possibility that her autonomy may be in question, in this regard the situation is somewhat ambiguous.

A different issue arises in situations wherein, from the point of view of nursing knowledge, what is best for the client is fairly certain but not what the client wishes. In such circumstances, beneficence is clearly in conflict with autonomy, and the problem of paternalism is especially apparent, as we shall see in the next case.

Case 2: Disagreement Between Nurse and Client

Respect for the client's right of choice anticipates the possibility that the client will choose something that the nurse believes less than optimal, if not positively harmful. Clients may reject or refuse a proposed plan of care for any number of reasons. Quality of life considerations might come into play. The client may be afraid of the proposed treatment because it will involve some pain. There may be concern about draining family resources and being a burden to others.

Whatever the basis of the difference of opinion, nurses find it difficult to care for a client who refuses to cooperate with the treatment plan that they think is best. Schultz and Schultz (1988, p. 46) make the point that conflict with a client makes health professionals feel vulnerable, both because the conflict may become a power struggle and because the client is rejecting what the health professional has to offer. Committed to benefiting the client, and feeling certain in their knowledge of what is best for the client, nurses may find themselves torn between acting paternalistically and respecting autonomy. The following case illustrates such a tension:

Mary Grange and Fran Lapointe work for the Victorian Order of Nurses (VON) and care for people in the community. One of their clients, Mrs. Black, is paraplegic and, among other things, needs help getting in and out of bed. Mary visits her in the morning to help her out of bed and into her wheelchair, and Fran returns in the evening to settle her for the night.

Recently, Mrs. Black developed a pressure sore on her buttock. Mary and Fran advised her to stay off of it in order to promote healing, but she adamantly refused. Meanwhile, the sore got larger. Mary and Fran became convinced that Mrs. Black needs a few weeks of bed rest in order for the sore to heal. Once again, they warned her of the seriousness of the situation, but to no avail. "It's my life," Mrs. Black responded, "and I'll live it my way!"

Mary and Fran are frustrated and would like to refuse to get Mrs. Black out of bed each day, thereby forcing her to stay off the area. However, they are not sure that this would be ethical.

Commentary

The main conflict in this case is between the nurses' desire (and duty) to do what they think is best for the client — to promote the healing of the pressure area — and the client's right to make decisions about her own care. The values in conflict are beneficence and respect for autonomy. The nurses are concerned about Mrs. Black's physical well-being, and rightly so. However, presuming her competence, they are also obliged to respect her right to make treatment decisions. It *seems* that the nurses cannot both respect her autonomy and act in accordance with beneficence at the same time. One value, it *seems*, can be realized only at the expense of the other.

Tragic choices, in which one must choose the lesser of two evils, are an unfortunate fact of life. However, sometimes what at first *seems* to be a tragic choice situation can be resolved in a happier way through careful and creative problem-solving. Whether this is possible in this case is difficult to say based on the limited information available. We lack a great deal of pertinent information about Mrs. Black. Does she live alone? Does she have a family? What supports are available to her in the community? Does she have a family physician who might be able to help or advise?

Any of these questions might have an important bearing on a satisfactory resolution of the issue. In situations of treatment refusal, it is advisable to begin by exploring the client's reasons or motivations for refusing treatment. Why is Mrs. Black refusing? By exploring this question with her, the nurses may find that the refusal is based on a misunderstanding that can be corrected. It may also be helpful to consult with others — perhaps family members or the family physician — to gain further insight into her character. What does staying in bed mean to Mrs. Black? What quality of life does she have while staying in bed? Are there ways that staying in bed could be made less of a burden to her? How exactly would her life be interrupted while in bed? What does staying in bed mean that she cannot do?

In the course of thoughtful and attentive dialogue with Mrs. Black, and further research into the issue, a happy solution might be worked out. Does the literature discuss alternative ways of treating pressure sores? Might there be some compromise treatment that will promote healing but still allow the client some mobility? Certainly all avenues in this direction should be explored.

However, dialogue with Mrs. Black may fail for one reason or another, and a compromise solution may not be feasible. In this event, the nurses will be faced with the dilemma of choosing between what they believe is best for Mrs. Black as concerns her illness and respecting her refusal of their well-informed advice.

Mary and Fran believe that, if the pressure sore on her buttock is to heal, Mrs. Black must stay in bed. Although they are not considering restraining measures, they would in effect be doing the same thing by refusing to help her out of bed. Should they so refuse, the pressure area would likely heal, and Mrs. Black may even later be grateful to them. However, it is also possible that being confined to bed, and especially against her wishes, would have negative psychological effects. Perhaps she would become depressed, or develop anger toward the nurses. At the very least, her relationship with Mary and Fran would probably change, and quite possibly for the worse.

Considerations having to do with the consequences of various options aside, what is owed Mrs. Black by way of respect for autonomy? Would it be justifiable for the nurses to impose on her their plan of care? Mrs. Black, after all, is an adult, and presumably of sound mind. What about her rights and her autonomy?

Yet, it is not clear that respect for autonomy means that a client has the right to active support in situations where nurses believe that what they are being asked to do is harmful. For example, if a client advised to rest an injured leg decides to get up and walk about, is the nurse obliged to assist? One might argue that preventing the client from walking is one thing, and actually helping him or her to walk is another. Respect for autonomy no doubt requires noninterference in someone else's self-regarding choices, but does it require one to assist others to do something one believes to be harmful?

The answer to the above question will depend in part on the extent of the harm one foresees arising from the client's choice. A choice that risks life is more problematic than one that risks inconvenience or minor discomfort. How much harm will come to Mrs. Black if she continues her present regimen? The nurses have informed her that the problem is "serious," but how serious is it, and according to whose standards?

Although the main issue in this case is between beneficence and autonomy, it also indirectly raises an issue of justice. Overriding someone's autonomy for reasons of beneficence is a different matter than doing so for reasons of justice. Mary and Fran have obligations to other clients besides Mrs. Black. If Mrs. Black does not allow her sore to heal and, consequently, requires more and more attention as the sore worsens, this would take time away from Mary's and Fran's schedules. Depending on how full their caseloads are, continuing to comply with Mrs. Black's wishes could mean that they will have less time to spend with other clients, who might therefore receive less than optimal care. Mary and Fran may feel less obliged to accept Mrs. Black's choice if doing so meant that other clients would be adversely affected.

Given the limited information available, in the case of Mrs. Black considerations of justice are only marginal. In the next case they are much more explicit.

Case 3: The Good of One Versus the Good of Many

Traditionally, the focus of beneficence in nursing, as in the health professionals more generally, has been the individual client. The *Code for Nurses with Interpretive Statements* of the American Nurses' Association (ANA, [1976] 1985), for example, states that "the nurse's primary commitment is to the health, welfare, and safety of the client" (Statement 3.1). The possibility exists, however, that the nurse's commitment to an *individual* client might come into conflict with his or her commitment to other clients, or more generally to society. How is the nurse to balance concern for the good of one against concern for the good of many?

The need for such balancing might arise in any number of circumstances. For example, pressed for time, a nurse might feel that he or she can do what is best for a particular client only at the expense of others who are also in need. In such cases, beneficence and justice overlap, as the following case shows:

While working in the community, a number of nurses recognized the need for a daycare centre for people with Alzheimer's disease. After much hard work, a program was organized. One man, Mr. Dobbs, who would otherwise be alone all day, has been attending. The problem is that when he is taken home at the end of the program each day, he sometimes does not recognize his home and refuses to stay. There is a gap of two hours before his daughter comes home. Several nurses, including the program supervisor, are concerned that not only Mr. Dobbs but the whole program is being put at risk by leaving him alone outside of his home. They have raised the matter with Mr. Dobbs' family and asked them to take charge of him for the two-hour period. The family refused to do so, claiming that their father is just "pretending" and will be perfectly safe. After much discussion about the problem, the supervisor is reluctantly considering discharging Mr. Dobbs from the program altogether.

Commentary

In this case there appears to be a conflict between the obligation to provide benefit for one individual as against providing benefit for a greater number. A similar issue might arise with regard to discharging clients from acute treatment facilities when needed resources are unavailable in the community. A particular client may be deriving minimal benefit from the treatment available but, given the lack of other options and resources, this may be the best care that he or she can get. At the same time, however, by using resources the client may be depriving others of treatment who may be in a condition to benefit more. What is the responsibility of the nurse to advocate for the needs of the individual client over the needs of the many who may be waiting? Ought the nurse to compromise his or her commitment to the individual client in consideration of possible benefit to others?

In this case, it is feared that, if Mr. Dobbs continues in the program and is left unattended at the end of the day, he may come to some harm. This could cause bad publicity for the program, and perhaps even law suits. Ultimately, the program could be cancelled. Should this happen, all those people who benefit from the program would be deprived of this benefit, as would those who might benefit in the future. On the other hand, discharging Mr. Dobbs from the program would be to deprive him of a benefit. If there is a risk that he might come to harm in the space of two hours between the end of the program day and the arrival of his daughter, the risk is even greater if he is left alone all day. Moreover, if the program risks negative publicity in keeping him as a participant, it surely risks bad publicity in the event that, having discharged him, he comes to some harm.

Whichever option is chosen, some harm might come to Mr. Dobbs, and the program might be jeopardized. How ought these options to be weighed? Adopting a utilitarian approach, the nurses would choose the option that, all things considered, would produce the greatest good for the greatest number. This would involve calculating the balance of benefits and harms that would follow as consequences from each option to determine which had the greatest net benefit. Such a calculation might well tip the scale on the side of discharging Mr. Dobbs from the program. Yet having already established a relationship with Mr. Dobbs, this would be to fail in one's duty to him. On the other side of the issue, however, the nurses also have a duty to others in the program, and to others who might benefit from the program in the future.

Neither option identified above is ideal, but fortunately there may be a happy way out of the dilemma of choosing between them. The family is of crucial importance in this regard. The opinion on the basis of which they are unwilling to assume some responsibility for their father seems quite bizarre. Given Mr. Dobbs' condition, the fact they believe he is just "pretending" not to recognize his house requires some explanation. It suggests either denial or profound ignorance on their part. How have they arrived at this opinion?

The case information does not indicate exactly what took place in the initial meeting, but another carefully planned meeting with the family could prove to be more fruitful. Clearly they could benefit from education about their father's condition. To this end, it might be helpful to involve a representative or advocate from some support group who might be able to give the family better insight into Alzheimer's disease. At the very least, it should be possible to persuade them that their father is in danger if left alone. If they could be brought to see this, and to appreciate as well that the future of the program is at stake, it is likely that they would agree to assume some responsibility for their father after he is discharged each day.

Failing the family's cooperation, other resources may be available in the community to give interim care to Mr. Dobbs. Perhaps a homemaker or some kind of "sitter" or "companion" could be arranged to cover the two-hour gap. Some reasonable arrangement should be possible. If not, however, and if it is decided that Mr. Dobbs is jeopardizing the program, a decision will have to be made between the good of Mr. Dobbs and the good of others who benefit and will benefit from the program's continued existence.

Conclusion

The health good of clients is rightly regarded as a matter of primary concern for those who are trusted with the duty to promote health and provide health care. In this chapter, we have seen that caring for others in a manner befitting professional nurses poses considerable challenges. In some cases, there may be uncertainty about how much giving and caring beneficence requires of the nurse. In other cases, there may be uncertainty or disagreement about which course of action will be the most beneficial. In yet other cases, the commitment to the good of an individual may be in conflict with the commitment to the good of others.

Even when the requirements of beneficence are relatively clear to the nurse, other ethical issues may arise when other values are also at stake in the situation. The client's values and wishes may be incompatible with the nurse's values, or with the plan of care the nurse believes to be most beneficial. In such situations, the nurse must weigh concern for the client's health good against respect for the client's autonomy or right to choose. Unchecked, the nurse's commendable desire to do good can easily slide into paternalism. Ethics may not forbid paternalism, but at the very least it requires that one be prepared to give justifications if one puts the client's autonomy second to the client's good.

Notes

1   The word "benevolence" is closely related in meaning to beneficence, but whereas beneficence has to do with *good deeds or acts*, benevolence has to do with *good wishes or intentions*. Reeder (1982) distinguishes the two as follows: "Benevolence, as I use it, names a disposition to desire and act so as to increase good and decrease evil for human beings; beneficence signifies a principle or ideal of conduct" (p. 83).

2   The rhetoric of caring, particularly as "caring" is set against "curing," has been increasingly called into question in recent years. For example, see Diers (1988) and Levine (1989).

3   The standards document from which this definition is extracted is currently being revised.

4   A more complete discussion of various means by which duty can be grounded or derived is given in Abrams (1982).

5   For example, the introduction to the American Nurses' Association ([1976] 1985, iii) *Code for Nurses with Interpretive Statements* expresses the obligations of the nurse in terms of a contract with society.

6   Jameton (1984, pp. 214-216) analyzes this issue with reference to the concept of justice.

7   In answering this question, one must also consider the possibility of "burn-out," for if this happens the nurse will not be much good to anyone.

8   Jameton (1984, p. 216) suggests that the nurse consider several points before undertaking personal risk, such as the degree and urgency of client need as weighed against the gravity of the risk as *assessed realistically*. This is good advice, especially when one considers issues that have arisen in connection with Acquired Immunodeficiency Syndrome (AIDS) and often exaggerated concerns about personal risks in caring for people with AIDS. For a discussion of the rights and responsibilities of nurses caring for person's with HIV, see Yeo (1995).

9   Debra Shogan (1988) expresses the same distinction in terms of "caring about" and "caring for." She points out:

> One can care for (tend to) someone or something and not care about the person or thing and one can care about someone or something and not care for (tend to) it. Those in the 'helping professions,' for example, tend to (care for) others as part of their work responsibilities; they may not care about these people, although often they do. (pp. 7-8)

Buchanan (1982, pp. 35-36) also has an insightful discussion of these two aspects of beneficence.

10   This definition has since been updated (see Spasoff et al., 1987, p. 1).

11   For a discussion of a definition of health that has been very influential in Canadian nursing, see Kravitz and Frey (1989).

12   Shogan (1988, p. 17), for example, restricts beneficence to include only concern for the welfare of others, and uses the term "caring" to encompass concern for the other in a broader and more inclusive sense.

References

Abrams, N. (1982). Scope of beneficence in health care. In E.E. Shelp (Ed.), *Beneficence and health care* (pp. 183-198). Dordrecht, Holland: D. Reidel.

American Nurses' Association. ([1976] 1985). *Code for nurses with interpretive statements*. Kansas City: Author.

Beauchamp, T.L., & Childress, J.F. (1989). *Principles of biomedical ethics* (3rd. ed.). New York: Oxford University Press.

Benner, P., & Wrubel, J. (1989). *The primacy of caring: Stress and coping in health and illness*. Menlo Park, CA: Addison-Wesley.

Buchanan, A.E. (1982). Philosophical foundations of beneficence. In E.E. Shelp (Ed.), *Beneficence and health care* (pp. 33-62). Dordrecht, Holland: D. Reidel.

Callahan, D. (1973). The WHO definition of "health." *Hastings Center Studies, 1* (3), 77-87.

Canadian Medical Association. (1990). *Code of ethics*. Ottawa: Author.

Canadian Nurses Association. (1987). *A definition of nursing practice, standards for nursing practice*. Ottawa: Author.

Canadian Nurses Association. (1991). *Code of ethics for nursing*. Ottawa: Author.

College of Nurses of Ontario. (1990). *The standards of nursing practice for registered nurses and registered nursing assistants*. Toronto: Author.

College of Nurses of Ontario. (1995). The ethical framework for nursing in Ontario. In *Guidelines for professional behaviour* (pp 6-17). Toronto: Author.

Diers, D. (1988). On clinical scholarship — again. *Image: Journal of Nursing Scholarship, 20* (1), 2.

Dworkin, G. (1971). Paternalism. In R.A. Wasserstrom (Ed.), *Morality and the law* (pp. 107-126). Belmont, CA: Wadsworth.

Gadow, S.A. (1985). Nurse and patient: The caring relationship. In A.H. Bishop & J.R. Scudder Jr. (Eds.), *Caring, curing, coping: Nurse, physician, patient relationships* (pp. 31-43). Birmingham, AL: University of Alabama Press.

International Council of Nurses. ([1973] 1982). *Code for nurses: Ethical concepts applied to nursing.* Geneva: Author.

Jameton, A.L. (1984). *Nursing practice: The ethical issues.* Englewood Cliffs, NJ: Prentice-Hall.

Jamiesan, E.M., Sewall, M.F., & Suhrie, E.B. (1966). *Trends in nursing history: Their social, international and ethical relationships.* Philadelphia: W.B. Saunders.

Kravitz, M, & Frey, M.A. (1989). The Allen nursing model. In J.J. Fitzpatrick & A.L. Whall (Eds.), *Conceptual models of nursing: Analysis and applications* (2nd ed., pp. 313-329). East Norwalk, CT: Appleton & Lange.

Levine, M. (1989). The ethics of nursing research. *Image: Journal of Nursing Scholarship, 21* (1), 4-6.

MacPherson, K.I. (1989). A new perspective on nursing and caring in a corporate context. *Advances in Nursing Science, 11* (4), 32-39.

Pellegrino, E.D., & Thomasma, D.C. (1988). *For the patient's good: The restoration of beneficence in health care.* New York: Oxford University Press.

Reeder, J.P. Jr. (1982). Beneficence, supererogation, and role duty. In E.E. Shelp (Ed.), *Beneficence and health care* (pp. 83-108). Dordrecht, Holland: D. Reidel.

Schultz, P., & Schultz, R. (1988). Discussion group summary; Family and community dimensions of the ethics of care with chronically ill persons. In J. Watson & M.A. Ray (Eds.), *The ethics of care and the ethics of cure* (pp. 45-48). New York: National League for Nursing.

Shelp, E.E. (1982). To benefit and respect persons: A challenge for beneficence in health care. In E.E. Shelp (Ed.), *Beneficence and health care* (pp. 199-222). Dordrecht, Holland: D. Reidel.

Shogan, D.A. (1988). *Care and moral motivation.* Toronto: OISE Press.

Spasoff, R.A., Cole, P., Dale, F., Korn, D., Manga, P., Marshall, V., Picherack, F., Shosenberg, N., & Zon, L. (1987). *Health for all Ontario: Report of the panel on health goals for Ontario.* Toronto: Author.

Veatch, R.M., & Fry, S.T. (1987). *Case studies in nursing ethics.* Philadelphia: J.B. Lippincott.

Watson, J. (1979). *Nursing: The philosophy and science of caring*. Boston: Little, Brown, and Company.

Yeo, M. (1995). ED personnel's safety vs. a duty to treat. In K.V. Iserson, A.B. Sanders, & D. Mathieu (Eds.), *Ethics in emergency medicine* (2nd ed., pp. 406-12). Tucson, Arizona: Galen Press.

STUDY QUESTIONS: BENEFICENCE

Case 1: Nurse-Client-Family Conflict

1. In deciding what to do in this case, ought Nurse Dunn to weigh considerations about what is good for the family as a whole alongside considerations about what is good for Mrs. A.? (That is, assuming that the two goods may not be convergent.)

2. The health care system is designed to deal specifically with health concerns and problems. Is Mrs. A.'s problem, strictly speaking, a health problem — or a health problem *only*? Are there components of her problem that fall outside the scope and mandate of the health care system?

3. Suppose Nurse Dunn is a committed feminist and is contemptuous of what she believes is a "pattern of domination" in the A. family. Should her beliefs and values about such things enter into her relationship with the family and in her decision-making?

4. Imagine that in the course of further discussion, Mrs. A. confides to Nurse Dunn that her husband is sometimes physically abusive with her. How would this change the issue?

Case 2: Disagreement Between Nurse and Client

1. Discuss the statement: "The very fact that the nurses are unable to persuade Mrs. Black to accept their advice is itself indicative of a major failure on their part."

2. The boundaries between "informing," "persuading," "manipulating," and "coercing" may be fuzzy. Discuss this problem with reference to possible strategies the nurses might adopt in presenting their plan of care to Mrs. Black.

3. Suppose that the consequences of treatment refusal were life-threatening. Would this justify a more aggressive approach on the part of the nurses?

4. Would it make any difference if this case took place in a nursing home or hospital setting rather than in the client's home?

Case 3: The Good of One Versus the Good of Many

1. What are the rights and responsibilities of Mr. Dobbs' family?

2. If the situation continued the same, and Mr. Dobbs came to serious harm, would the daycare centre be to blame for this? Would anyone?

3. Not much information is given to indicate Mr. Dobbs' decision-making capabilities. What relevance would such information have to the issues at hand?

4. What bearing might the mission statement and terms of reference of the daycare program have on the resolution of this issue?

AUTONOMY

I am the master of my fate
I am the captain of my soul.

— William Ernest Henley, *Invictus*

Autonomy means self-determination, the right to make indepen-
dent decisions concerning one's own life and well-being. When
the client's exercise of autonomy seems inconsistent with health
goals, health professionals — educated and oriented primarily
toward restoring, maintaining, and preserving health — may be
tempted to impede the client's autonomy in one way or another.
Under what conditions is it justifiable to impede or restrict client
autonomy? Issues of autonomy are sometimes complicated when
there is uncertainty whether the client is mentally competent to
assess various treatments or procedures and to give a properly
informed consent.

The cases in this chapter include a conflict between a nurse and
a client whose dietary preference poses a serious health risk; a
challenge for a nurse working in a residential facility in which
client autonomy is not highly valued; and an informed consent
problem arising in a research context in which the client is at the
same time a research subject.

The Nature of Autonomy

In the past, health professionals, and physicians especially, were entrusted with broader authority for decision-making in health care than they are today. Often the wishes of the client were not solicited, and even if known were sometimes ignored. Frequently, information was withheld or presented in a misleading way in order to avoid causing the client worry or harm. The early development of nursing as an adjunct to medical care made nurses partners in these practices. Many nurses today can remember when as students they were instructed not to give clients such basic information as their temperature, blood pressure, or even the name of their medication.

Such practices were supported and rationalized in terms of the paternalistic notion that "the doctor knows best." However commendable the motivation behind this paternalism, it is no longer acceptable today. Over the past forty years, clients have come to demand greater autonomy, and respect for autonomy has been enshrined in the codes of ethics of the various health professions. Payton (1979, p. 23) cites three main factors leading to this increase in the perceived value of autonomy in health care: a more educated and informed public, the recognition of the personal and collective power of clients, and increased awareness of the hypocrisy of promoting the rights of the individual while treating the individual as a helpless nonentity.

Literally, autonomy means self-rule. In ancient Greece, it had a predominantly political meaning. A political state would be autonomous only if it determined its own laws. A state would not be autonomous if, like a colony, it was ruled by another state and governed by laws it did not give itself. At the level of the individual, we could say that children lack autonomy insofar as they are not sufficiently mature to be trusted to govern themselves and so are subject to rules unilaterally laid down by parental authorities.

In the broadest sense, autonomy means self-determination, but several more specific meanings can be distinguished. Since these meanings are often confused, it is helpful to be able to sort them out. Borrowing from Miller (1981, pp. 24-25), we can specify four main meanings of autonomy: (1) autonomy as free action; (2) autonomy as effective deliberation; (3) autonomy as authenticity; and (4) autonomy as moral reflection.[1]

1. Autonomy as Free Action

This is probably the most common meaning of autonomy, both in health care contexts and more generally throughout society. Conceived as free action, autonomy is very similar in meaning to liberty. It means being able to do what one wishes to do, or conversely not being forced to do what one does not want to do. My autonomy is diminished when someone or something presents itself as an obstacle to my freedom. Sickness may be such an obstacle or impediment insofar as it reduces abilities or powers. Having had a stroke, one may no longer have the freedom to do certain things once taken for granted. After a hip injury, an elderly person may become considerably less independent. Much rehabilitation involves helping someone to restore diminished powers, or to cope as best as possible with what abilities remain intact.

The obstacle or impediment to autonomy may also be another person. I want to go outside for a walk, so I put my coat on and go outside. I have done what I wanted to do. If a young child wants to go outside for a walk, the matter is different. The child may have to ask a parent. The parent, for one reason or other, may say no, or otherwise curtail the child's freedom.

In the health care context, there are a number of circumstances in which clients may be deprived of freedom by others. The mental health setting provides the clearest examples. Locked doors and barred windows in a psychiatric hospital are designed to prevent residents from doing what they have a mind to do. In some instances, a client may be forced to take a sedative against his or her will. In these contexts especially, autonomy is often discussed in terms of rights, such as the right to refuse treatment. Interference with autonomy (in the basic sense of liberty or free action) is usually justified by the claim that the client is not autonomous in some other sense, such as one of those considered below.

2. Autonomy as Effective Deliberation

This sense of autonomy has to do with the rationality of a person's thought process. Has the person arrived at the choice through a process of reasoning that is at least minimally rational? Are the means of action chosen consistent with the end or outcome desired? Might the person have erred in deliberation and so be confused about how best to accomplish what he or she intends?

In some instances, the integrity of the thought process may be compromised by false assumptions or lack of information. Consider someone suffering with terminal brain cancer who has expressed the goal of dying peacefully and with as much dignity as possible. Suppose that the person refuses a certain palliative treatment believing that it will only prolong life and work counter to desired goals. If in fact the person is mistaken in this belief, the treatment refusal would not be consistent with the outcome desired. To this extent the treatment refusal, since following from reasoning based on a false premise, would not be autonomous. Similarly, someone trying to decide between various treatment options would not be able to deliberate effectively if information relevant to an informed decision were lacking.

The thought process itself may also be impaired by various causes such as mental illness. A young girl with anorexia nervosa who refuses to eat because she does not want to get fat is not thinking rationally. A person suffering from schizophrenia may not understand or intend the consequences of an entertained course of action.

3. Autonomy as Authenticity

Autonomy as authenticity has to do with the relationship between a given choice of action and one's total being or character. Is the choice expressed consistent with the settled dispositions, values, and character of the person? Does it express who the person really is in some deep and abiding sense, or is it something of an anomaly, perhaps less an expression of the person's true self than of some momentary influence?

Pain or sickness may constitute a major assault and cause someone to behave "out of character." In such circumstances, what the person wants to do may be less an expression of character or identity than of the pain or sickness. Autonomy may be compromised by such factors to the extent that the person is no longer being his or her self.

4. Autonomy as Moral Reflection

Choices express values, and one may be more or less self-conscious about the values expressed in one's choices. Moral reflection involves becoming aware of the values dimension of one's choices, and choosing consistently with values and principles that have been subjected to thoughtful examination. Have the values informing the choice been freely and deliberately chosen, or have they been adopted unconsciously and uncritically?

Autonomy as moral reflection is similar in meaning to autonomy as authenticity, but in addition to consistency requires a certain measure of self-examination. People who fail to consider the impact of their decisions on others may be acting authentically provided this is consistent with who they typically are, yet they may not be autonomous in this sense insofar as they have not reflected on the values guiding their action. Do they know they are being selfish or arrogant? Has an explicit choice been made to be that sort of person?

In the context of health care, autonomy may be used in one or several of the senses distinguished above.[2] This may give rise to confusion. Arguments about issues rooted in autonomy may be at cross-purposes if different people have in mind different meanings of the concept.

Autonomy, Competence[3], and Informed Consent

Issues having to do with autonomy are mainly of two sorts. Sometimes what is at issue is *respect* for the client's autonomy. Given that the client is capable of acting autonomously in some relevant sense, what obligations do health professionals have to help facilitate or promote action in accordance with autonomy? What is required as concerns making available to clients the means (e.g., information, treatments) by which they will be able to realize their autonomy? Conversely, under what circumstances is it justifiable for health professionals to stand in the way of or not cooperate with clients seeking to realize their autonomous choices?

In other instances, what is at issue is not how or whether to comply with or promote the client's autonomy but rather whether the client is really autonomous or capable of making autonomous choices. Even when a client expresses a will to do something, and seems determined to do it, it may be doubtful whether this is what he or she *really* wants, or whether the choice was *really* made autonomously. Is there evidence of some cognitive deficit or emotional problem that might have diminished the capacity for rational deliberation? Could the person be ignorant of certain things relevant to an informed choice? Is there any evidence of coercive influences? Thinking along these lines leads quickly to controversy. How is the nurse to decide what the client really wants? By what criteria might the nurse pronounce a client's choice sufficiently nonautonomous as to stand in the way of its enactment?

Most accounts of autonomy specify that to act autonomously one must have both a certain minimum of relevant knowledge or information and the freedom to act on the basis of one's choices. Accordingly, respect for autonomy in health care settings may be expressed both in terms of the ideals of information-sharing and client involvement in health care planning. Informed consent is closely linked to autonomy insofar as it promotes both of these ideals.[4]

Informed consent, like autonomy, has both a cognitive (informational) and a volitional (decisional) aspect.[5] The cognitive aspect of informed consent has to do with how well the client understands things related to the choice in question. How can the practitioner decide whether the client really does understand the options? How much information about proposed treatments and alternatives, and about risks and benefits, is the practitioner obliged to disclose? What constitutes a truly *informed* choice?

The volitional aspect of informed consent has to do with the voluntariness of the choice. What situational factors might impinge on the voluntariness of the choice? Are other people in a position to exert a coercive influence? How can we distinguish such things as coercion, manipulation, persuasion, influence, and advice? What constitutes a truly *voluntary* choice?

Both in terms of understanding and voluntariness, informed consent admits of degrees. One can be more or less informed, and can act more or less voluntarily. What degree of understanding is required for informed consent? What degree of voluntariness?

Questions related to mental competence are particularly relevant as concerns the cognitive aspect of informed consent. Competence is closely linked in meaning to autonomy in the sense of capacity for effective deliberation. It has to do with the mental capacity for informed choosing. Is the person mature enough to choose? Are reasoning powers intact?

Whether clients are mentally competent has a bearing on how much authority they should be given or allowed in decisions concerning their own welfare. Many issues, such as whether to comply with a client's decision, reduce to the question, "Is the client competent to choose?" Respect for autonomy does not require health professionals to comply with substantially nonautonomous choices.

Assessing Competence or Capacity

Given that treatment issues often turn upon whether the client is competent, standards used to measure, determine, and test competence are bound to be controversial. Appelbaum, Lidz, and Meisel (1987) analyze competence in terms of the client's ability to meet one or more of four tests: "evidencing a choice; actually understanding the information about the treatment under consideration; engaging in decision-making in a rational way, with an appreciation of potential outcomes; and making a decision about the treatment that is itself reasonable" (p. 88). Some of these standards are stricter than others. A client who satisfies one standard may not satisfy another.

Which standard, or combinations of standards, is most appropriate? Some writers have proposed a sliding scale for assessing competence, the standard to vary according to the consequences of the decision at hand. Thus a high standard of competence would be used for a decision with grave consequences and a lower standard for one upon which little hung in the balance (Drane, 1988). Moreover, different standards of competence may be appropriate in different contexts. Someone may be competent for some purposes (e.g., treatment refusal) but not for others (e.g., the management of financial affairs).

As a matter of fact, and regrettably so, providers sometimes form opinions about a client's competence based not on any explicit standard of competence but rather based on whether the client's views about treatment converge with their own. The client who is non-compliant, or who elects for an option contrary to what is recommended, is therefore deemed to be incompetent. In such instances, the client's apparently "irrational" decision is taken as evidence of incompetence under the presumption that no one in his or her "right mind" would make such a decision.

This line of thinking is not defensible. That someone makes a decision that appears foolish or stupid to others, or that a client disagrees or refuses to comply with the plan of care favoured by the health team, does not by itself prove that he or she is incompetent. For example, it could be that the decision, although "irrational" from the point of view of others, is consistent with his or her religious or cultural beliefs. Granted, some might further charge that these cultural or religious beliefs are themselves irrational. However, in a multicultural, pluralistic society, it is inappropriate for the health care system or those working within it to decide which beliefs are rational and which are not.

To be sure, the fact that a client chooses something apparently "irrational" from the standpoint of the health professional may be a good reason for deciding that an assessment of competency would be appropriate. However, indications that signal the need for a competency assessment ought not to be confused with legitimate tests of competence to be used in such assessments.

To understand competency assessment it is important to distinguish the *outcome of a given decision-making process* (the decision itself) from the *process by which the decision is reached*, including the context and constraints that bear on the process. Competency assessment gages the latter; not so much the *what* as the *how* of decision-making. The task of assessment is to determine if the person, given his or her mental state and other possible constraining factors, is *capable* of making an informed choice.

To emphasize this element of capability, some commentators use the term "capacity" in place of the term "competence", and this is the legal term of choice in some jurisdictions (for example, Ontario).[6] Understood in this way, a person would be deemed to be competent, or to have the capacity for informed choice, if he or she

a) *understands* information relevant to making a decision about the specific treatment

b) *appreciates* the reasonable foreseeable consequences of the decision or of failing to making a decision.

Both conditions or criteria must be met for a positive assessment. These general criteria can be further elaborated. With respect to information, it needs to be determined whether the client understands

- his or her condition for which treatment is recommended

- the nature of the recommended treatment

- the risks and benefits of the recommended treatment

- the alternative treatments, including no treatment

In addition, it is also necessary to establish that

- the person acknowledges that treatment is recommended

- the person understands that and how the proposed treatment or lack of treatment can affect his or her quality of life

- the person's decision is not substantially based on a delusional belief

It is important to keep in mind that these criteria are intended to establish whether the client is *capable* of making a rational choice and not whether whatever choice the client might make is rational.

Mental illness is often linked with incapacity, but not always or necessarily so. Being mentally ill does not automatically mean that the person cannot deliberate effectively and process information with understanding and appreciation. For example, many people with schizophrenia live independently in the community and, notwithstanding that they have a diagnosed mental illness, nonetheless have the capacity to decide their affairs in much the same way as everyone else does.

In this regard, it should be noted that competence or capacity can fluctuate over time. For example, the schizophrenic who goes off medication may as a consequence become impaired to the point of losing the capacity to make specific treatment choices. A person with Alzheimer's disease may exhibit the "sundowning effect": The ability to reason and deliberate is relatively intact in the morning but diminishes considerably toward the end of the day.

Ordinarily, capacity should be assumed unless there is good reason to doubt that the client is capable of making an autonomous decision. Evidence of confused or delusional thinking, severe pain or anxiety, severe depression, and impairment by drugs or alcohol do not alone establish that the client lacks capacity. However, such signs may be reason enough to question whether the client has the capacity for informed choice and serve thereby as indications that a capacity assessment might be appropriate.

Deciding For Others

If a client lacks the capacity for informed choice, it falls to others to decide on his or her behalf. Depending on the circumstances, this substitute decision-maker may be a family member, a friend, a lover, or even a court-appointed guardian.

There are two standards by which substitute decision-making may be guided. One is to decide in accordance with the client's wishes, the other with reference to the client's best interests.

1. Client's Wishes and Advance Directives

Autonomy has chiefly to do with being in control of one's life and as far as possible being able to shape one's life in accordance with one's own desires, hopes, beliefs, and values. That someone loses the capacity to make informed choices does not mean that autonomy is no longer a consideration in decision-making about him or her. In such instances, and indeed perhaps especially in such instances, respect for autonomy remains a central value. This is so not because the client who is now incapacitated may at some later point be restored to autonomy. In some cases, this may be extremely unlikely or even impossible. Rather, respect for autonomy continues to be of importance because or insofar as the client once was autonomous, and such desires, hopes, beliefs, and values as he or she affirmed at that time may continue to be relevant.

The substitute decision-maker exhibits respect for autonomy to the extent that he or she is guided by the client's wishes. Faced with a decision about treatment for an incompetent person, the substitute decision-maker's ideal is to decide as the client would if the client had the capacity to decide.

The substitute decision-maker will be in a better position to approximate this ideal the better he or she knows the client and the more information he or she has about the client's wishes. Living wills or advance directives can be effective ways for people who are now competent to express their wishes concerning how they would like to be treated in the event of becoming incapacitated.[7]

Such directives usually have two components. The proxy component designates the person who is to act as substitute decision-maker. The directive component provides instructions to the substitute decision-maker about the person's wishes. This instruction may in a general way indicate the client's wishes or values relevant to treatment decisions — such as how he or she feels about risk-taking or quality of life issues — or may be very specific about particular conditions that might arise and preferences regarding treatment options for those conditions.[8]

2. Client's Best Interests

When prior wishes are unknown, the substitute decision-maker must make a decision based on the person's best interests. This means asking the following sorts of questions:

- will the person's situation be improved by the treatment?

- will the person's situation improve or likely improve without the treatment?

- will the expected benefits outweigh expected risk of harm to the person?

- is the proposed treatment the least harmful, invasive and restrictive treatment that meets the requirements listed above?

Obviously, there is an element of subjectivity in all these considerations, but this is unavoidable. Regardless, the point is that when the client's wishes are unknown the guiding goal of the substitute decision-maker is to promote the client's best interests, as best as these interests can be determined.

Informed Consent in Practice

Informed consent raises numerous issues, and may put nurses at odds with other health practitioners. In the past, there has been considerable resistance to informed consent in the medical profession, as there has been to autonomy more generally. Some physicians (e.g., Ingelfinger, 1972) have argued that clients are largely incapable of understanding the sometimes complex science behind treatment options. Others, openly paternalistic, have expressed the worry that if given a choice the client may choose "the wrong thing," or that the information may somehow be harmful (Loftus & Fries, 1979).

Largely because of legal and institutional strictures, attitudes are changing. Even so, the process of obtaining informed consent often amounts to little more than an empty ritual enacted to satisfy the letter of the law. For this reason, Beauchamp (1989, pp. 181-182) distinguishes what he calls "legal" or "institutional consent," which may have little to do with promoting autonomy, from consent for which the client has given "autonomous authorization," and which truly does promote autonomy.

In some circumstances, nurses are responsible for obtaining informed consent, but more often they are involved less directly. Davis (1988, pp. 91-92) describes five main roles that nurses play in the informed consent process: Watchdog, advocate, resource person, coordinator, and facilitator. The nurses interviewed in her study are probably quite typical. They assisted by means such as deepening the client's understanding of the options and responding to specific questions. Often, they explored with clients the meanings of words that appeared on consent forms or that their physicians used.

In her study, Davis found that nurses tend to view informed consent as a process that occurs over time rather than the one-time, all-or-nothing affair to which institutional consent frequently amounts. It is telling that in many of the examples she gives nursing involvement occurred only *after* informed consent, in an official or institutional sense, had been solicited and obtained. This underscores the fact that nurses may view informed consent somewhat differently than it is institutionally understood and practised. Indeed, many nurses interviewed claimed that "assessment of patient comprehension was usually superficial and perfunctory" (Davis, 1988, p. 90).

Whatever role they adopt, nurses must make decisions about what, how, and when, to tell clients by way of facilitating informed participation in their plan of care. Such decisions may be complicated by the fact that the nurse's relationship with the client is part of a complex set of relationships that includes others on the health care team, the institution, and the client's family and significant others. The legally defined roles, wishes, and expectations of these others must be considered in decision-making, and conflicts may arise under a number of different circumstances.

Autonomy, Advocacy, and Empowerment

Nurse involvement in promoting autonomy may be more or less active, depending in part on how broadly he or she conceives autonomy. The consumer model of health care, for example, tends to conceive autonomy in relatively narrow terms as free action, and thus reduces the nurse to an instrument of the client's wishes. Respect for autonomy means little more than noninterference. Concerned above all to avoid paternalistic intervention, the nurse declines to participate in decision-making other than to provide information or technical assistance. The client is viewed primarily as a bearer of rights and is left alone to make decisions. Consumerism says to the individual, "You have been informed about your options, now do what you like."

More active roles for the nurse in promoting client autonomy tend to build on deeper conceptions of autonomy which link it with such notions as empowerment, control, and authenticity. "Respect for patient autonomy," Storch (1988) writes, "essentially means that patients be kept as much in command of themselves, their symptoms, and their situation as possible" (p. 215). Viewed along these lines, the nurse's role is to assist the client to assume command in a situation in which, for any number of reasons, he or she may feel very much out of control. Implicit here is a graduated conception of autonomy incorporating the possibility that the client, at least initially, may not be in a position fully to exercise autonomy. Perhaps disoriented by sickness or the loss of control that sometimes comes with being in an alien environment, the client may need help to regain autonomy.

Gadow's (1980) notion of existential advocacy is another example of how respect for autonomy can be construed in more active terms. "The ideal which existential advocacy expresses," she writes, is "that individuals be *assisted* by nursing to *authentically* exercise their freedom of self-determination" (p. 85). Existential advocacy views the nurse as co-experiencing the situation with the client in order to assist him or her to make an authentic decision.[9] Gadow continues:

> It is the effort to help persons *become clear about what they want* to do, by helping them discern and clarify their values in the situation, and on the basis of that self-examination, to reach decisions which express their reaffirmed, perhaps recreated, complex of values. (p. 85)

In this view, advocacy goes beyond merely ensuring that the client's wishes are considered and respected (e.g., as in accordance with consumerism) to include helping the client to clarify relevant values, and in this light to decide what he or she really wants to do.[10]

The kind of depth interaction Gadow proposes can not be equally attained with all clients, and in some cases is not possible at all. This is especially obvious with so-called "silent patients" who are unable to express their preferences. Gadow (1989, p. 535) notes that in our dealings with silent patients the concept of autonomy may seem inappropriate, and "other moral approaches such as utilitarianism and beneficence are tempting alternatives" to autonomy-oriented advocacy. If autonomy is represented in the image of the fully alert and mentally competent adult processing information and weighing alternatives, it is clear that silent patients are not autonomous, and advocating on behalf of their autonomy would make no sense. However, autonomy can also be interpreted in terms of authenticity and consistency with one's values. Although silent patients obviously can not assess treatment options in light of preferred values, those who make choices on behalf of silent patients can, insofar as they know enough about the individual to project what he or she would decide if able now to do so. Respect for autonomy, in such cases, requires that decisions now taken on behalf of the individual be consistent with what is known about his or her values.

Limiting Autonomy: Paternalism and Justice

There is much controversy about conditions under which it is justifiable to limit, restrict, or otherwise interfere with someone's autonomy. The issue is complicated by the fact that what constitutes an infringement of autonomy depends on how autonomy is defined.

In general, health professionals infringe on client autonomy in two main ways: through information control (e.g., withholding information, equivocation, and deception) or through impeding the client's ability to act upon his or her wishes (e.g., refusal to assist, constraint, and compulsory treatment). In the past, one of the major affronts to client autonomy was the practice of deception. Increased respect for autonomy in health care settings has gone hand-in-hand with the enhancement of the value of truthtelling.

In considering limitations on autonomy, it is important to distinguish reasons for infringing autonomy which appeal to the good of the person whose autonomy is being limited from reasons that appeal to the good of some other party. Restricting or limiting people's autonomy for their own good is what is meant by paternalism.[11] The circumstances under which paternalism arises as an issue may vary widely, and accordingly we can distinguish different varieties of paternalism, some of which are more acceptable than others.

A widely accepted variety of paternalism is what Feinberg (1971) calls "weak paternalism," which justifies intervention in order to prevent someone from causing himself or herself harm. In this view, it is right "to prevent self-regarding harmful conduct only when it is substantially non-voluntary, or when intervention is necessary to establish whether it is voluntary or not" (p. 113). If people are not autonomous, or if there is reason to doubt that they are, paternalistic intervention is justified to prevent harm to them or at least to do further assessment.

Closely related to weak paternalism is what Komrad (1988) calls "limited paternalism." Limited paternalism takes into account the possibility that the autonomy of the sick person may be greatly diminished because of sickness, and justifies paternalistic intervention insofar as its ultimate end is the restoration of autonomy. "The restitution of diminished autonomy," Komrad writes, "is the only rationalization of medical paternalism that does not profane autonomy" (p. 147).

These two forms of paternalism share in common the condition that the autonomy of the person being treated paternalistically is somehow or other in question. Under such conditions, paternalism is widely accepted in *principle* throughout our society. In *practice*, things are less clear cut. Autonomy can be interpreted in a number of different ways. What meaning of autonomy is being applied? Determining the voluntariness (or nonvoluntariness) of conduct is not an exact science. What criterion should be employed? There are many measures or standards for assessing competence to choose. Which measures should be used? In light of such ambiguities and uncertainties, it may be easy enough to raise doubts about someone's autonomy on some grounds or other. Indeed, the danger exists that this may done as pretext to conceal less acceptable forms of paternalism.

The strongest form of paternalism, and the one most difficult to justify if plainly put, involves limiting liberty even in the case of someone whose autonomy is not in question (e.g., a mentally competent adult demonstrably capable of rational thinking). It is mainly this kind of "strong paternalism" in health care that has been the object of criticism in recent years. The classic attack on strong paternalism dates back to the nineteenth century philosopher John Stuart Mill. In *On Liberty*, Mill ([1859] 1975) asserted a very simple principle as a means of deciding whether the restriction of someone's liberty is justifiable:

That principle is, that the sole end for which mankind are warranted, individually or collectively, in interfering with the liberty of action of any of their number, is self-protection. That the only purpose for which power can be rightfully exercised over any member of a civilised community, against his will, is to prevent harm to others. His own good, either physical or moral, is not a sufficient warrant. He cannot rightfully be compelled to do or forbear because it will be better for him to do so, because it will make him happier, because in the opinions of others, to do so would be wise, or even right. (pp. 10-11)

Mill has been an extremely influential philosopher and was a major exponent of the liberal philosophy that has shaped modern society and politics. His principle of liberty established autonomy (in the sense of liberty or free action) as a higher value than beneficence. Concern for the good of the other is limited and held in check by respect for the other's autonomy.[12] Respect for autonomy trumps beneficence.

Mill's views, although widely held, remain controversial, especially in the context of health care. Beneficence has traditionally been the supreme value for health professionals. Several commentators, concerned that respect for autonomy is being given too much value in health care today, seek to restore beneficence to a position of higher value (e.g., Zembaty, 1986; Clements & Sider, 1988; Pellegrino & Thomasma, 1988). Might there be something special about the health care context — for example, the vulnerability of the sick — that justifies the subordination of respect for autonomy to beneficence? Alternatively, to what extent can beneficence be interpreted more broadly (and more favourably) so as to incorporate respect for autonomy?

Although Mill's principle ranks respect for autonomy as a higher value than beneficence, it also places a limit on autonomy, stipulating a condition under which it *is* justifiable to limit autonomy; namely, in order to protect someone else from harm. Although there is widespread agreement on this so-called "harm principle," difficult questions arise about its application.[13] When the harm to others that will follow from action is great, as when someone is violent, there is a clear case to be made for limiting autonomy in order to prevent the person from harming other people. However, the matter is less clear when the harm foreseen is less severe, or when there is uncertainty whether the harm will materialize. What degree of harm to others, and what probability that the harm will occur, is sufficient to warrant limiting someone's autonomy?

However, paternalism and concern to protect others from immediate harm are not the only bases upon which autonomy may be limited in health care. Justice too may be a consideration. Health care can be very expensive. What appears as a choice or option from the standpoint of the client shows up as a cost or expense for those whose job it is to keep their eye on the fiscal bottom line. As long as hospitals and other service providers were able to draw from what once seemed a virtually limitless supply of financial resources, the cost side of client choice was largely invisible, or at least not a subject of pressing concern.

The reality is different today. In these times of fiscal constraint, the cost dimension of choices is becoming more of an issue. Choices cost money, and given the current imperative of cost reduction it is likely that reducing costs will mean to some extent reducing choices.[14] This applies not only to expensive treatments and drugs but also to such basic provisions as accommodation. For example, reduced funding may translate into fewer spaces in long-term care facilities. This in turn may mean that elderly people will have fewer choices as concerns residence.

In general, cost reduction may constrain choices such that what the client might want, and perhaps even need, may not be provided as an option on the grounds that it is not affordable. Such constraints on choice are very different in kind than those sanctioned by paternalism or by concern to protect third parties from harm, but their impact on autonomy may be no less considerable.

End of Life Decisions

Issues of autonomy may arise for virtually any treatment decision but not all decisions are equally serious. For example, much more is at stake in the decision whether to have surgical or chemical treatment for breast cancer than whether to have a wart removed.

As a rule, autonomy issues are more pronounced the greater our stake in or the more we care about the consequences of the decision at hand. End of life decisions are therefore especially problematic from the standpoint of autonomy because they concern not just quality of life but life itself. Respecting autonomy may be challenging enough for nurses even when relatively minor things are at stake. When life and death hang in the balance, the challenges are much more considerable.

Dying can be a terrifying, lonely and painful experience, particularly for those who fear losing control of the decisions that will determine how and when they will die. Caring for the dying and trying to make their last days comfortable in physical, psychological and spiritual terms is noble work. When caring for the terminally ill, nurses may find themselves challenged about what respect for autonomy comes down to in practice and how and whether this duty should be limited.

1. Autonomy and Life-Sustaining Treatment

If client autonomy means anything at all, it means the right to accept or refuse treatment. This right is recognized and enshrined in law and in various codes of ethics in nursing. Providing that the client is competent, and the decision is informed and voluntary, the client's decision must be respected.

However, when the consequence of treatment refusal is death, other professional values beside respect for autonomy may come into play, and in particular values having to do with respect for life itself. Thus decisions about life-sustaining treatment may be very problematic for nurses. Generally, it is easier for a nurse to accept and comply with client wishes in these matters the more he or she agrees that the decision is a good one. Thus a decision by a young woman with anorexia nervosa to refuse food is more troubling than that of an elderly person recovering from a serious stroke who indicates a wish not to be resuscitated in the event of cardiac arrest.

Life-sustaining treatment is any intervention or treatment, no matter how simple or complex, that is essential for the maintenance of life.

Depending on the circumstances, this may include food, water, a venti-lator, a feeding tube, or any number of other interventions.

The case of Nancy B. brought issues concerning life-sustaining treatment to the fore in Canada. Nancy B. was a twenty-five year old woman with Guillain-Barré Syndrome suffering from extensive muscu-lar atrophy. She was paralysed and ventilator-dependent. Her request to have her respirator disconnected, after having been confined to bed for two years, created uncertainty among those caring for her about whether to respect her wishes.

The administration at the hospital in which Nancy B. was a patient, the Hotel-Dieu Hopital in Quebec City, sought guidance from the courts about how to proceed. They wanted to know whether compli-ance with her wishes would violate legal sanctions against homicide and assisted suicide. The case made its way to the Superior Court of Quebec, which ruled that compliance with her wishes should be con-strued in terms of her right to refuse treatment, and not in terms of either homicide or assisted suicide.

The case of Nancy B. clarified the legal issues surrounding refusal of life-sustaining treatment and helped shape professional consensus. It confirmed that Canadians have a legal right to refuse even life-sustain-ing treatment, including feeding tubes, surgical operations, blood transfusions and cardio-pulmonary resuscitation. To fail to respect a person's wishes and give treatment without consent is the legal offence of battery.

2. Autonomy, Assisted Suicide, and Euthanasia

Euthanasia literally means a "good death" but the term evokes consid-erably more than that in contemporary parlance. Euthanasia issues are difficult not just because so much is at stake about which people care deeply but also because the terminology in which these issues are couched is so slippery.

The CNA (1994a), borrowing from the Law Reform Commission, defines euthanasia as "the act of ending the life of a person from compassionate motives, when the person is already terminally ill or when the person's suffering has become unbearable" (p.5). When the act is carried out in accordance with the person's wishes, this is called voluntary euthanasia. Involuntary or non-voluntary euthanasia, by contrast, is sanctioned not by the person's *wishes* but rather by what someone else believes to be in his or her *best interests*.[15]

The distinction between voluntary and involuntary euthanasia is clear enough, and virtually everyone would agree that it has at least some moral relevance. The situation is different as regards another common distinction used in debates about euthanasia, namely, that between passive and active euthanasia.

One way of making this distinction emphasizes the nature of the action involved. Thus passive euthanasia would apply to passive actions, such as omitting to do some thing that would keep the person alive. This could be construed as "letting die." Active euthanasia, on the other hand, means doing something to deliberately hasten the person's death, such as administering a lethal injection.

One problem with distinguishing active and passive euthanasia along these lines is that it is difficult to classify which kinds of actions belong in which category. For example, disconnecting a respirator may be classed as being either passive or active depending on precisely how one defines these terms. Furthermore, supposing that we are clear about the difference between actions and omissions, the question arises whether this difference makes a moral difference. Morally speaking, if the intent of one's intervention is the same, what moral difference does it make whether the action that fulfills this intention is active or passive?

Most commentators recognize that intention does make a moral difference and incorporate intentions into the distinction between active and passive euthanasia. Along these lines, passive euthanasia may be defined as action (or omission) the intent of which is something other than the death of the person (e.g., the relief of suffering) but which will likely lead to the person's death. Active euthanasia, by contrast, would include any action (or omission) the intent of which is to hasten or cause the death of the person.

In these terms, whether disconnecting the respirator in cases like that of Nancy B. should be classified as active or passive euthanasia would depend on the intentions of those involved. If the intention was to hasten her death, it would be active euthanasia. If the intention was to respect her autonomy by honouring her treatment refusal, the situation would be construed as passive euthanasia, death being an unintended effect of the intended action.

However, there is reason to question whether the case of Nancy B. should be construed as a euthanasia issue at all. Nancy B. was a competent adult who refused treatment. She had a right to thus refuse, and those responsible for her care were duty-bound to honour her wish. Viewed in this way, one might argue, it only muddies the issue to conceive her situation, and situations of treatment refusal in general, as instances of euthanasia.

Whether one classes the actions of health professionals in cases like that of Nancy B. as respecting a client's decision to refuse treatment or as assisting the client to die will depend on issues of conceptualization and terminology. The debate reduces to one of semantics. However, everyone concerned will agree that the debate moves to a new level in situations where the right to refuse treatment does not come into play at all. The case of Sue Rodriguez is an excellent case in point.

Ms. Rodriguez suffered from Amyotrophic Lateral Sclerosis (known as A.L.S. or Lou Gehrig's disease). She requested assistance to die at such time as her terminal condition became intolerable to her. The request was dismissed by the British Columbia Supreme Court, the British Columbia Court of Appeal, and by a five to four majority decision of the Supreme Court of Canada in 1993. In February, 1994, she died with the assistance of a physician, who administered a lethal injection.

In Sue Rodriguez's case there can be no doubt that the physician's intent was to cause or hasten her death and so the case is clearly one of active euthanasia or assisted suicide. The issue is whether such action should be legal. Presently it is not. The *Criminal Code* (section 221b) prohibits intentional killing or assisting someone to die.

In 1995, a Senate Commission reviewed the issues concerning assisted suicide with an eye to whether the law about these matters should be changed. In keeping with the line of argument developed in the case of

Nancy B., the Commission distinguished between respecting a person's wish to refuse life-sustaining treatment and assisting someone who wishes to die. The Commission recommended that assisted suicide should not be legalized.[16]

Sue Rodriguez asked that someone take steps to help her end her life. For most people who support legalizing such assistance, the fact that she was a mentally competent adult who requested help to die makes a great deal of moral difference. Along these lines, it is instructive to contrast her case with that of Tracy Latimer.

Tracy Latimer was a twelve-year old girl suffering from cerebral palsy caused by brain damage at birth. She was a quadriplegic, unable to speak or to recognize her own name, and had vision problems. She suffered seizures and extreme pain from muscles tensing, which required several operations. It was uncertain whether or to what extent further surgery would alleviate her pain, and whether her family would be able to continue looking after her at home.

Tracy's father, feeling certain that his daughter's condition would not improve sustantially and with the intention of ending her pain and suffering, ended Tracy's life by carbon monoxide poisoning. In 1995, he was found guilty of second degree murder. A crucial difference between this case and the other two discussed earlier is that Tracy did not express any wishes in the matter, and indeed lacked the capacity to do so.

The progression from the case of Nancy B. to Sue Rodriguez to Tracy Latimer spans the range of issues concerning end of life decision-making. In Nancy B.'s case, the issue concerned whether to comply with her express wishes in the matter of treatment refusal, given that doing so would hasten her death. In the case of Sue Rodriguez, the issue cannot be construed in terms of the right of a competent person to refuse treatment because the act she requested did not involve her treatment and was clearly intended to cause her death.

Even so, the Nancy B. and the Sue Rodriguez cases are alike in that both involved competent persons and raise questions about limits to the duty to respect autonomy. The case of Tracy Latimer, by contrast, cannot be construed in terms of autonomy at all, since Tracy did not ask her father to end her life and was not in a position to do so.

Summary

Respect for autonomy is a challenging commitment for nurses. Autonomy has several different meanings, and sometimes there is confusion about what respect for autonomy entails. There may be doubt as to whether a particular client is autonomous, or about what course of action will best promote autonomy. When emphasis is placed on the client's right to make decisions, difficulties may arise if the option selected is incompatible with the nurse's professional judgement, with the agency or institution's policy or practices, or with the physician's plan of care. In some cases, advocacy on behalf of the client's autonomy may seem to require action that exceeds the nurse's role as legally or institutionally defined relative to other health professionals.[17]

Acknowledgment of the client's right to participate in decisions affecting his or her health and welfare carries a corresponding obligation for the nurse to assist the client to access and understand relevant information. However, the degree of responsibility that either the public or the profession expect the individual practitioner to assume in order to ensure that the client's wishes are considered and implemented is sometimes uncertain.

Moreover, nurses need to be sensitive to the fact that Canada is a multicultural society. In Western countries, personal freedom is highly valued, not infrequently above the welfare of others or of the community. Many ethical problems are framed as conflicts between the rights of one person or group and the rights of another person or group. However, for some ethnic groups respect for individual autonomy is not an ethical priority. Consideration of the well-being of family and community may be immensely important to these clients. In such situations, nurses may find themselves conflicted as concerns their commitment to respect client autonomy.

The cases that follow examine some of the difficult issues that arise in connection with autonomy, and illustrate how respect for autonomy may come into conflict with other values cherished in nursing.

Case 1: Client Choice Versus Client Good

In most circumstances, respect for autonomy is compatible with beneficence — the commitment to do good for the client and to do no harm.
Indeed, things like helping the client to understand treatment options
and to clarify values may serve therapeutic purposes. Moreover, when
given the freedom to choose, clients usually use this freedom in ways
compatible with a treatment or plan of care that is also favoured by the
nurse.

However, if the freedom to choose is genuine, it means that the client
may also choose something different from what the nurse believes is
beneficial, and perhaps even something positively harmful. In such
instances, respect for client autonomy is in conflict with beneficence.
This conflict may be very difficult for nursing staff to deal with, as the
following case illustrates:

> *Mrs. Wright, a fifty-five year old woman with advanced multiple
> sclerosis, was admitted to the chronic care unit of a hospital. As
> part of the admission routine, a full diet was ordered. At lunch
> time, Nurse Klein observed that Mrs. Wright was eating very
> slowly and appeared to have difficulty swallowing some of the
> foods on her dinner tray. Mrs. Wright explained that she needed
> to chew the food well in order to avoid choking. After staying
> with her until she finished her meal, Nurse Klein told Mrs. Wright
> that she was going to fill out a special diet requisition for a soft
> diet.*
>
> *At dinner time when her food tray was presented, Mrs. Wright
> became very angry and upset. "I don't want baby food!" she
> asserted. "Bring me some real food that I can enjoy." Nurse Klein
> patiently explained to her why it was best that she eat a soft diet
> and informed her about the risks of choking and aspiration. She
> also pointed out that the nursing staff would have limited time to
> spend assisting her with meals. Even so, Mrs. Wright was
> adamant. "It's my life and I will live it the way I want!" she insist-
> ed.*

The next day arrangements were made for nursing staff to meet with Mrs. Wright and her husband. During the discussion, it became clear that Mr. Wright supported his wife, and that the couple had thoroughly explored the options and were prepared to accept the consequences of their decision. They had also discussed the implications their decision would have on family members. Having realized that the Wrights were not going to change their decision, the nursing staff approached Mrs. Wright's physician and convinced him that it would be in her best interest to order her a soft diet. This only further angered Mrs. Wright.

Commentary

From the standpoint of nursing knowledge, Mrs. Wright's choice seems unwise, and likely to bring her harm. Nurses are committed to doing good for their clients, and at the very least to avoid doing harm. However, they are also committed to respecting client autonomy. If respect for autonomy means allowing Mrs. Wright to eat what she wants, then the nursing staff will be in a dilemma, torn between beneficence and respect for autonomy. A first question to ask, then, is whether in this case respect for autonomy does indeed mean allowing the client to eat what she wants.

In deciding this question, it is important whether Mrs. Wright is being autonomous in refusing the recommended diet. If her refusal is not autonomous, nursing staff are not obliged to honour her choice. However, there is no evidence of mental incompetence or lack of capacity. Moreover, nursing staff have discussed the risks with her, and her decision appears to be properly informed. Mrs. Wright and her husband are prepared to accept both the short and long term consequences of this decision.

Having established that Mrs. Wright's choice was indeed autonomous, the nursing staff, while not coercing her outright, manipulated the situation in order to "persuade" her to comply with the recommended diet. They did this by enlisting the support of her physician, perhaps hoping that she would defer to the physician's stature and authority. For many clients, "doctor's orders" carry a great deal of weight.

In enlisting the physician's support, the nursing staff apparently were attempting to circumvent Mrs. Wright's choice. In doing so, they were acting paternalistically, assigning to their conception of her good a higher value than respect for her autonomy. Whether this intervention was morally justifiable can be debated. In any event, it did not work. Mrs. Wright, sensing that she was being manipulated, only became angry and more resolved to live her life on her terms.

The information we are given is that, initially, "Nurse Klein *told* Mrs. Wright that she was going to fill out a special diet requisition for a soft diet." Presumably, Mrs. Wright was not invited to discuss and agree to this as an option. This would indicate an insensitivity on the part of Nurse Klein that could have compromised the trust relationship from the very beginning.

Switching to soft food carries immense psychological meaning for Mrs. Wright, and it would have been appropriate to probe Mrs. Wright's feelings about the matter more carefully. Given what has happened, it may be very difficult to restore trust, but if this is at all possible it would be advisable to discuss with Mrs. Wright issues concerning maintaining dignity, self-respect and control over her life while living in an institution.

The ideal solution to the conflict between beneficence and respect for autonomy in this case would be one that satisfies the requirements of both. It might help to address some of Mrs. Wright's concerns in the nursing care plan. Perhaps a nutritionist working with Mrs. Wright could develop a diet plan to satisfy both her dietary preferences and her safety needs. Perhaps Mr. Wright, other family members, or friends would be available to help Mrs. Wright at meals, thereby addressing at least one of the nursing staff's reservations about honouring her choice.

If everything else fails, the nursing staff will have to choose between complying with Mrs. Wright's wishes and doing something even more blatantly paternalistic and offensive to autonomy, such as refusing to bring her any meals other than ones they think are appropriate. As knowledge base for such a decision, it is important to determine as precisely as possible the risks to Mrs. Wright if she is permitted to eat what she wishes. It is also important to project the consequences that might follow if these risks were to materialize. If, for example, Mrs. Wright were to choke or aspirate, would the nursing profession and the law judge the nursing staff to have fulfilled their advocacy obligations to her?

Although the main issue in this case is between autonomy and beneficence, considerations of justice also come into play. Approaching the case from this angle, an argument can be made for limiting Mrs. Wright's autonomy on other than paternalistic grounds. Her choice, after all, would have consequences affecting other people. Mealtimes are very busy, and if Mrs. Wright were to have her way, the nursing staff would have to spend more time with her. This could mean spending less time with other clients, to whom nursing staff also have a duty. What about the good of these other clients? Concerns about Mrs. Wright's good aside, would it be fair to allow Mrs. Wright her choice if this must come at the expense of other clients?

This case has a subplot about how autonomy may be limited for clients living in institutions. These facilities are their homes. Sadly, for residents, they are often more like prisons. Schedules, policies and practices may rob them of meaningful choices and of dignity. Clients who try to maintain lifelong habits and preferences run the risk of being labelled difficult and having uneasy relationships with nurses, who they must rely on for their basic needs,

Respecting client choice when the client is so heavily dependent requires nurses to be especially sensitive to the vulnerability of their clients. It may also require nurses to work for changes in institutional practices and policies that thwart dependent clients from gaining greater control over their lives and maintaining their dignity.

Case 2: Advocating on Behalf of Voiceless Clients

The case of Mrs. Wright presents difficult questions for nursing and illustrates a key feature of the concept of autonomy. Focusing on instances of treatment refusal or disagreement between clients and health practitioners, however, ought not to obscure other less dramatic aspects of the concept of autonomy. Respect for autonomy is much more complex and goes a lot deeper than honouring the wishes of the clearly competent client, as important as that may be. It also comes into play with respect to clients whose autonomy is in question, or who for one reason or another cannot make their preferences known.

Individuals who are unable to identify or articulate their needs and preferences may be at risk of being ignored or deprived of adequate care. With such clients, the nurse's advocacy role may be especially appropriate, perhaps complementary to the role of substitute decision-maker taken on by a family member or legal guardian. In this decision-making, consideration should be given to any known preferences or wishes of the client.

An especially difficult challenge is presented by clients whose autonomy is merely diminished or otherwise impaired, and who may be capable of some measure of autonomy. In such instances, respect for autonomy may require a special effort to determine what clients really wish, perhaps by empowering them to become more assertive and helping them to achieve greater control over their situation. The task may be increased by the fact that some institutional arrangements are less conducive than others to the flourishing of client autonomy. In some institutions, clients may be treated in ways that effectively disempower them and suppress autonomy, as the case below illustrates:

> *I am a recently graduated RPN who has just begun working in a nursing home. I feel that nursing staff are sometimes too mechanical in the way we give care. When residents are restless and call out for a nurse, nursing staff often ignore their cries. Sometimes I have stopped and talked with one of these residents, and this tends to quieten them down. Often the resident will cling to my*

hand, clearly indicating a desire that I remain. Recently I read an article about how important conversation is to older people, and I believe that nursing staff should spend more time talking with them.

When I expressed my feelings about this to my charge nurse, she agreed in principle that nurses should have more time to talk with clients but pointed out that there was not enough nursing staff to allow for this. We are indeed short-staffed, and there is never enough time to do all the work that needs to be done. Even so, I believe that communication is an essential part of nursing care, and as important as physical care. What should I do?

Commentary

The RPN's problem in this case stems from her belief that the clients for whom she is responsible are not getting the kind of care they deserve. Considered in terms of beneficence, it could be argued that the institution is failing to promote the good of these clients, perhaps even to the point that neglect and social isolation may be doing them harm. Along these lines, one would focus on the duty of the nursing staff to advocate for the good of the residents.

Alternatively, this issue can also be approached in terms of respect for autonomy. Nurses should be aware of the impediments to the realization of client autonomy and act in ways that will increase the opportunities for clients to become more autonomous. Are the residents getting the kind of care they would choose if they were able to choose for themselves? Do the institutional arrangements have the effect of holding residents back from speaking up for themselves? Might the diminished autonomy of residents be in part a result of the way the institution treats them? Perhaps there is a vicious circle at work here: The residents are not treated as autonomous individuals because they are not acting autonomously, but they are not acting autonomously because of the way they are treated.

Let us assume that the RPN is correct in her assessment. The reality is that respecting autonomy and providing excellent care can take time, and may be costly. Treating clients like objects may be more economical than treating them as human beings. Furthermore, the value of respect for autonomy and dignity is hard to measure. The results of physical care, on the other hand, are often very tangible, and can more easily be calculated as benefits on a balance sheet. The issue is a general one in contemporary health care, as insufficient time and resources to respect client autonomy and to provide proper care is a reality in many employment settings. What will best promote autonomy may not be affordable.

The RPN in this case may be able to find some creative way to express and act on her commitments within the institution. Perhaps she could win the support of other nursing staff who may also be dissatisfied with the status quo. Perhaps she could enlist the support of her supervisor to begin a program whereby volunteers from the community would come in and spend time talking with the residents. Any such planning should of course be done in partnership with the residents and their families. To plan groups and activities and present them as *fait accompli* to residents may be well-intentioned, but it is paternalistic. At the institutional level, establishing patient councils and patient representation on committees would be another way of allowing residents to gain greater autonomy over their lives

Failing her ability to arrive at an acceptable solution, however, the RPN would be faced with an issue of professional integrity. As a relatively new member of the profession, she is experiencing the phenomenon that Kramer (1974) describes as "reality shock." No doubt she has heard and learned about client advocacy and clients' rights, and so forth, but she has entered a world in which things appear to be far from ideal. She is at risk of being socialized into a nursing culture where such rights appear to be ignored. The practice environment in this facility may very well be incompatible with good nursing. By all standards, talking with clients is an essential component of good nursing, as this RPN has probably been taught in her nursing program.

In choosing how to respond to this issue, the RPN is also choosing what kind of practitioner she will become. If she chooses to conform to the behaviour of the other staff, she may win their acceptance. The pressure to be accepted may be considerable, but conformity will mean sacrificing her personal and professional ideals. The quality of care she is able to give, job satisfaction, and her professional integrity will suffer.

If, however, she chooses to continue to speak out on behalf of her clients, she risks being rejected by her colleagues and possibly her supervisors. As employees, nurses are expected to provide good quality care with the resources available. To complain that the resources are not adequate, or that the care is unsafe, or that the way clients are treated is unethical, may label an employee a troublemaker, and perhaps even put continued employment at risk. In this case, to stand up for what is morally right could threaten the RPN's job security, or at least reduce her quality of life in this workplace.

Neither alternative available to the RPN is very attractive. Kramer (1974) identifies this sort of dilemma as a major reason why nurses leave the profession. It would be understandable if, forced to choose between unacceptable alternatives, the RPN decided to leave this agency for employment in a setting where she could practise the kind of nursing that she has been taught and in which she can take pride. Still, this would not help the residents of *this* facility, who would remain unable to speak for themselves and lack an advocate to articulate and amplify their voices.

Case 3: Autonomy in the Research Context

Autonomy is a central value in the research context as well as in health care. The research context gives rise to some slightly different sorts of issues. Research is essential to the goal of furthering knowledge, and such knowledge in turn is important in order to promote health and help people who are sick.

The good to be gained from research, however, must be balanced against concern for the subjects of research. Such concern is directed not only to the good of the research subjects conceived in terms of possible harms and benefits, but also more broadly to their autonomy.

Over the years — and against the background of publicized abuses — ethical guidelines for research involving human subjects have been drafted by many institutions and a number of different professions.[18] The Canadian Nurses Association (CNA, 1994b) *Ethical Guidelines for Nurses in Research Involving Human Participants* is one of several useful documents that offers guidance for nursing research. Invariably, such documents emphasize the importance of respect for autonomy in the research context.

The main problem area in research ethics has to do with protocols for informed consent. The CNA (1994b) specifies that an "informed consent procedure must consider the principles of disclosure (sharing of information), comprehension (ablity to understand), competence (ability to make rational decisions), and ability to consent freely (voluntary agreement)" (p. 7). All of these conditions for informed consent, however, need to be interpreted with reference to particular cases. Such an interpretation is not like the application of a mechanical formula. There are grey areas.

Research involving human subjects may be divided into two main kinds: Therapeutic and nontherapeutic.[19] Nontherapeutic research holds out no benefit for the research subjects, who, therefore, have no self-interest in participating. Therapeutic research, on the other hand, does offer research subjects a possibility of benefit, and this prospect may be decisive in motivating them to participate in the research.

The ethics of therapeutic research are especially complex. As

Thomas (1983) points out, such research introduces the possibility of a serious role conflict. In the context of therapeutic research, the *research subject* is also a *client*, the *researcher* may also be a *caregiver*. The caregiver-client relationship is a different game than the researcher-research subject relationship. The foremost concern of the caregiver is the good of the client; the foremost concern of the researcher is the success of the research.

If roles become blurred and relationships overlap, problems may arise. The trust conferred upon someone by virtue of his or her caregiver role might carry over if the same person happens also to relate to the client as a researcher. The client may fear that refusal to participate in research may jeopardize the quality of care. Elements of coercion, intended or not, may come into play and compromise the integrity of the informed consent process.

Competence to consent is a focal point of concern in the research context. The assessment of competence can be especially difficult when, as is often the case, the client's status varies from time to time, or when he or she is deemed competent to make some but not all decisions. Elderly clients present special problems because they often have diminished autonomy and may be more vulnerable or disempowered than other populations.

The following case concerns a double-blind study in which neither the RPN giving the medication nor the research subject/client knows whether the experimental drug or a placebo is being administered. It illustrates some of the difficulties and issues discussed above:

> *Dr. Muhit has been granted approval to run clinical trials of a new medication using the residents of a health care facility as research subjects. When Shirley Brooks, RN, initially spoke with Mrs. Clements to obtain her consent to participate, Mrs. Clements said, "That's fine dear. Anything that you and Dr. Muhit say is fine with me."*
>
> *A number of times when Nancy Goldman, RPN, has approached her with the medication, Mrs. Clements has asked, "Tell me again, dear, what is this medication for?" Ms. Goldman*

knows that some of the residents are receiving placebos and that others are receiving the experimental drug, but she does not know who is receiving which.

Commentary

In their discussion of informed consent and nursing, Carpenter and Langsner (1975) point out that "practically speaking, there are two problems in informed consent, inadequate informing and inadequate consenting" (p. 1049). This case appears to present both of these problems.

In the first place, there is reason to doubt whether Mrs. Clements has made an *informed* choice, and even whether she is competent to do so. Informed consent requires that the subject be informed about the nature, risks, and possible benefits of the research or therapy, and of reasonable alternatives where this is applicable. Mrs. Clements appears to know very little about the research in which she is involved, having left the decision-making up to those she perceives as her care providers.

There is also reason to doubt whether Mrs. Clements' consent is truly *voluntary*. She has complete confidence in Nurse Brooks and Dr. Muhit. It is not clear whether Nurse Brooks is herself involved in the research. If she is responsible for Mrs. Clements' care, it could be argued that she was not an appropriate person to obtain consent. We know that Dr. Muhit is involved in the research, but we do not know if he is also responsible for Mrs. Clements' care.

In any event, Mrs. Clements appears not to realize that Dr. Muhit at least is relating to her as a researcher, and as such may not champion her best interests as much as would someone who was exclusively her physician. Moreover, one could construe Mrs. Clements' remarks to Nurse Brooks as indicating concern to get the best care possible: for example, "If I agree to participate, you and the doctor are more likely to look after me." *Ethical Guidelines for Nurses in Research Involving Human Participants* (CNA, 1994b) advise that "manipulative tactics (e.g., the expectation of benefits), threats, coercion and/or the fear of adverse consequences (e.g., prisoners, students, patients) should never be used to influence consent " (p.8). Has it been made clear to Mrs. Clements that quality care is in no way conditional upon her consent to participate in the research?

Ms. Goldman appears to have doubts whether Mrs. Clements' consent is valid. This being so, she has several options. She could ignore or pass off Mrs. Clements' questions, and continue to administer the medications. However, if in fact the consent is not valid, to do so would be to continue a violation of Mrs. Clements' autonomy. This would contravene the express ethical norms of the nursing profession.

Another option would be to respond to Mrs. Clements' questions each time on an ad hoc basis and help her to understand better her involvement. If done in an encouraging and supportive manner, responding to her questions with openness and honesty would probably ensure Mrs. Clements' continuing participation in the clinical trials. However, this course of action would also fail to address the root problem, which is that the consent may not be valid.

Moreover, it would be difficult to answer Mrs. Clements' questions without providing some necessary background as well. For example, a thorough answer to the question, "What is this medication for?" could get very involved and complex, making reference to placebos, the nature of double-blind clinical trials, and so forth. In effect, Ms. Goldman would have to provide her with the kind of information she should have been given in the first place in the process of obtaining a properly informed consent. How much does Ms. Goldman know about the research, and how competent is Mrs. Clements to understand the information relevant to making an informed choice?

The course of action that would best promote Mrs. Clements' autonomy would be to address directly the issue of the validity of the consent. Along these lines, Ms. Goldman could report her observations and concerns to Nurse Brooks. Together they could then explore the meaning of Mrs. Clements' behaviour. It may also be appropriate to raise the issue with Dr. Muhit.

A good case could be made that Mrs. Clements should be reassessed in the matter of her consent. This much, it could be argued, would be sound practice as well as good ethics. Ongoing assessment and determination of preferences for care and treatment should be done on a routine basis.

If further exploration confirms that Mrs. Clements' consent is not valid, a decision will have to be made about her continued participation in the research. In the context of making this decision it would be appropriate to raise questions about who should be involved in any subsequent efforts to obtain informed consent (or refusal) from Mrs. Clements.[20] If nursing staff are to participate, they should have the knowledge and expertise necessary to assist the client to understand the nature of the research and any associated risks and benefits.

The case of Mrs. Clements would be a good occasion and opportunity for a general review of the consent provisions of the research protocol. Mrs. Clements may be typical, and the problem raised may be symptomatic of a larger problem. How many other residents in the nursing home are in a similar situation? How adequate are the informed consent provisions in the research protocol?

The goals of research are important. If progress is to be made in building the knowledge base for health care, it will be necessary to run clinical trials in order to determine the relative effectiveness of different forms of treatment. However, the rights of clients are also important and ought not to be ignored or lost sight of in pursuit of the goals of research. Whatever course of action she decides upon, Ms. Goldman should be guided by a clear understanding that her primary obligation is to her clients, both in terms of their welfare and their autonomy.

Conclusion

Being committed to promoting and respecting autonomy is one thing; knowing how and being able to put this commitment into practice is another. Sometimes it may not be clear exactly what respect for autonomy entails. Often the situation of clients with respect to autonomy is ambiguous. Autonomy may come into conflict with other values such as beneficence and justice. When respect for autonomy can be realized only at the expense of some other value, it may be difficult to decide which value should take precedence.

These challenges may be made even more difficult by the fact that most nurses are employees in health care facilities and have an obligation of fidelity to their employers, not to mention a prudential interest in getting along well with the powers that be.

The traditional idea of the physician as captain of the health care team may also operate as a constraint. This idea carries with it the expectation that the nurse will promote compliance with the medical plan of care. In some instances, such compliance may conflict with the duty of the nurse to advocate on behalf of client autonomy.

If respect for client autonomy is not to be a mere slogan, nurses will have to think carefully about these matters. It is essential to weigh respect for autonomy as a value together with other possibly conflicting values and to develop sound judgement in determining how best to advocate for the client.

Notes

1   The analysis that follows expands on and slightly diverges from Miller's analysis. For a more detailed analysis of the concept of autonomy, and of the various meanings the concept has taken on, see Dworkin (1988).

2   While the first three senses of autonomy distinguished typically apply to clients, autonomy as moral reflection (otherwise known as moral autonomy) tends to be applied more to health professionals. This is discussed in greater detail in the chapter on integrity.

3   In what follows, competence refers to the mental competence of the client. However, in the context of nursing, competence is also used in the sense of professional competence, as when questions are raised about a nurse's competence to do a given job. This is a very different sense of competence, and is not to be confused with the sense intended throughout this chapter.

4   There is some difference of opinion in the literature as to whether informed consent should be thought of and justified primarily in terms of autonomy or in terms of beneficence. Proponents of the latter view (e.g., Appelbaum, Lidz, & Meisel, 1987) emphasize the therapeutic value of informed consent, presenting clinical evidence that participation in decision-making serves clinical goals and is in fact good for the client. Informed consent is to be valued in health care insofar as it serves the goals of beneficence. Proponents of the former view (e.g., Faden & Beauchamp, 1986) tend not to put as great an emphasis on the therapeutic value of informed consent, arguing that it promotes autonomy and is valuable for that reason alone — even if it should turn out to be contratherapeutic.

5   For a detailed account of informed consent geared to practitioners, see Appelbaum, Lidz, & Meisel (1987). For a more philosophical account, see Faden & Beauchamp (1986).

6   For a more detailed analysis of capacity and related issues in the Ontario context, see Dickens, 1994; Singer & Choudry, 1992; and Weisstub, 1990.

7   Molloy, 1992, and Singer, 1993, are excellent examples of advance

directives. For a discussion of directives, see Downie, 1992.

8   The legal status and weight of advance directives varies from one jurisdiction to another. In Ontario, advance directives have been given considerable statutory weight in recent consent legislation. Indeed, this legislation goes so far as to authorize forcing treatments and procedures upon unwilling, incompetent people who, while competent, indicated that they would wish to be thus treated. This legislation is shaped by the case of *Fleming v. Reid* (1990), in which the Ontario Court of Appeal decided that a mentally incapable person voluntarily detained in a mental hospital could not be treated contrary to previously expressed wishes even if such treatment was now in the person's best interest.

9   Gadow uses the concept of authenticity somewhat differently than does Miller, whose view we considered earlier. What Gadow means by autonomy is closer in meaning to what Miller calls "moral reflection."

10   This ideal of advocacy, according to which the client's carefully considered values (and not merely his or her expressed wishes) are at the centre of nursing practice, is consistent with the "Man-living-health" framework described by Parse (1981).

11   More precisely, acting on behalf of people's own good can be broken down into acting to prevent harm to them and acting to provide benefit for them. As a justification for limiting autonomy, the latter is obviously much more contentious. Similarly, limiting someone's autonomy on behalf of the good of others may be done either to prevent harm to others, or to provide benefit to others. Here too the latter is much more contentious.

12   Mill makes it clear that he does not intend this principle to apply to people who are not autonomous (e.g., people not of legal age, people with serious mental problems, and so forth). Frequently, issues of paternalism hinge on whether the person really is autonomous; that is, on whether the principle applies at all.

13   Mill's principle is further complicated by the distinction between actions that would harm only oneself and actions that would harm other people. This distinction between so-called "self-regarding" and

"other-regarding" actions may be blurred (e.g., see Ten, 1975). For example, a father's decision to refuse treatment may indirectly risk harm to others in the family as well as to himself.

14 Reducing choices may save money in the short term, but whether this is so if one takes a long view is open to debate. Even in the short term, there are at least some instances — end of life decision-making may be a case in point — in which increasing choices may actually reduce costs.

15 This is assuming, as *per* the definition above, that euthanasia is done from "compassionate" motives. In this regard, it is important to note that the term euthanasia is sometimes used more broadly to cover acts of terminating life even when the motives are not compassionate (e.g., euthanasia in Nazi Germany).

16 However, the Commissioners were divided about this issue. Four Senators rejected permitting assisted death under any conditions and three recommended protection under the *Criminal Code* for those who assist in suicide under strict conditions.

17 For further discussion of the legal and institutional limitations on client advocacy, see Carnerie (1989).

18 The CIA-sponsored research done at the Allan Memorial Institute in Montreal on the effects of hallucinogenic drugs is a chilling example of the abuse of human subjects in research in the Canadian scene. For a discussion of this research, see Weinstein (1988). For a more general discussion of research abuses, see Beecher (1959; 1966).

19 Some commentators (e.g., Levine, 1983) argue that the distinction between therapeutic and nontherapeutic research is misleading. This may be true, but here at least it serves a clear purpose.

20 This is a difficult question that goes beyond the immediate case at hand. If someone involved in client care is responsible for obtaining consent (or refusal), there is a chance that the client will consent out of fear that refusal to participate will jeopardize his or her care. Moreover, a direct caregiver may not be familiar with the details of the research and may not be able to respond adequately to any questions and concerns raised by the client. On the other hand, if someone from the research team is involved in obtaining consent, the pos-

sibility exists that the researcher's obvious interest in securing subjects for the research may give rise to subtle forms of coercion or
deception in the informed consent process. One commentator
(Harrison, 1990) has suggested that the way out of this dilemma is for
someone involved neither in direct care nor in the research to be
responsible for the informed consent process.

References

Appelbaum, P.S., Lidz, C.W., & Meisel, A. (1987). *Informed consent: Legal
theory and clinical practice*. New York: Oxford University Press.

Beecher, H.K. (1959). *Experimentation in man*. Springfield, IL: Charles C.
Thomas.

Beecher, H.K. (1966). Ethics and clinical research. *The New England Journal
of Medicine, 274* (24), 1354-1360.

Beauchamp, T.L. (1989). Informed consent. In R. Veatch (Ed.), *Medical ethics*
(pp. 173-200). Boston: Jones and Bartlett.

Canadian Nurses Association. (1994a). *A question of respect: Nurses and end
of life treatment decisions*. Ottawa: Author.

Canadian Nurses Association. (1994b). *Ethical guidelines for nurses in
research involving human participants*. 2nd revised edition. Ottawa:
Author.

Carnerie, F. (1989). Patient advocacy. *The Canadian Nurse, 85* (11), 20.

Carpenter, W.T., & Langsner, C.A. (1975). The nurse's role in informed consent. *Nursing Times, 71* (27), 1049-1051.

Clements, C.D., & Sider, R.C. (1988). Medical ethics' assault upon medical
values. In R.B. Edwards & G.C. Graber (Eds.), *Bioethics* (pp. 150-158). San
Diego: Harcourt Brace Jovanovich.

Davis, A.J. (1988). The clinical nurse's role in informed consent. *Journal of
Professional Nursing, 4* (2), 88-91.

Dickens, B. (1994). Medical consent legislation in Ontario. *Medical Law
Review, 2* (Autumn), 283-301.

Downie, J. (1992). Where there is a will, there may be a better way. *Health Law
in Canada, 12* (8), 73-80, 89.

Drane, J.F. (1988). The many faces of competency. In R.B. Edwards & G.C.

Graber (Eds.), *Bioethics* (pp. 169-177). San Diego: Harcourt Brace Jovanovich.

Dworkin, G. (1988). *The theory and practice of autonomy.* Cambridge: Cambridge University Press.

Faden, R.R., & Beauchamp, T.L. (1986). *A history and theory of informed consent.* New York: Oxford University Press.

Feinberg, J. (1971). Legal paternalism. *Canadian Journal of Philosophy, 1*(1), 105-124.

Fleming v. Reid. (1990). 82 D.L.R. (4th) 289 (Ont. C.A.) at 316.

Gadow, S.A. (1980). Existential advocacy: Philosophical foundations of nursing. In S.F. Spicker & S.A. Gadow (Eds.), *Nursing: Images and ideals* (pp. 79-101). New York: Springer.

Gadow, S.A. (1989). Clinical subjectivity: Advocacy with silent patients. *Nursing Clinics of North America, 24* (2), 535-541.

Harrison, C. (1990). Ensuring voluntary consent to research. Presented at the annual meeting of the Canadian Bioethics Society, Quebec City, PQ.

Ingelfinger, F.J. (1972). Informed (but uneducated) consent. *The New England Journal of Medicine, 287* (9), 465-466.

Komrad, M.S. (1988). A defense of medical paternalism: Maximizing patient autonomy. In R.B. Edwards & G.C. Graber (Eds.), *Bioethics* (pp. 141-150). San Diego: Harcourt Brace Jovanovich.

Kramer, Marlene (1974). *Reality shock: Why nurses leave nursing.* St. Louis: C.V. Mosby.

Levine, R.J. (1983). Clarifying the concepts of research ethics. In J.E. Thomas (Ed.), *Medical ethics and human life* (pp. 198-213). Sanibel, FL: Samuel Stevens.

Loftus, E.F., & Fries, J.F. (1979). Informed consent may be hazardous to health. *Science, 204* (4388), 11.

Mill, J.S. ([1859] 1975). *On liberty.* In D. Spitz (Ed.), *On liberty: A Norton critical edition* (pp. 1-106). New York: W.W. Norton.

Miller, B.L. (1981). Autonomy and the refusal of lifesaving treatment. *Hastings Center Report, 11* (4), 22-28.

Molloy, W. (1992). *Let Me Decide.* Toronto: Penguin Press.

Palmer, M.E., & Deck, E.S. (1987). Teaching your patients to assert their rights. *American Journal of Nursing, 87* (5), 650-654.

Parse, R.R. (1981). *Man-living-health: A theory of nursing.* New York: John Wiley.

Payton, R.J. (1979). Information control and autonomy: Does the nurse have a role? *Nursing Clinics of North America, 14* (1), 23-33.

Pellegrino, E.D., & Thomasa, D.C. (1988). *For the patient's good: The restoration of beneficence in health care.* New York: Oxford University Press.

Singer, P. (1993). The University of Toronto Centre for Bioethics Living Will. *Ontario Medical Review,* (January), 35-41.

Singer, P., & Choudry, S. (1992). Ontario's proposed consent laws: Consent and capacity, substitute decisions, advance directives and emergency treatment. *Canadian Medical Association Journal, 146* (6), 829-832.

Special Senate Committee on Euthanasia and Assisted Suicide (1995). *Of life and death: Report of the Special Senate Committee on Euthanasia and Assisted Suicide.* Ottawa: Queen's Printer.

Storch, J.L. (1988). Ethics in nursing practice. In A.J. Baumgart & J. Larsen (Eds.), *Canadian nursing faces the future: Development and change* (pp. 211-221). St. Louis: C.V. Mosby.

Ten, C.L. (1975). Mill on self-regarding actions. In D. Spitz (Ed.), *On liberty: A Norton critical edition* (pp. 238-246). New York: W.W. Norton.

Thomas, J.E. (1983). The physician as therapist and investigator. In J.E. Thomas (Ed.), *Medical ethics and human life* (pp. 213-221). Sanibel, FL: Samuel Stevens.

Weinstein, H. (1988). *A father, a son, and the CIA.* Toronto: James Lorimer.

Weisstub, D. (1990). *An enquiry on mental competency. Final report.* Ontario: Queen's Printer.

Zembaty, J.S. (1986). A limited defense of paternalism in medicine. In T.A. Mappes & J.S. Zembaty (Eds.), *Biomedical ethics.* (2nd ed., pp. 60-66). New York: McGraw-Hill.

Study Questions: Autonomy

Case 1: Client Choice Versus Client Good

1. In most cases, respect for autonomy is consistent with, if not promotive of, the health good of the client and of good nursing. Might this be so in this case?

2. Sometimes, concern for the "best interests" of the client can mask other less noble reasons for interfering with autonomy (e.g., the interests of nursing staff; cost considerations). Discuss this possibility with reference to the case under consideration.

3. Does Mrs. Wright have any duties or responsibilities that ought to be brought to bear in this case?

4. Of what relevance are considerations such as the probability and severity of the anticipated risk in deciding what is morally right in this case and others like it?

Case 2: Advocating on Behalf of Voiceless Clients

1. In recent years, many commentators have drawn attention to the neglect of elderly people in the health care system. Some writers have suggested that elderly people are often the victims of "ageism" (discriminatory treatment based on age). What bearing does age have on how the elderly are generally treated in residential facilities?

2. State whether and why you agree or disagree with the statement: "Autonomy is wonderful, but it is not cheap. The sad reality is that sometimes we just cannot afford autonomy." How might your response vary depending on the interpretation of autonomy applied?

3. Discuss ways in which institutions and institutional factors, structures, policies, or rules, may either promote or suppress autonomy.

4. "The more autonomous people are, the harder it is to control them." Discuss this statement with reference to health care, stating in what ways you agree and in what ways you disagree.

Case 3: Autonomy in the Research Context

1. Researchers and caregivers have different responsibilities and wear different hats, so to speak. Describe some issues that may arise if the same person wears both hats at the same time?

2. Suppose it is decided that Mrs. Clements is not mentally competent to give consent. Under what conditions, if any, would it be morally permissible for her to continue in the research?

3. The case provides no information about the possible harms and benefits of the experiment. What moral relevance might such information have? Would informed consent be less important if the risk of harm was minor, or the promise of benefit great? How would this case be different if the medication being studied had no promise of benefit for Mrs. Clements at all?

4. In general, state how the therapeutic and the research contexts are different in relation to respect for autonomy. To what extent may the goals of therapy and the goals of research be in conflict?

TRUTHFULNESS

The truth is rarely pure, and never simple.

—OSCAR WILDE

The paternalism that has for so long been entrenched in the health professions has been especially pronounced in matters of truthfulness and truthtelling. New attitudes toward death and dying, increased emphasis on personal autonomy, and the recognition of a right to informed consent have all called such paternalism into question. The general presumption today is in favour of openness and the disclosure of information to clients. How to tell the truth is as important as what to tell. Obfuscation, talking in jargon, ambiguity, and communicating in mixed signals may be impediments to the honest communication of the truth. Cultural and religious differences may also be barriers. Issues of disclosure and truthtelling are especially complicated in nursing because in many settings a "no-new-information" policy inhibits nurses from disclosing information to clients that has not already been communicated by physicians. The limited autonomy of the profession in this area poses ethical and political challenges.

Case studies in this chapter explore the ethical difficulties a nurse encounters when a client asks for diagnostic information she is not charged to give; the problems that arise because a physician has been cajoled by the parents of a young woman to withhold a cancer diagnosis from her; and the dilemma faced by a nurse whose client does not want to know information that could have serious consequences for her newborn baby.

Truthfulness and Truthtelling in Health Care

Health professionals possess much general knowledge about the functioning of the body and the symptoms of and treatments for various conditions, as well as salient information and opinions about the health status of clients. The imbalance of knowledge and expertise between health professionals and their clients gives rise to a number of difficult ethical issues, especially with respect to information related to diagnosis and prognosis or that otherwise bears on a client's ability to make informed choices. Given that the practitioner possesses knowledge of concern to the client, what are the ethics of concealing and revealing this information? Under what circumstances, if any, is it justifiable to withhold information from or lie to a client? How important is being truthful as weighed against other values?

Historically, the health professions expressed little concern for truthfulness in their ethical codes (Bok, 1978, pp. 223-224) and are indeed somewhat unique with respect to norms of truthtelling. While it would be unacceptable for lawyers or accountants to deceive their clients, in medicine deception has been widely practised, if not prescribed. To understand why this has been so, one must look at the value system that informs and has shaped the health professions.

Until recently, the good of the client was the overriding concern. In the hierarchy of values, truthfulness was assigned a subordinate place in relation to benefiting the client and preventing harm. Decisions about what, when, and whether to tell clients the truth about their medical condition were based on what would be best for the client's own good. Health professionals subscribed to what Veatch (1976, pp. 206-209) refers to as a special sort of "utilitarianism," in which the anticipated harms and benefits of being either truthful or untruthful are compared to determine which will result in the greatest net benefit. Since in so many instances the disclosure of the truth has been associated with harmful consequences such as anxiety and distress, truthtelling often lost out to the primary concern to do good for the client (beneficence), or at least to do no harm (nonmaleficence).

Attitudes toward truthtelling among health professionals have undergone much change in the last several decades, as is apparent when one compares surveys conducted on the topic over the years.[1] For example, in a 1961 study, 88 per cent of 219 physicians surveyed said that they did not as a rule inform their patients of a cancer diagnosis (Oken, 1961). By comparison, a 1977 study based on an almost identical questionnaire reported that 98 per cent of 278 physicians surveyed said that it is their general policy to disclose this information (Novack et al., 1979).[2] This data is dramatic evidence of a profound attitudinal shift that is by no means limited to communications about cancer.[3]

Several factors may account for this change in attitude. In the first place, being truthful with clients is less associated with harm than it used to be. In the case of people who are gravely ill, this is partly because there is greater openness about the once taboo topic of death and dying (Goldberg, 1984, p. 949). Today, there is a greater recognition of the therapeutic *benefits* of information disclosure in general. Even from the perspective of the client's good as the primary concern, there is reason to be more truthful.

Still more important, however, is the fact that the perspective of beneficence is no longer accorded the primacy it once had in the health professions. In the last few decades, the traditional paternalistic style of practice has been superseded by a more cooperative approach which places greater emphasis on client autonomy, client education, and informed participation in health care decision-making. Beneficence — especially as associated with paternalism — has been devalued in proportion to the ascent of client autonomy as a value.

The ethical consensus today, although by no means unanimous, is that clients have a right to know the truth, even if disclosure is likely to be harmful. There may be rare occasions when less than full and frank disclosure is morally defensible, but as a rule "erring on the side of telling the truth is the safest—and most ethical — policy that caregivers can follow (Wagner, 1991, p. 68).

Arguments For and Against Truthfulness in Health Care

Sociological and historical considerations aside, it is important to consider the arguments that can be cited both for and against openness and truth disclosure in the health care context. These will be considered below. The main arguments on either side of the issue depend on how one situates truthfulness in relation to two other values; namely, beneficence and respect for autonomy. Two lesser considerations, one based on the nature of the practitioner-client relationship and the other on the knowledge gap between health professionals and clients, will also be considered.

1. Truthfulness and Beneficence

The main argument given in defence of limited disclosure and even deception is that health professionals have a duty to prevent harm to clients, and telling the truth may very well cause harm. This argument is usually made with reference to information that may cause the client distress.

One response to this argument is to point out that, although the duty to do no harm is important, health professionals have other duties as well, such as being truthful with clients and respecting their autonomy. If a disclosure will have harmful consequences, truthtelling is indeed at odds with beneficence (or nonmaleficence). The greater the harm foreseen, the more serious the conflict between the obligations. Argued in these terms, the issue depends on how one weighs these duties relative to each other.

Another way of responding to this argument, however, would be to challenge the association of disclosure with harm. There is reason to doubt the factual basis of the worry that disclosure will result in harm, or in balance will result in greater harm than benefit. Granted, in some cases disclosure of information *will* prove to be harmful, but to what extent is the practitioner able to *predict* this in advance with any accuracy? A blanket assumption that disclosure will prove harmful is dubious at best.[4] In its review of the subject, the President's Commission for the Study of Ethical Problems in Medicine and Biomedical and Behaviourial Research (1982) found that the fears of health professionals about the negative consequences of disclosure tend to be exaggerated:

> Despite all the anecdotes about patients who committed suicide, suffered heart attacks, or plunged into prolonged depression upon being told "bad news," little documentation exists for claims that informing patients is more dangerous to their health than not informing them, particularly when the informing is done in a sensitive and tactful fashion. (p. 96)

The Commission's point about informing patients in a "sensitive and tactful fashion" is an important one. To the extent that disclosure *may* have harmful consequences, the harm can be minimized, if not avoided altogether, by the development of a thoughtful and sensitive bedside manner.

Indeed, much can be said in support of the claim that the consequences of disclosure, rather than being harmful, or in addition to being harmful, may be beneficial. Bok (1978) writes:

> The damages associated with the disclosure of sad news or risks are rarer than physicians believe; and the *benefits* which result from being informed are more substantial, even measurably so. Pain is tolerated more easily, recovery from surgery is quicker, and cooperation with therapy is greatly improved. The attitude that "what you don't know won't hurt you" is proving unrealistic; it is what patients do not know but vaguely suspect that causes them corrosive worry. (p. 234)

Other benefits could be added to Bok's list. Disclosure makes it possible for clients to express their feelings, and this alone may have therapeutic value. Knowing what is wrong and what to expect can remove needless fears and anxiety, and may enhance the client's ability to cope (Freel, 1985, p. 1019).

2. Truthfulness and Autonomy

Although the main arguments supporting limited disclosure and deception tend to centre on beneficence (or nonmaleficence), those supporting greater openness and disclosure tend to focus on respect for autonomy. For example, grounding the duty to tell the truth in human dignity, the American Nurses' Association (ANA, [1976] 1985) states that "truth telling and the process of reaching informed choice underlie the exercise of self-determination, which is basic to respect for persons" (Statement 1.1). Clients need relevant information in order to fully exercise their autonomy. In this regard, arguments for openness and disclosure parallel those in support of informed consent. Thus the ANA claims that "clients have the moral right to determine what will be done with their own person; to be given accurate information, and all the information necessary for making informed judgments" (Statement 1.1). In order to be self-determining in matters of their own health care, clients require adequate and reliable information. The health professional is often in a position to present information that is relevant to a client's choice, and may do so more or less truthfully. In being truthful, health professionals enable clients to make informed choices on the basis of the truth presented. Conversely, lack of information, or false information, impedes the client's capacity to make rational choices.

A closely related point is that truthfulness also promotes autonomy by helping clients to maintain a sense of control over their lives. The dying, in particular, have an obvious interest in planning whatever time remains to them, and knowing the truth about their situation affords them the opportunity to plan (Lokich, 1978, p. 18).

On the other side of the issue, it is sometimes given as a justification for deceiving or withholding information that some clients, particularly when the medical problem is severe or fatal, do not want to know about their condition (Collins, 1983). In such cases, telling clients the truth may be not only harmful, but would also fail to respect their autonomy. The crucial question raised by this argument concerns what counts as evidence that the client does not wish to be told the truth. A clear statement to this effect from the client is one thing; an inference based on a generalization is another. It would not be sufficient simply to assume or project that the client does not wish to know, especially as there is evidence that in general people do want to know the truth.[5]

3. Truthfulness, Trust, and the Practitioner-Client Relationship

Arguments based on beneficence and autonomy aside, another approach to the issue of disclosure is to ground the practitioner's obligations in the practitioner-client relationship.[6] This approach tends to conclude in favour of openness and disclosure.[7] The concept of trust plays a pivotal role in analysis along these lines. It is emphasized that the practitioner-client relationship is a fiduciary one based on mutual trust. Such trust requires that the partners in the relationship relate to each other in a truthful manner. Clients are expected to disclose all relevant information fully and frankly, and practitioners are expected to be truthful in return (Weir, 1980, p. 111). Deception or the withholding of information would endanger this trust and jeopardize the relationship.[8]

4. Truthfulness and the Practitioner-Client Knowledge Gap

The difference between health professionals and clients with respect to their ability to assess, understand, and interpret information is often used as a basis for arguments in support of deception or limited disclosure. One argument, which is sometimes raised in connection with informed consent, takes as its major premise that the information in which health professionals trade is too difficult for lay people to understand. A related argument has it that health professionals are sometimes unable to tell clients the truth with regard to their exact condition or prognoses because they themselves do not know this. Practitioners may be uncertain about the meaning and implications of the information available to them, and reluctant to communicate information that may be misinterpreted or lead the client to jump to unwarranted conclusions. The field of genetic counselling, which is fraught with uncertainty, is a special case in point (Weir, 1980).

Although the knowledge gap between practitioners and clients is undeniable, the fact that such a gap exists is not a sufficient reason for being untruthful. Because clients are unable to understand things as deeply or in as great detail as practitioners does not mean that they are unable to understand anything at all. Being truthful with clients does not require that practitioners communicate in five minutes everything that they know, but only what is relevant to the client's wishes, needs, and interests. It is important to distinguish between *complete information* and *accurate information* (Curtin, 1982, p. 328). The fact that our knowledge may be incomplete or uncertain does not exempt us from the duty to be open and accurate about what we do know. To be sure, the communication of this knowledge will sometimes pose a challenge, but this is part of the professional role. To the extent that the practitioner feels incapable of communicating relevant information to the client in an understandable way, he or she is deficient in a very important clinical skill and should seek to become more competent in communicating with lay people.

Truth, Truthfulness, and Untruthfulness

In the previous section we considered arguments bearing on whether or why one should as a rule tell clients the truth. On balance, these arguments tend to support a general presumption in favour of openness and disclosure. Such a presumption, however, does not dispense with the need for judgement. What is morally appropriate in matters of disclosure will depend very much on the particular situation in which the communication of information is at issue. A presumption in favour of openness and disclosure does not mean that there are no exceptions, but it does mean that exceptions must be justified.

A different issue arises with respect to what it means to tell the truth in the first place. What is truth? Weir (1980, p. 98) points out that in the medical literature the nature of the truth is often taken to be "self-evident" or unproblematic. The truth is equated with "the facts," and telling or not telling the truth is reduced to being "accurate" or "inaccurate" in presenting clients with information about their medical condition.

Such a framework is much too narrow. A *factually true statement* is not necessarily a *truthful statement*. A statement may be accurate as judged against the facts, but deceptive, as when a practitioner speaks in jargon knowing that the client will not understand what is being said. Similarly, we can be truthful although stating something that is factually untrue, as when we are unknowingly in error. Considerations such as these demonstrate the need to distinguish between truth in an empirical or *factual sense* and truth in a *moral sense*, to which Bok (1978, p. 6) applies the term *"truthfulness."*[9] Truthfulness is not so much a matter of accuracy as it is of honesty. Thus Bok insists that the "moral question of whether you are lying is not *settled* by establishing the truth or falsity of what you say. In order to settle this question, we must know whether you *intend your statement to mislead"* (p. 6).

The moral status of practices such as withholding information, equivocating, being ambiguous, communicating mixed signals, misleading, and outright lying can be ascertained only if we go beyond the factual accuracy of what is said to consider the communicative context in which it is said. This context encompasses not only the intentions of the speaker, but also the wishes, interests, expectations, and cognitive competence of the listener. What are the listener's interests in the matter? What or how much does the listener want to know? Under the circumstances, how is the listener likely to interpret what is said? What does the speaker intend the listener to understand or infer from what is said?

Along these lines, Jameton (1984, p. 172) distinguishes the verbal act from its effects on others. What is literally said may be one thing; how it is likely or predictably to be interpreted in the context may be something altogether different. This difference between what is said and what will be understood or inferred can be exploited for the purpose of deception.

Even without saying anything inaccurate, our statements (and silences) can have the deliberate effect of creating or confirming a false belief, allowing a false belief to go uncorrected, or otherwise keeping the truth concealed. We can deceive just as surely by telling the literal truth as by telling a literal lie. In what Veatch calls the "truthful lie," health professionals superficially fulfil the duty to tell the truth by using medical jargon, knowing that the client will be unable to decipher from what is said the truth the practitioner knows (Veatch, 1976, p. 222). The language may be factually accurate, but the communication is untruthful to the extent that its intended effect is not to reveal the truth but to conceal it from the client.

To be truthful — as opposed to merely uttering something that is true — is to communicate with the intent that, on the basis of our communication, the listener will understand what we ourselves know or believe to be true about some matter of concern. To be untruthful, on the other hand, is to intend as the effect of our communication that what we know or believe to be true is and remains concealed from the other. Lying, in which we say something we know to be untrue for the purpose of deceiving another, is but an extreme instance of a phenomenon that includes gestures, false clues, understatement, exaggeration, manipulation, the use of jargon, withholding information, evasion, and silence. For example, by withholding or omitting information we are untruthful to the extent that by remaining silent we are *deliberately* concealing something from the other.

Dialogue and Beneficent Truthtelling

Presuming that one intends as a rule to be as truthful with clients as possible, other questions arise about how best to achieve this. Untruthfulness is not the only barrier to the communication of truth. A practitioner may say something false believing it to be true, and in so doing will be speaking truthfully or honestly. Nevertheless, the *effect* of the communication will be that the client will not learn the truth. Certainly the intention to speak the truth is important, and clients are generally owed this much at least, but clients are entitled not just to honesty but also to reliable information. The practitioner's commitment to the client requires that efforts be made to ensure accuracy as well as honesty.

Even if the truth is presented honestly and accurately, communication may still fall short of an important goal insofar as information is presented in a manner that is not *understandable* or relevant to the client. The truth at issue in clinical situations may be very difficult for clients to understand, especially if their mental competence is diminished or they are in the grip of powerful emotions. The truth is more than an impersonal body of facts and statistics, and must be tailored to the specific context or circumstances of the client.

In order to ensure that the client understands, practitioners need not only good intentions and a reliable knowledge base but also good clinical skills in understanding and communicating with clients as the unique individuals that they are. Although some clients will be limited in their ability to understand by intelligence and education, and will be overwhelmed by too much detail, others will be very keen to understand and will appreciate being given as much information as possible. Especially if the truth amounts to "bad news," various psychological factors such as denial or intellectualization may impede the client's ability to understand what is being said.

Goldberg (1984, p. 953) recommends that we conceptualize truthtelling not as a single event but as a process or part of an ongoing dialogue. The objective of such dialogue is not simply to impart information to clients but to help them to understand over time what the truth means to them in their particular circumstances. An honest communication of the facts may not be enough, since the client will be concerned to know what the facts mean.[10] In a sense, the practitioner and client could be viewed as "co-interpreters" of the truth. Ongoing dialogue makes it possible for practitioners to base their decisions about what, when, and how to communicate information on the specific wishes, interests, and capacities of the individual client.

The truth that is at issue in many clinical situations is of a sort that may be very painful and hard to bear. This may not be a good enough reason to be untruthful with the client, but it is nonetheless important.

The resolve to communicate the truth does not mean that one must do so in a blunt or insensitive manner. As far as possible, one ought to communicate the truth in such a way as to preserve one's duty to benefit and prevent harm to the client.

To this end, matters such as word choice and the timing and setting of disclosure may be critical. The Canadian Nurses Association (1991) emphasizes how important it is to be sensitive to context in these matters: "Whenever information is provided to a client, this must be done in a truthful, understandable and sensitive way. The nurse must proceed with an awareness of the client's needs, interests, and values" (Value II, 7). Ongoing dialogue with clients provides practitioners with an understanding of their wants, needs, and capabilities in light of which information can be communicated not only truthfully, accurately, and understandably, but also in accordance with concern for the client's good.

A further point to be raised in discussing the clinical-ethical interface concerns the cultural variability of norms and expectations about truthfulness and truthtelling. In some cultures and faiths, the provision of information to people who are seriously ill or dying is in many cases forbidden. Some elements of the Jewish faith, for example, remain primarily oriented around beneficence (Herring, 1984; Schindler, 1982).[11] As defensible as the norms that have evolved in North American society may be, they are not universally embraced. In a multicultural society such as ours, it is important to be sensitive to the wishes and expectations of people who do not share our values, and to avoid imposing these values on others.

Truthfulness and the Predicament of Nursing

Thus far truthtelling has been discussed generically as an issue for all or any health professionals. In nursing, truthtelling presents particular challenges because the role of nurses in the health care system often places them between the physician and the client. In hospital settings, the *client* is also a *patient* of one or more physicians. Ideally, the roles of physicians and nurses will be complementary, but in some instances they may conflict.

Information disclosure is a matter about which conflict between the nurse and the physician often arises. While the nurse and the physician alike may possess or have access to information of concern to the client, the disclosure of much of this information is primarily the prerogative of the physician. Jameton (1984, p. 167) points out that many nurses are institutionally bound by a "no-new-information" policy, according to which they are not permitted to give any medical information to clients that has not already been given to them by physicians.

To the extent that nurses are bound by such a policy, they can become caught in some very difficult predicaments. The nurse may feel obliged to communicate certain information to the client, yet be forbidden to do so, or able to do so only at the price of conflict with the physician. The fact that in many situations nursing work is performed in continuous proximity with clients makes the predicament more acute. Clients and their loved ones often direct their questions to nurses. How should nurses respond when they possess the information necessary to answer questions accurately and appropriately but are bound not to because such disclosures are deemed to be the exclusive prerogative of the physician?

When the roles of nurse and physician are differentiated according to a "no-new-information" policy, the nurse's ability to act in accordance with the duty to be truthful is limited. Although it is understood that role differentiation is necessary, in the area of psycho-social care there is room for debate about exactly how these roles should be differentiated, especially with regard to truthtelling. Granted, one should not speak beyond one's competence, and whoever imparts information should understand what is being imparted so as not to misinform. However, these conditions are not enough to disqualify nurses from having greater authority with respect to information disclosure than they currently have in many settings.

Indeed, Jameton (1984) argues that in many ways nurses are ideally suited for communicating information to clients since they possess special training in client and family education. Because of differences in education, he claims, "nurses are likely to be better at communicating with patients than physicians are" (p. 174). Moreover, the closeness of their contact with clients makes it possible for them to establish the kind of "ongoing dialogue" that Goldberg (1984) rightly emphasizes is so important for communicating the truth.

Issues of truthtelling for nurses, as Freel (1985) points out, "are embedded in broader practice issues," such as "the scope of nursing practice and professional dominance" (p. 1023). Yarling (1978) makes a cogent argument that the decision to inform the client is "a moral decision rooted in the recognition of the patient's moral right to such information" (p. 49). The medical expertise of physicians, therefore, does not entitle them to a monopoly over these decisions. As far as morality is concerned, nurses and physicians stand as equals.

As compelling as arguments may be that nurses are entitled to greater decision-making authority with respect to the communication of information, at the present time, and in many circumstances, rules that may be less than ideal are in effect. Curtin (1982) cautions that even if the nurse has ethics on his or her side, "the physician through means of position power and coercive power generally will secure compliance in moral as well as medical decisions or assure disciplinary actions" (p. 333). The reality in many practice settings is that disagreement with the physician concerning disclosure may be costly to nurses, both personally and professionally.[12]

In deciding what is appropriate in a given situation, it is prudent for nurses to consider the professional and legal implications of communication that may be perceived as being beyond their scope of practice. "Until the entire profession of nursing adopts a mutually supportive stance and institutionalizes it through enabling legislation and agency policies," Curtin (1982) notes, "individual nurses will be placed in uncomfortable if not untenable positions when conflicts arise regarding professional prerogatives, moral and ethical duties and patients' rights" (p. 333).

Case 1: Responding to a Direct Request for Information

In some instances, health professionals are morally uncertain about exactly *what* to tell clients, and *when* to tell what. A morally appropriate disclosure will depend very much on the context, and the client's interest in disclosure. The disclosure issue appears differently depending on whether the client is aware of and asks for the information, is aware of it but does not ask for it, or does not ask for it because he or she does not even know it exists.

In the event that the client has explicitly asked for certain information, the issue is relatively clear. The matter of *what* to tell is precisely pinpointed by the client's question; the matter of *when* to tell receives urgency from the fact that the client is asking the question *now*. Direct questions put the practitioner on the spot because they narrow the options. If the practitioner knows the answer to the client's question, the choice is fairly clearly between revealing it and not revealing it.

For a variety of reasons, clients often look to nurses for answers to questions that may be deeply important to them. In such instances, the duty to be truthful requires nurses to give a direct answer to the question (provided they know the answer). Unfortunately, the issue is not quite that simple. Difficult situations arise for nurses when, as often happens, they are not charged to give the information about which they have been asked. In many instances, nurses will agree with the constraints that inhibit them from giving a direct answer, and in other instances they will disagree. Regardless, in such situations the duty to be truthful with clients generates a conflict for nurses, as the following case illustrates:

> *Nurse Morton is an experienced nurse working in the emergency room of a large inner city hospital. Shortly after night report, Mr. Moses, a thirty-five year old construction worker who has a fractured femur and is in traction awaiting transfer to the orthopaedic unit, puts on his call light to complain of trouble breathing. When Nurse Morton arrives he is grimacing and breathing rapidly. He complains of chest pain, but is otherwise only slightly distressed.*

case study

In taking an EKG on Mr. Moses, Nurse Morton notes that his heart rate is slightly elevated. Suddenly, there appears a clear abnormality in the tracing pattern. Nurse Morton checks the leads and continues the tracing. A few seconds later, two more apparent abnormalities appear. Nurse Morton is startled, and glances quickly at Mr. Moses. She knows that long bone fractures carry the danger of embolism. Mr. Moses, noting her worried look, asks "What do you see?" Nurse Morton, who has extensive experience in reading EKGs, feels certain that there is something wrong. At the same time, she knows and accepts that it is not her role to interpret EKG readings. How should she respond?

Commentary

In the course of taking an EKG, Nurse Morton has discovered an abnormality. Having correctly inferred from her behaviour that she has noticed something significant, Mr. Moses has asked her to tell him what she sees. At first glance, this may seem a direct and straightforward question, but upon analysis it becomes less so, and the problem of how to respond to it in a truthful and responsible way becomes more complex.

Were Nurse Morton to respond to the question by describing in graphic terms the image she sees on the screen, she would be speaking truly, and at a literal level would be answering Mr. Moses' question. However, it is obvious from the context that this would not be a truthful response, and would not be a proper answer. It is clear from the context that Mr. Moses is asking her about the *meaning and significance* of what she sees.

Viewed in these terms, the question is still not entirely unambiguous. One way of interpreting it further would be to reduce it to a question about Nurse Morton's psychological state. Mr. Moses has noticed that Nurse Morton was startled, and he wants to know why. Interpreted in this way, the most truthful response would be one that communicated what the pattern she saw *meant to her*. The truthful answer to *this* question would be to say what was in her mind. At the very least, it would be to say that she saw something she *believed* to be abnormal.

A case can be made for equating truthfulness with saying what one has in mind, but even thus defined a truthful or honest response may not be a proper answer to Mr. Moses' question. To the extent that Mr. Moses is interested in Nurse Morton's psychological state and the opinion that she has formed, this is because he believes that this has a bearing on the question that really interests him: What does this *mean for me*? Clients expect and deserve more than truthfulness from health professionals. They trust that practitioners will be competent as well as honest. For the most part, clients value honesty in practitioners because they expect that what practitioners believe to be the truth is the truth. It is *this* truth that is important to them, and not the *belief* of the practitioner *per se*. If Nurse Morton were to tell Mr. Moses what she believes, would she be giving him the truth that really interests and concerns him?

This will depend on the reliability of the belief or opinion she has formed. The Canadian Nurses Association (1991) offers the following advice that might be helpful to Nurse Morton:

> Nurses have a responsibility to assess the understanding of clients about their care and to provide information and explanation *when in possession of the knowledge required to respond accurately* [italics added]. When the client's questions require information beyond that known to the nurse, the client must be informed of that fact and assisted to obtain the information from a health care practitioner who is in possession of the required facts. (Value II, 7)

Following this advice, the issue would centre on Nurse Morton's competence to provide the kind of information about which Mr. Moses is really interested. What, after all, does she really know? Were Nurse Morton to come right out and say "You have a ST wave change, which may indicate a pulmonary embolism," she may be saying something that, although truthful, would be beyond her competence, and quite possibly inaccurate. Given the limited clinical evidence available to her, to say this much may be irresponsible.

Furthermore, even if she were capable of giving an accurate diagnosis at this time, or at least to suggest it as a hypothesis, to do so is not within the scope of her practice. She is not charged with the responsibility of interpreting the EKG readings and making a diagnosis. The health care delivery system is one in which various practitioners work within defined roles to provide the best care possible for clients. For the most part, this assignment of roles and responsibilities is based on training and competence. Although in some instances there may be disagreement about how roles are defined relative to one another, overall the system of delivery works best if practitioners keep within their assigned roles.

Nurse Morton knows and accepts that it is not her responsibility to give the information about which Mr. Moses is really interested, and, we can gather, she does not want to give it. Still, she is in a difficult situation. Inadvertently, she has communicated to the client that she has interpreted the reading, and this has understandably aroused his interest and concern. How can she respond in a way that is as honest and truthful as possible while at the same time not communicate information that she is not charged to give and which may very well be inaccurate?

A cautious response would be to tell Mr. Moses that it is not her job to provide EKG interpretations, and that it would be best for him to direct his questions to the doctor. In so responding, she would be saying what is true, but would be evading his question, and not speaking as truthfully as possible. It would be more truthful, but less cautious, to respond that she has noticed a pattern in his heart rhythm that she needs to bring to the doctor's attention. However, it is likely that Mr. Moses would then ask her what she thinks the pattern means, and she would be faced with the same problem of whether to reveal the opinion that she has formed.

Under the circumstances, it is difficult to imagine a response that would be both responsible and completely truthful. In this situation, as in so many others, the best solution that can be hoped for is likely to compromise one of the values at issue.

Case 2: Lying to Protect the Client

Health professionals may be less than fully truthful with clients for a number of reasons. Arguably, the most understandable and justifiable reason is one rooted solidly in the paternalistic tradition of medicine; namely, for the client's own good.

However, paternalism is not the exclusive preserve of health professionals. Families and the loved ones of clients can be and often are more paternalistic than health professionals. Indeed, since they generally know their loved ones better and have a greater stake in what happens to them, it can be argued that paternalism is more justifiable for family members.

The family is an important part of the therapeutic context. The support of family members can be valuable to clients, especially in times of crisis. Moreover, they have a legitimate interest in the outcome, and often seek to be involved in decision-making. In some instances, this involvement can complicate communication between practitioners and clients, as the following case shows:

Karen Scullion, seventeen years old, has been admitted for surgery to evaluate a soft tissue mass suspicious for sarcoma. Radical resection of the tissue mass along with extensive skin grafting was performed.

While Karen was in the recovery room, the physician saw her parents to inform them of the results of the surgery. They were understandably shaken. Both parents insisted that Karen not be told the results until she "gets stronger." The mother informed the physician that Karen's favourite aunt recently died of cancer. Karen became so upset that in a matter of months she went from being near the top of her class at school to being in danger of failing several subjects. Her parents expressed the fear that, if Karen learns that she has cancer, she will suffer an even more serious breakdown. At first the physician insisted that Karen must be told the truth, but, after considerable pressure from the parents, agreed to withhold the information from her.

A few days later when the physician was making rounds with Nurse Chan, Karen asked if the surgery went well. The physician assured her that everything was okay, and said that she should just focus on her physiotherapy and concentrate on getting home.

Nurse Chan and the other nurses feel that Karen has a right to know the results of the surgery as soon as possible, and are further concerned that without such knowledge she cannot give informed consent to the extensive post-surgery rehabilitation she requires. When Nurse Chan approached the physician about this, he responded that the parents probably know their daughter best, and said that he wants to wait until the parents "come around."

Commentary

The main issue raised in this case is not *whether* but rather *when* Karen should be told the truth. The family believes that she should not be told the truth *now*, and have pressured the physician into keeping the information from Karen for an as yet unspecified period of time.

If Karen had not put a direct question to the physician, the issue would have been one of withholding information until some time thought to be more appropriate. However, by putting a direct question to the physician Karen gave the issue a sharper focus. In order to continue to withhold the truth beyond that point, the physician had to lie: Everything is not "okay."

Lying, in which one says something one knows to be false with the intent to deceive, is by some standards more serious than simply withholding information, which involves not saying what one knows to be true. In lying to Karen, the physician also put Nurse Chan and the other nurses on the spot. They must interact with Karen on a regular basis, and she will likely direct further questions to them about her health status. The lie having been told, Nurse Chan and the other nurses must decide whether to uphold this lie. In thinking about this issue, several considerations come into play.

If beneficence were the dominant consideration, Nurse Chan would decide what to do by comparing the relative benefits and harms of telling the truth as against upholding the lie. This calculation would have to be based on *predicted* consequences, and in general there is reason to doubt the ability of practitioners to make such predictions accurately and objectively. The disclosure of bad news is often emotionally uncomfortable for health professionals, and this may give them an unconscious bias toward predictions that would justify withholding information.

In this case, however, it is the family's prediction that has set the stage for the issue. Although the physician is probably correct in pointing out that the family members know Karen best, this alone is no guarantee that their prediction will be accurate and objective either. Moreover, the parents appear not to have taken into account the benefits that could come from being truthful, and the harms that could result from not disclosing the information to Karen. Karen will eventually learn the truth, and when she does she will probably feel betrayed and angry.

Whether upholding the lie would produce the most good for Karen is immaterial when one examines the case from the perspective of respect for autonomy. Karen is young, and it may be difficult for her parents to recognize and accept that she is no longer the "child" they have known her to be for most of her life, but those relating to her in a professional manner are obliged to view her differently. Unless there is evidence to the contrary, at seventeen she is mature enough to be treated as an adult. The fact that she is asking questions indicates that she wants to know the truth, and it is a serious offense against her autonomy to lie to her about it.

Other considerations bearing on when the truth should be disclosed to Karen follow from the ethical and legal requirements of informed consent. In light of the lie that she has been told, there is reason to suspect that Karen's initial consent to the surgery may not have been valid. If it was valid, the possibility of a serious diagnosis should have been discussed with her, and her feelings about post-surgery disclosure solicited. In any event, further interventions will be necessary, and her consent will be required for these. At the very least, informed consent will require that she knows the truth before consenting to any further tests or treatments.

If the above considerations lead Nurse Chan to conclude that Karen should be told the truth as soon as possible, there remains the question of *who* should tell her. Ordinarily, this would be the prerogative of the physician. Unfortunately, the physician is in a difficult situation. However ill-advised it was to do so, he has agreed to act in accordance with the family's wishes on the matter, and feels bound by this agreement. Indications are that the physician would like to be released from this agreement, but this would require Karen's parents to change their minds.

To this end, Nurse Chan and the physician could discuss ways of approaching the family about the matter. In paediatric contexts (and from the parent's paternalistic point of view this is how this case appears) parents can sometimes be persuaded to tell their children painful truths themselves (with or without the support of the medical and nursing staff).[13] Karen's father and mother might similarly be persuaded and assisted to tell their daughter, or at least to permit the physician to do so, with the nurse providing support. Lokich (1978) advises that the families of clients with cancer also need counselling to "help them develop supporting structures to deal with the disease and the future" (p. 29). Moreover, he suggests that "the family who insists that the patient could not stand to know the diagnosis should be carefully informed of the pros and cons of disclosure as well as of the importance of honesty" (p. 29).

Should an attempt to persuade the parents fail, the physician will have to weigh the force of his agreement with the family against other considerations. In this regard, it is important that the physician realize that by lying to Karen he has also put nursing staff in a difficult predicament. Upholding the lie in this situation is in violation of their professional ethics, and indeed of the physician's as well.

Ideally (and probably), it should be possible to resolve this issue by thoughtful discussion with the family. Failing this, Nurse Chan has some very forceful arguments on her side by which to persuade the physician to remedy the problem. If it proves necessary, Nurse Chan may also be able to gain moral (and institutional) support from senior staff members, such as the head nurse or supervisor.

However, resolving the issue through either of these channels may take some time. If Karen raises direct questions about her health status with Nurse Chan or the other nurses during this time, this will force the issue. Provided that Nurse Chan is convinced that the process of resolving the issue is under way, it may be an acceptable compromise to be somewhat evasive in response to Karen's questions, or simply to say that these questions would be better directed to the physician. Such an approach would be less than fully truthful, but would not be deceitful if Nurse Chan was actively taking steps to ensure that the truth will be told.

Case 3: Respecting the Client's Wish Not to Know

One of the reasons ongoing dialogue is so important is that through such dialogue practitioners learn things that enable them to communicate both truthfully and effectively with clients. What are the needs, wishes, and interests of the client? What does (or would) the client want to know? The more that is known about the client's wishes concerning disclosure, the less ambiguous are questions about what, when, and whether to disclose.

When the wishes of clients about disclosure are known, considerations having to do with respect for autonomy are particularly compelling. One important way by which we express such respect is by acting in accordance with the client's wishes and preferences, sometimes even when we believe that this is not in his or her best interests.

Respect for autonomy is usually invoked in favour of a general presumption to tell the truth, but this is because the usual case is one in which the client wants to know the truth. However, if respect for autonomy means honouring the client's wishes, then telling the truth will be incompatible with respect for autonomy in those cases where the client does not wish to know the truth. Such is the case in the following scenario:

> *Margaret Hanson is a twenty year old single parent who gave birth to her first baby six months ago. The baby required extensive resuscitation efforts at the time of birth, and was mechanically ventilated for almost two weeks. After six weeks in hospital, the baby's condition improved, and he was discharged home. However, the baby has been extremely irritable, difficult to feed, has had two seizures, and is delayed in achieving some developmental milestones. Further evaluation of these problems from a medical perspective is ongoing.*
>
> *Nurse Jim Bannister has been caring for Ms. Hanson in the neonatal follow-up clinic over the last few months, and they have developed a good relationship. Ms. Hanson has shared with Nurse Bannister some of her concerns about the baby's condition*

and about what the future holds. Although depressed over the seizures and the baby's fussiness, Ms. Hanson is most concerned about the possibility of the baby being "mentally retarded." She feels that she cannot deal emotionally with the prospect of developmental problems while at the same time going through the stresses of learning to care for a baby with feeding difficulties and seizures. On one occasion, she has said to the physician and Nurse Bannister: "If you find out the baby is mentally retarded, please don't tell me. It would be more than I can bear at the present time. Please allow me to hope that my baby will be fine over the long term. I don't know what I would do if I thought that my baby would never have a normal life."

Recently, it has become clear to the physicians and to Nurse Bannister that, as feared, the baby is developmentally delayed. In view of the good relationship Jim has developed with the client over the past few months, the physician values his opinion on the matter a great deal, and has asked him if he thinks Margaret should be confronted with the truth on her next visit. The physician is worried that if the truth is kept from Margaret much longer, the consequences both for her and her baby may be serious. What advice should Nurse Bannister give?

Commentary

The main question in this case centres on the timing of disclosure. A number of ethical (as well as clinical) considerations bear on this question. From the standpoint of beneficence, the challenge is to determine *when* Margaret would best be able to face the reality she fears. Certainly, for her own good she will have to come to terms with her baby's condition. This will be traumatic for her, but it may be less of a trauma at some future time. Letting her come to the realization slowly and at her own pace may be most beneficial for her. At some level, she may already know or at least suspect the truth, and be preparing herself to face it more directly.

Continued support can be given to help Margaret become emotionally and psychologically prepared to face the reality, but if she continues to resist the truth beyond a certain optimal time, concern for her good would require that the truth be told regardless of how well-prepared she is to receive it. Indeed, it may be that enough time has already elapsed to conclude that her problems will only worsen if the moment of direct disclosure is deferred much further.

In any event, the clinical assessment of what would be best for Margaret is subject to ethical scrutiny. From an ethical point of view, considerations about her best interests must be weighed with respect for her autonomy. As Gadow (1985, p. 37) stresses, not just *paternalistic deception* but *paternalistic honesty* as well is morally reproachable.

From the standpoint of respect for autonomy, the challenge is to determine what Margaret really wishes.[14] She has said on a previous occasion that she does not want to know the truth, but it is not clear whether this remains her *present wish*. If it is determined that her previous statement still remains valid, arguments to the effect that she has a *right to know* the truth do not apply. By indicating that she does not want to know the truth, she has in effect waived this right. To insist on telling her would be to confuse a *right* to be informed with an *obligation* to be informed (Yarling, 1978, p. 45). As the mother of a newborn who is dependent on her for care, Margaret may indeed have such an obligation. Even so, respect for autonomy does not go so far as forcing people to live up to their obligations.

A third consideration bearing on this case is fidelity to promise. As was discussed earlier, a presumption in favour of telling the truth can be derived from the nature of the fiduciary relationship between client and practitioner. However, in this case withholding the information would not be a violation of trust as long as this remains what Margaret wishes and expects from those caring for her. It is significant that Nurse Bannister and the physician agreed to withhold the truth from Margaret, or at least did not indicate that they would do otherwise. This particular practitioner-client relationship, therefore, is built on an implicit promise not to tell the truth. It can be argued that Nurse Bannister and the physician should never have made such an agreement, but since they did they are obligated by it.

The arguments considered so far have centred on what is owed to Margaret. However, Margaret is not the only party involved. The good of Margaret's baby, to whom obligations are also owed, hangs in the balance as well. What would be best for the baby? How effectively can Margaret care for the baby while being unaware of the baby's condition? Conversely, how effectively could she care for the baby if she were "devastated" upon learning the truth?

If it were decided that it would be best for the baby if Margaret was told about the baby's condition at her next visit, there may be a conflict between respect for Margaret's autonomy and concern for her good as against concern for the good of the baby. However, it is by no means obvious what is owed to Margaret, or that telling Margaret the truth despite her wishes would be best for the baby.

The situation upon which Nurse Bannister must reflect is a complex one. He will have to weigh the various considerations discussed above, taking into account the clinical assessment of the situation (much of which is not given in the description of the case). In planning and evaluating his options, and perhaps in discussing these with the physician, the fact that Nurse Bannister has a good relationship with Margaret is important. It is likely that by working with Margaret a solution can be found that will be best for all concerned.

Whenever the truth is made known to Margaret, Nurse Bannister will be able to lessen the trauma by educating her about how to cope with the situation and assuring her that ongoing support will be available. Indeed, it may turn out that Margaret's fears were somewhat exaggerated, and that the reality proves easier to deal with than the fears that kept her from confronting this reality.

Conclusion

Issues of truthfulness and disclosure are among the most difficult and delicate ethical issues for health professionals. Because of changing values, health professionals are expected and obliged to be more open and truthful in communicating with clients than they were in the past.

The cases we have examined illustrate some of the challenges the commitment to truth and truthfulness present for health professionals, and especially for nurses. In assessing and evaluating one's options in light of this commitment, contextual factors are crucial. In matters of truthfulness and truthtelling, it is especially important that ethical sensitivity be backed up by good clinical and interpersonal skills.

Notes

1   Useful summary reviews of the empirical data can be found in Novack et al. (1979) and in Moutsopoulos (1988).

2   This attitudinal shift does not appear to be anywhere near as dramatic as concerns prognosis. Annas (1994) reports on a 1982 study in which fewer than half the physicians surveyed would offer a frank prognosis to patients "with fully confirmed diagnosis of lung cancer in an advanced stage" (p. 223). By contrast, 85 percent of Americans surveyed wanted a "realistic estimate" of how long they had to live if they had a type of cancer that usually led to death in less than a year.

3   Less research has been done on the attitudes of nurses with regard to truthfulness with clients. Jameton (1984, p. 169) has an insightful discussion of two studies (Popoff, 1975, and Sandroff, 1981) that are frequently cited, and the comparison of which suggests a trend toward greater truthfulness in nursing.

4   Moutsopoulos (1988) reports that, after an exhaustive review of the medical literature on disclosure, he was able to find only "one instance where a patient suffered acute physical or psychological reaction to the truth that led to harm, namely one case of suicide" (p. 99). He goes on to point out that the same study mentions the suicide of two patients "who had not been informed of their diagnosis."

5   Bok (1978) cites studies that "show that there is generally a dramatic divergence between physicians and patients on the factual question of whether patients want to know what ails them in cases of serious illness such as cancer" (p. 229). Patients tend to want to know more than their physicians think they do.

6   For examples of arguments along these lines, see Veatch (1976, pp. 218-222), Fromer (1981, pp. 333-335), and Moutsopoulos (1988, pp. 103-104).

7   Ellin (1981), who argues that the fiduciary relationship *does not* preclude deception, is something of an exception.

8   The consequences of deceptive practices may extend beyond the particular relationship to jeopardize the practitioner-client relationship more generally. If, as a result of the publicization of deceptive prac-

tices, it came to be believed that such practices were common, people entering therapeutic relationships would become more uncertain that they were being told the truth and hence more distrustful.

9   Weir (1980) gives a very helpful gloss on Bok's distinction:

> For a person to be able to "speak the truth" depends upon that person's knowledge of a certain sphere of information and ability to give an accurate representation of that knowledge....to "speak truthfully" depends, in contrast, not on that person's knowledge or professional competence in some field, but on the person's moral choice to be honest and straightforward in speech. (p. 100)

10   Truth is never entirely objective, as is evident if one considers that facts are always embedded in some context. A study of people with lung cancer done by McNeil, Pauker, Sox, and Tversky (1982) showed that the preference between the alternative therapies of radiation and surgery depended very much on *how* the information was presented to clients.

11   Hattori et al. (1991) present research on the attitudes of Japanese physicians and their clients towards information disclosure. Several cultural differences stand out in this study, such as the fact that in Japanese society the family plays a much more important role in information disclosure than it does in North American society.

12   Jameton (1984, pp. 166-170) describes a publicized case that underscores some of the personal and professional hazards of communicating more or different information to clients than has been communicated already by their physicians.

13   For a discussion of truthtelling issues as they arise with children, see Leikin (1981) and Foley (1989). Foley says that "the philosophy today is to provide every child with an honest and complete explanation of his or her diagnosis, treatment, and prognosis based on cognitive abilities" (p. 110).

14   Given her psychological and emotional state, however, there may be some doubt whether her choice really was autonomous. If, or to the extent that it was not, respect for autonomy does not require that the choice be honoured.

References

American Nurses' Association. ([1976] 1985). *Code for nurses with interpretive statements*. Kansas City: Author.

Annas, G.J. (1994). Informed consent, cancer, and truth in prognosis. *The New England Journal of Medicine, 330* (3), 223-25.

Bok, S. (1978). *Lying: Moral choice in public and private life*. New York: Pantheon Books.

Canadian Nurses Association. (1991). *Code of ethics for nursing*. Ottawa: Author.

Collins, J. (1983). Should doctors tell the truth? In S. Gorovitz, R. Macklin, A.L. Jameton, J.M. O'Connor, & S. Sherwin (Eds.), *Moral problems in medicine* (2nd ed., pp. 199-202). Englewood Cliffs, NJ: Prentice-Hall.

Curtin, L.L. (1982). Case study XIV: A patient's right to know, a nurse's right to tell. In L.L. Curtin & M.J. Flaherty (Eds.), *Nursing ethics: Theories and pragmatics* (pp. 321-335). Bowie, MD: Robert J. Brady.

Ellin, J.S. (1981). The solution to a dilemma in medical ethics. *Westminster Institute Review, 1* (2), 3-6.

Foley, M.K. (1989). Children with cancer: Ethical dilemmas. *Seminars in Oncology Nursing, 5* (2), 109-113.

Freel, M.I. (1985). Truth telling. In J.C. McCloskey & H.K. Grace (Eds.), *Current issues in nursing* (2nd ed., pp. 1008-1024). Boston: Blackwell Scientific Publications.

Fromer, M.J. (1981). *Ethical issues in health care*. St. Louis: C.V. Mosby.

Gadow, S.A. (1985). Nurse and patient: The caring relationship. In A.H. Bishop & J.R. Scudder Jr. (Eds.), *Caring, curing, coping: Nurse, physician, patient relationships* (pp. 31-43). Birmingham, AL: University of Alabama Press.

Goldberg, R.J. (1984). Disclosure of information to adult cancer patients: Issues and update. *Journal of Clinical Oncology, 2* (8), 948-955.

Hattori, H., Salzberg, S.M., Kiang, W.P., Fujimiya, T., Tejima, Y., & Furuno, J. (1991). The patient's right to information in Japan: Legal rules and doctor's opinions. *Social Science and Medicine, 32* (9), 1007-1016.

Herring, B.F. (1984). *Jewish ethics and halakhah for our time: Sources and commentary*. New York: Ktav Publishing.

Jameton, A.L. (1984). *Nursing practice: The ethical issues*. Englewood Cliffs, NJ: Prentice-Hall.

Leikin, S.L. (1981). An ethical issue in paediatric cancer care: Nondisclosure of a fatal prognosis. *Paediatric Annals, 10* (10), 37-45.

Lokich, J.J. (1978). *Primer of cancer management*. Boston: G.K. Hall.

McNeil, B.J., Pauker, S.G., Sox, H.C., & Tversky, A. (1982). On the elicitation of preferences for alternative therapies. *The New England Journal of Medicine, 306* (21), 1259-1262.

Moutsopoulos, L. (1988). Truth telling to patients. In R.B. Edwards & G.C. Graber (Eds.), *Bioethics* (pp. 93-105). San Diego: Harcourt Brace Jovanovich.

Novack, D.H., Plumer, R., Smith, R.L., Ochitill, H., Morrow, G.R., & Bennett, J.M. (1979). Changes in physicians' attitudes toward telling the cancer patient. *Journal of the American Medical Association, 241* (9), 897-900.

Oken, D. (1961). What to tell cancer patients: A Study of medical attitudes. *The Journal of the American Medical Association, 175* (13), 86-94.

Popoff, D. (1975). What are your feelings about death and dying? Part 1. *Nursing 75, 5* (8), 15-24.

President's Commission for the Study of Ethical Problems in Medicine and Biomedical and Behavioral Research. (1982). *Making health care decisions: A report on the ethical and legal implications of informed consent on the patient-practitioner relationship* (Vol. 1). Washington, DC: Government Printing Office.

Sandroff, R. (1981). Is it right? Protect the MD ... or the patient? Nursing's unequivocal answer. *RN, 44* (2), 28-33.

Schindler, R. (1982). Truth telling and terminal illness: A Jewish view. *Journal of Religion and Health, 21* (1), 42-48.

Veatch, R.M. (1976). *Death, dying and the biological revolution*. New Haven, CT: Yale University Press.

Wagner, M. (1991). A question of informed consent. *Nursing 91, 21* (4), 66, 68.

Weir, R. (1980). Truthtelling in medicine. *Perspectives in Biology and Medicine, 24* (1), 95-112.

Yarling, R.R. (1978). Ethical analysis of a nursing problem: The scope of nursing practice in disclosing the truth to terminal patients (Part II). *Supervisor Nurse, 9* (6), 40-50.

Study Questions: Truthfulness

Case 1: Responding to a Direct Request for Information

1. Is it morally justifiable to withhold information when one is uncertain whether it is true or accurate?

2. Give an example of how Nurse Morton might speak *truly*, but not *truthfully* in response to Mr. Moses' question.

3. Suppose that Mr. Moses' question concerned a diagnosis already charted by the physician but not yet disclosed. How would this change the issue?

4. To what extent might it be an abdication of moral responsibility to respond to direct questions with the words "I am not charged to provide such information"?

Case 2: Lying to Protect the Client

1. What moral relevance does Karen's age have on the issue raised by this case?

2. What input are families entitled to as concerns decision-making affecting their loved ones?

3. How might it help or hinder the resolution of this issue to view the family as client?

4. How would you distinguish between lying and withholding information, and how would you evaluate the moral seriousness of each?

Case 3: Respecting the Client's Wish Not to Know

1. Is it ever advisable for health professionals to agree in advance to withhold information from clients at their request?

2. Suppose that Margaret were married, and she insisted that her husband also not be told the truth. How would this change the issue?

3. "Respect for autonomy does not mean giving people license to be irresponsible." Discuss this statement with reference to this case.

4. Develop the argument that the fact Margaret has said that she does not want to know the truth means that she is not being autonomous.

CONFIDENTIALITY

*I ... will hold in confidence all personal matters committed to
my knowledge in the practice of my calling.*

— FLORENCE NIGHTINGALE PLEDGE

---

*Clients must be able to trust health professionals to preserve con-
fidentiality. Otherwise, they would not be as open about themselves as is necessary for health professionals to provide appropriate and effective care. Breaches of confidentiality, even when
apparently harmless, can undermine the trust of clients in health
professionals. Nevertheless, in some instances health professionals have an ethical obligation to warn innocent persons that they
are at serious risk. Also, they are required by law to disclose confidential information when the health and safety of another person is at stake.*

*In the case studies in this chapter, issues of confidentiality are
discussed involving a nurse working in an occupational health
unit whose superior demands the health record of an employee
asking for sick leave; a fertility clinic team working with a client
who tests positive for the HIV virus and wants this fact concealed
from his wife; and a nurse working in a small town who in social
settings is asked to share information about clients.*

Health Professionals, Persons, and the Personal

Persons are defined and define themselves in different relationships and roles: employee, employer, colleague, acquaintance, friend, lover, spouse, parent, child, and so on. In whatever role we exist, we selectively reveal and conceal different parts of ourselves. In a relationship with a spouse we reveal things we conceal, or at least remain silent about, with colleagues; our children know things about us that we would never share with acquaintances. If our lives are like stories, we are not open books; different pages and chapters are open to different people.

That we open and close ourselves selectively does not mean that we are deceitful, although it can mean that. Rather, it attests to the fact that persons are multidimensional, and the power in some measure to choose which dimensions will be open to which people is an essential condition of being a person. It ensures the sacredness of what is most intimate and private to us. In the fullest sense, to be a *person* is to hold some things *personal*.

Privacy and confidentiality are closely interrelated.[1] Westin (1968) defines privacy as "the claim of individuals, groups or institutions to determine for themselves when, how and to what extent information about them is communicated to others" (p. 7). Winslade (1978, p. 195), who also links privacy and confidentiality, defines the latter in terms of the protection of and control over information *privy* to persons in special relationships. In general, privacy concerns the right of the client to limit access of other persons to his or her personal information. Confidentiality, by contrast, pertains to the obligation of those who have become privy to such personal information not to disclose it without authorization.

Privacy and confidentiality are especially important in the health care context. Health care institutions reach further into intimate and private dimensions of our lives than do most other institutions. In the interest of promoting, preserving, and restoring health, we allow health professionals access to knowledge about ourselves that we otherwise guard as being private or personal. We reveal our bodies naked to be probed and examined. We open pages of our lives that are sometimes unknown even to those with whom we are most intimate. In doing so, we become very vulnerable. Our personal well-being and dignity may be threatened. Information revealed or otherwise gleaned, if more publicly revealed to certain others outside the therapeutic context, may cause us harm.

Because health care reaches so far into our personal lives and makes us vulnerable, it is imperative that health care professionals be respectful of our privacy and hold in confidence knowledge disclosed in the therapeutic relationship. The situation may be conceived as a kind of contract. Clients open personal dimensions of their lives to health professionals, who in turn promise to hold in confidence what is disclosed to them. Without the expectation that this promise will be honoured, clients would not reveal what it is necessary to know for therapeutic purposes.

Breaches of Confidentiality

Historically, respect for privacy and confidentiality has been a major value in the health professions, as evidenced by such ancient sources as the physicians' Hippocratic Oath. Florence Nightingale regarded respect for confidentiality as being an integral part of the practice of nursing. In contemporary nursing, this respect is enshrined in the various promissory statements — ethical guidelines, codes of ethics, and legislation — that govern the profession.

Professional promise and official statements notwithstanding, in practice respect for confidentiality has often been honoured more in the breach than in the observance. Fleck (1986) writes that "the frequency with which casual breaches of confidentiality occur in hospitals ... suggests that relatively few health care professionals regard confidentiality as a matter of serious moral concern" (p. 18). In Ontario, Krever (1980) chronicled some disturbing — if not shocking — breaches of confidentiality in the health care system. Many of these occurred in connection with claims investigations undertaken by insurance companies, in which confidential information was often obtained under false and even fraudulent pretences. Partly as a result of the kind of scrutiny Krever brought to bear on these matters, in Ontario and elsewhere, checks and controls to preserve confidentiality have been tightened.

Generally, breaches of confidentiality may be either deliberate and intentional or inadvertent and unintentional. Intentional breaches of confidentiality, which will be the focus of the next section, occur when health professionals, quite aware that confidentiality is in question, knowingly and deliberately decide to subordinate confidentiality to some other good or value. The duty to respect confidentiality, for example, may come into conflict with the duty to prevent harm, as when a nurse learns something from or about a client that bears on the safety of others. Some classic cases of this involve people with communicable diseases, those who subject others to physical abuse, and people such as airline pilots whose health status has a direct bearing on the safety of others.

Inadvertent or unintentional breaches of confidentiality, by contrast, occur when health professionals do not realize that they are breaching confidentiality or engaging in practices that may result in improper disclosures. A conversation among nurses overheard in a cafeteria, an unguarded answer to a seemingly innocuous question about a client, a chart or record left momentarily unattended, are but a few examples.[2] Such violations are typically the result of carelessness or thoughtlessness, and to a great extent can be avoided by an increased resolve to guard confidential information.

In some instances, however, there may be uncertainty whether information really is confidential, or who has the rightful control over information. What constitutes a breach of confidentiality? A breach of confidentiality occurs when two conditions are met: information about someone must be shared with or made available to others without the client's authorization; the information shared must be confidential. Either of these conditions may be difficult to apply in a given case.

1. Information Sharing and Client Authorization

At first glance, the condition that information-sharing be authorized by the client seems simple enough. Given that the ultimate authority over confidential information is the client, the sharing of confidential information is authorized or not depending on whether the client agrees or consents to it. If confidential information is released to someone with the client's consent, then no breach of confidentiality has taken place.

However, this does not mean that the client must specifically agree to and authorize every instance of information-sharing in the health care setting. In a modern health care facility, this would be extremely tedious and would compromise the delivery of quality care. Historically, confidentiality has been understood by the nursing profession to permit information-sharing on a "need to know" basis with other health professionals who have a part in the care of the client. It is assumed (more or less explicitly) that the client authorizes this information-sharing as long as it is needed for the purpose of giving care.[3] In this regard, it is important to distinguish between *implied* and *expressed* (or explicit) consent to the disclosure of information.

The trend toward a team-based approach to health care (which requires greater information-sharing) presents new difficulties and challenges of confidentiality.[4] Furthermore, teams in hospitals work with community-based colleagues from admission to discharge. The persons involved may include nurses, physicians, chaplains, home care workers, nutritionists, speech therapists, physiotherapists, laboratory technicians, management and clerical staff. They do not all need to know the full information in the client's health record. It is enough for each to know only what he or she needs to know in order to contribute effectively to the client's care. For example, on a "need to know" basis, nursing staff in a nursing unit would have access to client laboratory reports but clerical staff would not. However, in some cases deciding what information is needed for care purposes and by which care-givers can be quite difficult.

As a rule, the greater the number of people with authorized access to confidential information, the greater the risk of unauthorized people gaining access. As hospitals move toward comprehensive computer and health information management systems, new challenges with respect to protecting confidentiality arise.

2. Determining Whether Information is Confidential

Closely related to the issue of authorization to disclose confidential information is the issue of determining whether a given item of information is in fact confidential to begin with. Suppose that in a hospital maternity ward Mrs. Smith asks the nurse if Mrs. Jones (who earlier was moved to the delivery room) has delivered yet, or whether she had a boy or a girl. Ought this information to be considered confidential? Or suppose that in an occupational setting Mr. Simpson's boss asks the nurse to provide a log indicating when and how often (but not why) Mr. Simpson has been to the health unit in the past six months? Is this information confidential?

Part of the difficulty in deciding these questions in the abstract is that what stamps a given item of information as being confidential is not merely a function of the nature of the information alone. The context or understanding in which it is initially acquired or made available is also decisive. For example, nothing about the fact that Mrs. Jones had a baby boy, or that she chose cauliflower with dinner instead of carrots, stamps it as being intrinsically confidential. Indeed, it is hard to imagine how or why it would be.[5]

Even so, if I am made privy to this information in an understanding or context in which the client has reason to assume that I will not reveal it to others, it is for that reason confidential. Along these lines, information about a client is confidential if it is learned in a context (e.g., a professional relationship in a hospital setting) wherein the client has reason to expect (e.g., a promise has been made) that it will be treated as being confidential.

However, such an "understanding" or "promise" may be more or less explicit, and problems might arise from this. Someone may share something that he or she regards as being confidential without explicitly asking the person with whom it is shared not to reveal it to anyone else. The promise of confidentiality in such a situation is implied or assumed. Alternatively, it may be implied or assumed that certain information is not confidential. It may be that Mrs. Jones does not mind if Mrs. Smith is told that she had a baby boy. Indeed, she may even prefer that Mrs. Smith be told. However, it may also be that, for reasons we could hardly anticipate, she does not want Mrs. Smith to know.

The role of contextual factors in stamping information as being confidential or not confidential introduces uncertainty, and with this uncertainty the possibility of misunderstanding or misconstruing the situation. The more that is assumed or left implicit between nurse and client, the greater the risk of misunderstanding (e.g., "But I assumed that you would treat *that* as being confidential between us!"). The nurse can guard against such misunderstanding and potential complications by being as explicit as possible with the client about what sorts of things will or should be protected under the umbrella of confidentiality. This is especially important in cross-cultural exchanges, as sensibilities about privacy and confidentiality vary between cultures.

Exceptions to the Rule of Confidentiality

It is with good reason that confidentiality is valued as highly as it is in health care. A sense of control over personal information may be vital to a client's integrity and well-being. This control alone may have therapeutic value.

Moreover, the nurse needs access to information about the client in order to provide care. If the client cannot trust the nurse to keep such information confidential, he or she will be less cooperative in granting access to personal information, or indeed may decline to participate in programs or services. From the perspective of the client, confidential information is a double-edged sword: It may be used to help, but it may also bring harm.

As important as it is for the sorts of reasons given above, the value of confidentiality in health care is not absolute. The duty to preserve confidentiality can come into conflict with other duties. Confidentiality is not an absolute value and must be weighed alongside other values, as is widely acknowledged by the health professions. There are exceptions to the rule of confidentiality and conditions under which it is justifiable to breach confidentiality. Indeed, under certain circumstances the nurse is required by law to disclose confidential information.

Considerable controversy exists around the issue of what constitutes a legitimate or justifiable exception.[6] The least controversial exception is when preserving (or promising) confidentiality conflicts with the concern for the good or safety of others (beneficence). A landmark legal case here is that of Tarasoff v. Regents of the University of California.[7] A young woman was murdered by a person who at the time was under psychiatric care. The murderer/client had previously confided to his psychologist an intention to kill his former girl friend. Although the psychologist took some steps to protect against this danger, and at one point had the client detained by the university police, he did not communicate the threat to the woman. Obviously, he did not do enough to prevent harm from coming to her. After the young woman was murdered, her family took the matter to court, arguing that she should have been warned of or otherwise protected from the danger. In effect, the court ruled that, if in the course of a therapeutic relationship the therapist is given reason to believe that the client may present a danger to others, he or she has a "duty to warn" of this danger.

The "duty to warn" remains a subject of some controversy for health professionals, especially when extrapolated to cases involving people with Acquired Immunodeficiency Syndrome (AIDS). Consider, for example, the case of a sexually active man who has no intention of informing his wife that he has AIDS. Does a health professional who is aware of the situation have a responsibility to warn the woman that she is in danger, even though this would mean disclosing information gained in confidence?

The ethical codes of the various health professions agree that under certain conditions it is justifiable, if not obligatory, to disclose confidential information in the interests of averting harm. For example, the

Canadian Nurses Association (1991) states the following limitation to the duty of confidentialty:

> The nurse is not morally obligated to maintain confidentiality when the failure to disclose information will place the client or third parties in danger. Generally, legal requirements or privileges to disclose are morally justified by these same criteria. In facing such a situation, the first concern of the nurse must be the safety of the client or the third party. (Value III, Limitation)

One of the noteworthy things about this statement is that, going beyond concern for the safety of third parties, it also includes concern for the safety of the client as a justifiable reason for disclosing confidential information. Some would object to this inclusion on the grounds that it is paternalistic. The difference between harm to the client and harm to third parties, it can be argued, is morally relevant. If the client is willing to assume the risk of personal harm rather than disclose certain information, that is the client's decision to make. Unsuspecting third parties, however, have no choice in the matter, and so the argument that there is an obligation to intervene on their behalf is more cogent.[8]

A major weakness in the prevention of harm argument is that the idea of harm is vague and uncertain. Harm encompasses a broad range of phenomena. Harms can be distinguished along a continuum ranging from the very minor, such as a pin prick, to the most serious, namely death. The more serious the harm foreseen, the more compelling is the case for breach of confidentiality. How serious does the harm foreseen have to be in order to warrant a breach of confidentiality? Moreover, there may be some uncertainty whether the harm foreseen, however serious, will materialize. One must consider not only the *magnitude* of the harm, but also its *probability*, which may range from being very low to very high. The psychologist whose client confided an intention to kill his former girlfriend apparently believed that the probability of the event was low. What degree of probability assigned to the harm foreseen is sufficient to justify breaching confidentiality?

Both the magnitude and the probability of the harm foreseen are morally relevant and have to be weighed together, but they cannot be combined to yield a simple formula for mechanically deciding the conditions under which it is justifiable to breach confidentiality. One cannot dispense with the need for health professionals to cultivate good judgement in these matters.

This need is explicitly acknowledged in various codes of ethics. The International Council of Nurses ([1973] 1982) asserts that "the nurse holds in confidence personal information and *uses judgment* [italics added] in sharing this information." The American Nurses' Association (ANA, [1976] 1985) states: "The right to privacy is an inalienable human right. The client trusts the nurse to hold all information in confidence. This trust could be destroyed and the client's welfare jeopardized by *injudicious disclosure* [italics added] of information provided in confidence" (Statement 2.1).

Granted the resolve to keep confidences, there may be uncertainty about what is and is not confidential, or whether a competing duty weighs heavily enough in the situation to over-ride one's duty to hold information confidential. In these grey areas there can be much room for latitude in decision-making.

With regard to this latitude, and indeed anywhere grey areas are left to individual judgement or discretion, it is important that the rules of the game be known in advance.[9] Clients are entitled to know, at least in a general way, the conditions under which confidential information about them might be released to others without their consent. In this regard, nurses should be aware — and as appropriate make their clients aware — of any laws that might require nurses or other health professionals to disclose confidential information. For example, Ontario and many other jurisdictions nurses are bound by law to report suspected abuse to the Children's Aid Society.

Indeed, if clients are informed in advance of the conditions under which personal information about them might be disclosed, it could be argued that subsequent disclosure under those conditions would not constitute a breach of confidentiality at all. No promise to the contrary would have been made. If I refuse to promise unconditionally to keep something secret, and on this understanding the person tells it to me regardless, I have not broken my promise if later I disclose it to someone else.

A moral that might be extracted from this discussion: Be very careful what you do and do not promise; above all, do not make promises on which you may later feel you have to renege.

Confidentiality in the Age of Information

New technologies in health care pose new challenges with respect to privacy and confidentiality. The use of smart cards and computer information systems raises apprehensions that every detail of client interactions with the health system will be monitored by "big brother". In addition, reports of computer hackers breaking into databanks prompt worries about how secure supposedly protected data really is.

Rapid developments in genetic testing raise yet other concerns. The information gleaned from such testing may be very revealing, and very sensitive. There are a variety of reasons why such information might be of interest or even importance to third parties, including employers, insurance companies, the police, and family members.

Although the information age in which we live increases the urgency of concerns about privacy and confidentiality, the key moral questions and issues arising are not new. What rights do clients have over their personal health information? Who is entitled to have access to such private information? Under what circumstances might it be permissible, or perhaps even obligatory, for a health professional to disclose confidential information without the consent of the client?

Moral questions and issues concerning privacy and confidentiality appear in an especially interesting and important perspective when viewed in light of public health and the control of communicable diseases. In the Middle Ages, when the Black Plague swept through Europe, a sign on the door told neighbours that someone in the house was infected or had died. Often the family was put in quarantine or driven out of town when the news was thus announced for all to see. Infected persons and persons suspected of being plague carriers would suffer discrimination, persecution, and in some cases be put to death.

Many of the same prejudices and practices that have surrounded infectious, deadly diseases for centuries can be discerned in our society's response to AIDS. However, today's society is also different from previous ones as concerns the importance it assigns to human rights. Concerns about privacy and confidentiality have shaped our society's response to this disease from the beginning.

There is a great deal about HIV and AIDS that we do not know. Even so, such clinical facts about testing and treatment as bear on issues of privacy and confidentiality are for the most part well-established. It is known that HIV is transmitted through contact with body fluids infected with HIV. The main modes of transmission are through sexual contact and sharing intravenous drug needles. Approximately 3000 Canadians contracted the virus through transmission of blood products before they were screened for HIV starting in 1985. With recent treatment advances, some persons with HIV are living longer, but no cure is in sight.

In addition to being a deadly disease, HIV can be described as a social disease. Persons with HIV must deal with discrimination and stigmatization and may incur serious social and financial losses. Given the magnitude of these harms and risks, consent for testing, and confidentiality in the matter of test results, are especially important. When consent is sought for testing, the client must be told clearly what will happen to the test results. If the client does not approve of the disclosure procedure, he or she may decide not to be tested. In other words, consent for HIV testing is mandatory but testing is voluntary.

Given the serious harm that can follow disclosure of HIV tests results, voluntary, anonymous HIV testing has been made available in some jurisdictions, including Ontario. The security of anonymity enables clients to learn whether they have HIV without fearing that this information may become known to someone else and subsequently used against them. Since the people who come forward for anonymous testing are offered counselling and education about prevention and safer lifestyles, it also helps reduce the spread of HIV. In addition, the statistical, non-nominal information that is gathered from anonymous testing helps public health agencies to plan education and prevention programs.

If anonymous testing were not available, and fewer people therefore agreed to be tested for fear of reprisal, epidemiological knowledge would not be as complete as it is. Anonymous testing demonstrates that provisions and protections respecting privacy and confidentiality also make good sense from a public health point of view.

The concept of confidentiality, although fairly straightforward in some ways, is in other respects very subtle. The following cases elaborate on some of these subtleties and exhibit some of the main issues raised in connection with confidentiality.

Case 1: Confidentiality in a Nontraditional Therapeutic Setting

Increasingly, nursing is practiced in settings outside of the acute care hospital. Nurses work in clinics, in the community, in industry, in schools and in remote outposts. The principles that guide nurses in matters of confidentiality evolved and were designed to govern in traditional settings and nurse-client roles. Outside the traditional setting, certain factors can make the application of these principles considerably more difficult. Different expectations and assumptions may come into play. Roles and relationships take on different meanings. The world of the factory is different from the world of the hospital. Similarly, the client's home sets a different milieu for nursing than does the hospital.

Occupational health nursing is a field in which the nurse's commitment to confidentiality may be tested as a result of factors that are not present in traditional settings. The occupational health nurse typically works alone, and often without the support of other health professionals on site. Colleagues and managers may lack knowledge and appreciation of the fundamental values of health care. In health care settings it is understood that the interests and well-being of the client are the top priority. However, in industry and business, other goals and values may be at the fore. Even within a health care setting, the values that govern the care of *patients* may be different than the values adhered to when the clients are *employees* of the institution.

Organizational factors may also challenge confidentiality in the practice of occupational health nursing. Corporate health services are often part of the human resources department. This may lead to conflict, since the two departments may have different perspectives on employee information. Occupational health settings are also unique because the client and the nurse are both employees of the same company or institution. Occupational health nurses can be in an ethical dilemma when they are expected to represent both the management's and the client/employee's interests.

The following case shows how these complicating factors may come into play and helps to elucidate some general features of the concept of confidentiality.[10]

John Le Blanc is the nursing manager of an occupational health unit in a large urban hospital. He reports to the Vice-President of Human Resources, Rose Christie. From past experience, John knows that Rose does not attach as much value to confidentiality as he believes she should. Even so, this difference in point of view has never been tested in their working relationship. Today, however, Rose has asked him for the health record of Evelyn Green.

Evelyn Green is a registered nurse who has been employed by the hospital for twenty years and has an excellent employment and attendance record. Unbeknownst to others, she developed a serious alcohol problem after her husband died a year ago.

Last week, Evelyn came to the occupational health unit and asked John to help get her into a recovery program as soon as possible. John immediately arranged for her to be assessed by an Alcohol and Drug Addiction Program contracted with the hospital, upon which plans were made for her to enter a recovery program the following week. John also filled out a form on Evelyn's behalf certifying that she had an illness and would need to be granted sick leave for six months. In keeping with accepted procedure, the form did not indicate the nature of the sickness. This omission was very important to Evelyn, who feared that she might lose her job if her employer learned about her drinking problem.

John knows that Rose is concerned about the high costs of replacing Evelyn for six months. Rose feels that she has a right to more information about the reason justifying sick leave for Evelyn, which is why she requested her health record.

However, John has a duty to preserve confidential information. He explains to Rose that the information she has requested is confidential and cannot be provided. Hearing this, Rose becomes angry. She reminds John that he is also an employee of the hospital and as such owes loyalty to their employer. Furthermore, she claims that the hospital owns the record and therefore has a right to review it.

After politely hearing her arguments, John reaffirms his initial stand. Rose responds, "I want that information on my desk by tomorrow morning. And if you won't get it for me, you can be replaced by someone who will!"

Commentary

The issue raised by this case can be analyzed from more than one angle. In the first place, it could be expressed as a conflict between the employer's need to know and the employee's (Evelyn Green's) right to control private information. So conceived, the issue turns on how much weight should be given to each.

In deciding this, it makes a difference why the employer needs to know the information. For example, if the information were needed in order to prevent some serious harm, this would be a weighty reason. In this case, however, the employer needs to know for essentially economic reasons. Such reasons carry considerably less weight.

On the other side of the balance, it is pertinent that the information at issue, if released to the employer, is potentially harmful to the client. It is also relevant that the client, who initially made the information available to health professionals, would have had reason to expect confidentiality.[11] How disclosure to the employer would affect employee trust in the health service would also weigh in the balance. If other employees learned that personal information from the health service would be disclosed to the employer on demand, they might be discouraged from using the health service.

As described, however, the issue is only indirectly between the employer and Evelyn Green. More directly, it concerns the occupational health nurse, who is caught in the middle. Viewed from this angle, the focus is on the duties and responsibilities of the nurse. On the one side, as Rose has reminded him, John has a duty to their employer. On the other side, he has a duty to the clients of the Occupational Health Department, and in particular a duty to preserve information made-privy to him in the context of a professional relationship.

Were the issue between these two duties only, John should choose to preserve confidentiality. In so deciding, he would be acting in accordance with the nursing profession's code of ethics, standards of practice, and with the requirements of the law. However, a further complication stems from the fact that Rose has threatened him with the loss of his job if he fails to cooperate. It would be reasonable for John to be concerned for his interests and to weigh these in his decision-making. Moreover, duty to others (perhaps he is supporting a family) may be a serious concern for John.

Given this analysis, John's dilemma is that if he does what he believes is morally right, he puts himself, and employees who depend on the services of the occupational health department, in jeopardy. If he follows Rose's instructions and violates his ethical values by handing over confidential records, he may protect his job, but at the cost of sacrificing or compromising his integrity.

Moreover, this course of action would also involve serious professional risk. The disclosure of such information without the client's consent would be in contravention of professional norms and could make him vulnerable to charges of professional misconduct.

What options, then, does John have? He could discuss the issue with Evelyn Green and ask her to release the information voluntarily. Under the circumstances, however, such a request would be coercive. The knowledge that John could lose his job might burden Evelyn with a sense of guilt or responsibility, especially if John approached her directly.

A better alternative would be for John to discuss the matter further with Rose. Although Rose happens to work in a health setting, she is not a health professional but an administrator. Apparently, she has not been sensitized to regard confidentiality as a primary value.

To explain his position, it might prove effective for John to provide Rose with information about the professional norms and constraints under which nurses and other health professionals practice. Guidelines published by the Ontario Occupational Health Nurses Association (1987), for example, state that access to confidential information "should be confined to the occupational health physician and the occupational health nurse," and, moreover, explicitly advise that "health records should be located separately from general personnel files"(p. 2).[12]

Informing Rose about these legal and professional norms might be enough to win her to his side. However, the mindset of health care (oriented around client well-being) and that of business or administration (more oriented around the proverbial bottom line) are somewhat different. Rose may not be a very good student of health care ethics.

Even so, perhaps from within her mindset John could persuade Rose of the importance of preserving confidentiality. She may be receptive to the argument that employee trust in the health service would be undermined if the promise of confidentiality were not guaranteed. This in turn would have adverse consequences for the hospital.

John's next step could be to approach a senior nursing administrator, who may have a broader perspective on the issue. Moreover, the administrator might be able to intervene and convince Rose that the policy of preserving confidentiality is in the best interest of employees and, in the long run, of the hospital. It might also prove useful to remind Rose of Evelyn's excellent employment record and of the costs of losing such a valuable employee.

If these options prove to be dead ends, there may be yet other options to try, such as contacting an outside person to mediate. Resources for John include nursing professional organizations and the provincial self-regulatory body.

It is also possible, however, that, in the end, John will find himself faced with no attractive options, and will have to make a tragic choice that may put his own job in jeopardy. There is little doubt that John has good arguments on his side, and in an enlightened workplace his position regarding confidentiality would prevail. Unfortunately, the reality is that many workplaces are less than ideal.

Case 2: Confidentiality in a Family Context

In the previous case, the third party who wanted confidential information was not an intimate and had interests clearly at odds with those of the client. Much more frequently, requests for confidential information come from family members or significant others who share with the nurse concern for the well-being of the client.[13] This intimacy and concern may seem to give these others a greater claim to confidential information. Indeed, usually the client is quite willing to share information with intimates, whose desire to know arises out of concern. Perhaps they are worried or anxious, and knowing more will help them to cope with the situation. Perhaps knowing more will put them in a better position to help, even if only by sharing with the client a personal crisis he or she is living through.

Sometimes, however, the client may not want family members or intimates to have access to health-related information. Or the client may want family to know some things, but not others; or perhaps may want only some family members to be informed. The client may be estranged from his or her family, or certain members of the family. He or she may want to protect family members from bad news or may feel guilty or ashamed. A variety of reasons may come into play.

Acquired Immunodeficiency Syndrome (AIDS) has presented many challenges to confidentiality. AIDS is mainly transmitted through sexual behaviour, and sexuality is a deeply personal and private part of our lives. Moreover, sexuality comes under a number of social norms and taboos. Consequently, this dimension of our lives can be shrouded in secrecy and deception. Indeed, some people conceal aspects of their sexual lives even from those with whom they are sexually and emotionally intimate.

Because AIDS is infectious, and its consequences are so grave, screening protocols to detect Human Immunodeficiency Virus (HIV, the virus thought to be the principal cause of AIDS) have been established in a number of areas in the health care system. Such screening may turn up information about clients' sexual history and behaviour about which they may be understandably apprehensive.

case study

The issue of confidentiality raised in the following case is further complicated by the fact that the testing has been done in the context of a treatment involving a married couple:[14]

After four years of trying unsuccessfully to have a baby, and numerous consultations, Valerie and Alan Joblonski have been referred to a fertility clinic. It is suspected that their inability to conceive is due to Alan having a low sperm count. In this event, the chances of conceiving would be greatly enhanced by undergoing a process wherein Alan's sperm would be collected and concentrated, later to be artificially inseminated in Valerie during the optimal period of her ovulation cycle.

The clinic screens couples for a number of medical indicators, and, after much debate, has recently added HIV to the list. During the screening process, it is determined that Alan is positive for the virus. In a post-test conference, Alan reveals that he has had several bisexual relationships, and moreover that Valerie is unaware of this.

According to clinic policy, if a client tests positive, treatment will be interrupted until a counselling team, including a social worker and a psychologist, have met with the couple. Alan is unwilling to do this. He wants the staff to withhold his test results from Valerie because he fears she will leave him if she learns of his extramarital affairs.

The day after the post-test interview with Alan, Valerie, who is unaware and unsuspecting of the problem, phones the clinic and asks when the treatment will be scheduled. The nurse who speaks with her evades the question because the nursing staff disagree about what they should tell her or how they should proceed. Some think that Valerie must be told, and if not by her husband then by staff. Others are concerned that this would violate confidentiality with Alan.

Commentary

Three main values figure prominently in this case: confidentiality, beneficence (more precisely, nonmaleficence), and truthfulness.[15] A number of different scenarios might eventuate, and in each scenario these values will combine to generate slightly different issues. The fact that more than one person is involved in the treatment adds further complexity to the health professional-client relationship. There is even some ambiguity about whether Valerie and Alan Joblonski constitute two discrete clients or are in some sense a single client.

Beginning with confidentiality, a first question that arises concerns the ownership of the information. Although it is clear that the information at issue is confidential, there may be some uncertainty whether Alan alone owns and has the exclusive right to control this information. After all, one might argue, Alan and Valerie presented at the clinic as a couple and not as two strangers. It is as a couple that they would be the subject of the treatment. Viewing them together as a corporate client rather than as two discrete clients, each would be privy to whatever information might be generated or otherwise brought to light in the course of the therapy.[16]

Certainly this line of argument stretches the concept of confidentiality as it is traditionally understood. In the paradigm case for confidentiality, the client is normally (and unambiguously) a discrete individual. The case of Valerie and Alan is clearly different.

In any event, the argument that Valerie is entitled to this information insofar as she is a sort of co-owner depends in part on the nature of the understanding and promise in light of which the couple began the program in the first place. If, for example, the clinic staff had made it clear from the beginning that any information made available to one would also be made available to the other, the argument for disclosure would be much more plausible.[17]

Suppose, however, that no such understanding of co-ownership had existed, and that, indeed, Alan had reason to believe that his wife would not as a matter of course be made privy to information about him. In this event, to disclose the information to Valerie would be a breach of confidentiality. The question then arises whether such a breach would be justifiable. Confidentiality, after all, is not an absolute value, and the duty to preserve confidentiality is not an absolute duty. Other values also come into play; in this case, beneficence and truthfulness.

Beneficence has to do with concern for the good of another. One of the things that sets this case apart from the previous case is that the good of someone else outside the confidential relationship is clearly at stake. There is a risk that Valerie may acquire HIV through the treatment. There is also a risk that their child thus conceived would acquire HIV. If keeping confidentiality with Alan, in addition to not disclosing the information to Valerie, meant going forward with the treatment, this would be at the expense of risking harm to others, and indeed to someone directly involved in the same professional-client relationship. Obvious questions of informed consent aside, this would violate the much venerated principle of health care ethics: *primum non nocere* (first, do no harm). This principle, nonmaleficence, is a modality of the general value of beneficence.

If indeed the issue were only between confidentiality and nonmaleficence, the question would centre on which of the two ought to be given more weight. Providing the clinic adheres to its policy, the issue will not come to that. The policy calls for counselling with the couple in this case, and information about Alan's HIV status would have to come out in any counselling process. In any event, Alan is unwilling to go for such counselling.

However, if Alan were to agree to counselling, and even after that he and Valerie decided they wanted to go forward in the program, a different issue would arise. Considerations of nonmaleficence would still be relevant because the treatment would still pose the same risk for Valerie and any future child. But nonmaleficence would need to be weighed not against confidentiality, but against autonomy. Should Valerie be allowed to choose a treatment that carries such a risk for herself? And who should speak for the future child?

On the other hand, if Alan continues to refuse the counselling, and insists on keeping the information from his wife, a different issue will arise. In this event, the treatment could not go forward, and Valerie (and any child that might be conceived) would not be at risk of acquiring HIV *as a result of treatment*. Nevertheless, the risk would still exist. Would the clinic then be morally required to disclose the information to Valerie? After all, there is a difference between causing harm to someone (as would be risked if the clinic continued the treatment) and not preventing harm (as would be the case if the clinic did not make Valerie aware that sexual activity with Alan puts her at risk). The latter, in effect a duty to warn, is less weighty than the former, but either may be serious enough to outweigh the duty of confidentiality.[18]

Given Alan's test results, there is reason to believe that Valerie is already HIV positive. Presumably, like Alan, she has been tested as *per* the clinic policy and the test has been negative. However, a negative test result would not afford certainty that she was not infected with HIV. There is a window period in which an infected person may nonetheless test negative. Since Valerie is having unprotected sex with with someone known to be HIV positive, she has been at risk of contracting HIV. Under the circumstances, a follow-up test would be appropriate. If Valerie is not told about Alan's HIV status, she will be unaware of her risk profile and unmotivated to pursue follow-up testing.

The argument for disclosure could also be made in terms of truthtelling. Putting aside questions about Alan's duty to Valerie (everyone will agree that *he* owes her the truth), is she owed the truth by the team? This question, like the ownership question posed earlier, is complicated by the fact that two people are involved in the treatment. We are accustomed to thinking about truthfulness in terms of an individual client, and what is owed to him or her. This case, however, concerns a shared situation in which two lives intersect. The truth in question is primarily about Alan, and only indirectly about Valerie.

The problem of truthtelling in the present circumstance is occasioned by Valerie's asking for and expecting some explanation about what is happening. Why is the treatment not going forward? What is the problem? The truthful answer to this line of questioning is less directly about Valerie than about Alan, and would require the disclosure of confidential information. Alternatively, maintaining confidentiality with Alan would mean being less than truthful with Valerie (e.g., lying to her, not telling her the whole truth, etc.).[19]

The fact that the staff disagree about how to proceed indicates that they need to sit down as a group and discuss their various opinions about the matter.[20] At the very least, they should agree that the first thing to do is to talk privately with Alan and make sure that he fully understands the nature of his condition and the risk of infecting others.

Learning that one is HIV-positive can be quite devastating. Understandably, Alan may be disoriented and confused. A referral to a self-help or support group might help him to come to terms with his problem. It is likely that proper education or counselling will be enough to change his mind about telling Valerie.

Whatever ensues in this case, it underscores some gaps in clinic policy and the staff could use it as a lesson from which to clarify and improve policy. Perhaps an improved policy would spell out in advance to clients what personal information, if any, would be made available to spouses. This certainly would have helped staff to avoid or resolve some of the issues raised in this case.

In light of this case, it might also be advisable to review the policy of testing couples for HIV. What purposes was it supposed to accomplish? At the very least, more thought needs to be given to the sorts of points to be covered in counselling, both before and after such a test.

Case 3: Confidentiality and Seemingly Innocuous Information

Frequently, confidential information concerns matters the client has an obvious interest in keeping from certain others, such as information that could rebound in harm to the client. The first two cases concerned information of this sort. However, much personal information about someone gained in a health care setting is not like that at all. Much of it seems innocuous because there is no obvious reason why the client might have an interest in keeping it from others. For example, there is no apparent reason why disclosure of the fact that Mrs. Smith in the next hospital room is a school teacher, or that Mr. Jones down the hall has three children, would matter to them.

With regard to such seemingly innocuous information, it may be tempting to relax the normal constraints concerning confidentiality. Indeed, such information may not be perceived as coming under the protective umbrella of confidentiality at all.

The following case raises some issues that may arise in connection with information of this kind. The context in which this information is being shared with others — among friends of the clients in a small rural community — adds another dimension to these issues:

Sandy Young grew up in a small town and went to a nearby city to study nursing. After graduating, she worked in a busy teaching hospital for three years and was laid off when the hospital restructured.

Unable to find work in another hospital in the city, she returned to her home town to live with her parents. After seeking employment there for two months, she accepted a position as a registered nurse in a small nursing home. She found herself caring for the parents and grandparents of her own friends. Some clients were mentally alert and others had varying degrees of cognitive impairment. Although her workload was heavy, she found time to talk to the clients and their families. She received many cards of appreciation from residents and their families.

Sandy became very active the social life of the community. At parties, community events, and in her volunteer work, she would often be approached by relatives and friends of her clients seeking "news" about their condition. Questions posed ranged from ones about the health and mobility of a client to questions about who came to visit the client, and how often.

Although she believed that these people were well-meaning and genuinely concerned, and moreover thought that her clients would probably approve, she nevertheless felt uncomfortable sharing this "news."

Sandy mentioned her feelings to her colleagues at the nursing home, but they didn't think it was a problem. Most of them had worked at the home a long time and couldn't recall any concern expressed by the residents. "Sandy, you're not in the big city anymore — things are a lot more friendly and informal here," one of the older nurses told her. Despite these assurances, Sandy continued to be troubled about the matter.

Commentary

Sandy is uncertain whether the information in question ought to be subjected to the normal constraints of confidentiality. Three related considerations might bear on her deliberations. In the first place, the information seems innocuous. No harm, it seems, is likely to come to her clients from its disclosure. Secondly, the people to whom she is disclosing the information are friends and relatives of her clients. In a small community such as this one, one might even think of them as an "extended family." They care about her clients, and their wanting to know seems motivated by genuine concern. Thirdly, Sandy believes that her clients would probably want these others to know the kind of information or "news" of which she is aware.

For the purpose of analysis, it will be helpful to express each of these considerations in the form of a rule for deciding the question that troubles Sandy. The first consideration might be expressed in the form of the following rule: Disclosure of personal information about a client is morally permissible if the information is harmless, or if the client has no interest in keeping it confidential.

The most obvious problem with this rule is that the judgement that a given item of information is harmless, or that a client has no interest in keeping it confidential, is fallible. The nurse may very well be mistaken. For causes or reasons the nurse could hardly imagine, seemingly innocuous information may turn out to be harmful. This is especially true given that what counts as a harm may be somewhat subjective.

In any event, it could be argued, if such a judgement is to be made, the client and not the nurse should make it. Another objection to this first rule is that, even if one could be certain that no harm could rebound from the information, there may still be reason enough for guarding it as being confidential. Even if I could know for certain that a secret entrusted to me in confidence would not come back to harm the person who entrusted it with me, I would nevertheless break my promise of confidentiality by revealing it.

The second consideration can be expressed as the rule that disclosure of personal information about a client is permissible provided it is disclosed only to family or friends of the client, who presumably have a genuine concern. One problem with this rule is that the nurse may be mistaken in distinguishing those who are genuinely concerned from those who are not. The fact that someone is a family member is not sufficient evidence that they are genuinely concerned about the client.

Moreover, even if they are genuinely concerned, knowing confidential information could still put them in a position to bring harm upon or violate the interests of the client (albeit unintentionally). Furthermore, even if the nurse could be certain that the person's concern was genuine, and that no harm could come from their knowing, the client simply may not want them to know.

The third consideration can be expressed as the rule that the disclosure of personal information about a client is permissible only if and to whomever the client wishes it to be disclosed. This rule puts the emphasis not on the nature of the information, or even the context in which it might be shared, but rather on the autonomy of the client, on his or her right to control the disclosure of personal information.[21] Given the importance of autonomy in contemporary health care, this rule has much to recommend it.

However, this rule does not obviate the need for sound judgement on the part of nursing staff. Client consent or authorization may be more or less explicit. The less explicit the authorization (e.g., based on what I know about the client, I think he would wish me to tell his good friend Charlie that he may not recover from his bout of pneumonia), the greater the possibility of error.

The surest and most cautious way of determining what the client wishes is to ask. Sandy might be able to resolve her problem simply by talking with her clients and soliciting their wishes on the matter. However, some of them are cognitively impaired. What about those unable to express their wishes? If unable to get explicit consent (or refusal), should Sandy play it safe and disclose nothing at all? Alternatively, might there be someone else who could speak for these clients?

It may be that her clients would in fact wish for "news" about them to be communicated in the social settings in which Sandy finds herself. People in small communities often pride themselves on their neighbourliness and caring attitudes, and feel distinct from people in large cities where "nobody knows anybody else." Some customs and rules that are appropriate in a big city climate of anonymity and indifference may not be as appropriate in a smaller community.[22] Informality and openness tend to be more highly valued in small towns than in large cities.

On the other hand, at least some of Sandy's clients may not wish "news" about them to be shared even with concerned friends and neighbours. Some clients might look on such exchanges of "news" as a kind of "gossip" in which they would rather not be mentioned.[23] Some may value their privacy more than others, and might regard a lack of privacy as being a negative feature of life in small towns. Indeed, such a lack of privacy is the reason some residents of small towns go elsewhere for health services or treatments about which they would rather not have their neighbours know.

In analyzing the issue that troubles her, it would be helpful for Sandy to reflect on some factors that combine to generate the issue in the first place. One such factor concerns a certain ambiguity about the status of the information in question. The people who approach Sandy for such information, and perhaps Sandy herself, appear to view this information as being "news." Viewed in this way, disclosure seems quite appropriate. However, this "news" happens also to arise in the context of a professional-client relationship, and as such is confidential. Viewing the information as "news" may obscure this important point.

A second factor contributing to the issue has to do with the relationship between Sandy's professional role, on the one hand, and her personal or social life on the other. The issue arises, after all, because Sandy appears in the same circumstance wearing two hats. At a social function, she is both a member of the community and a nurse privy to confidential information of interest or concern to those she encounters socially. Those who ask her for information, and perhaps Sandy herself, may blur or fail to differentiate these two roles. In her professional nursing role, Sandy assumes certain obligations to her clients. These obligations are binding even when she takes off her uniform and participates in the community. Clarifying and communicating this point to those who approach her for "news" will help Sandy to deal with the situation.

Clarifying the issue will also help Sandy to deal with her co-workers, who, it appears, are quite open about such informal disclosures. Having translated her initially vague feeling of discomfort into an analysis, Sandy will be in a better position to convince others at least that there *is* an issue that needs to be addressed. Sitting down with other nursing staff and exploring their views and beliefs on confidentiality could prove to be very productive. They might learn from each other, and also develop some guidelines or criteria for responding to issues of confidentiality arising within the community.

Conclusion

In the name of health and caring, nurses are afforded privileged access to what is otherwise private information about clients. With this knowledge, nurses also acquire power — a double-edged power that may bring ill as well as good upon clients. In turn, clients, already made vulnerable by illness, become even more so.

In such a relationship, trust is vitally important. In assuming this trust, the nurse should be as clear as possible about what he or she can and cannot promise by way of information disclosure, and about what the client can and cannot expect.

Granted, all human interaction takes place against a background of understandings and assumptions that can never be rendered fully explicit. But where the consequences of misunderstanding would be serious, nurse and client together should endeavour to make their shared understanding as explicit as possible.

Notes

1   Privacy is a broader concept than is confidentiality. In its own right, it raises many important concerns in health care. The right to privacy, for example, has been invoked in the context of the abortion debate. Arguments against mandatory screening (e.g., for genetic defects, for illicit drugs) and testing (e.g., AIDS, hepatitis B) are frequently couched in terms of "invasion of privacy." For a fuller discussion of privacy, see Rachels (1975), Greenawalt (1978), and Wasserstrom (1986).

2   Many inadvertent breaches of confidentiality occur in the context of what Glinsky (1987) calls "shop talk." Glinksy uses an interesting example to show how such "shop talk," although seemingly innocuous, may in fact result in harm.

3   In some institutions, information to this effect will be communicated to clients as a matter of policy (e.g., as part of the process of admission to hospital). Clarifying such things up front reduces the likelihood of issues arising down the line.

4   Siegler (1982) argues that confidentiality as traditionally conceived in terms of one-to-one relationships has become outmoded in contemporary health care, which requires that client information be widely shared with and made available to many different health professionals.

5   One way of deciding whether a piece of information should be considered confidential would be to imagine what harms (if any) might come to the client were it to be disclosed to certain others. However, there are problems with this approach. In the first place, one may fail to foresee a possible harm that might arise (e.g., suppose that, having learned from a nurse that Mrs. Jones gave birth to a boy, Mrs. Smith discloses this to Mr. Jones, whose wife wanted very much to tell him but had not yet had the opportunity). In the second place, the client (for whatever reason) simply may not wish the information to be shared with certain others, even if there is no possibility of harm.

6   Veatch and Fry (1987, pp. 141-154) distinguish three main justifications for breaching confidentiality: because required to do so by law; in order to protect the client from harm; in order to protect some

third party from harm. Their analysis of each of these possible justifications is insightful and sensitive to complexities.

7   The text of the court decision (majority opinion), which was recorded in 1976, can be found in Tobriner (1986). The dissenting minority opinion was given by Clark (1986).

8   For example, the American Nurses' Assocation ([1976] 1985) recognizes an exception to the rule of confidentiality "when *innocent* [italics added] parties are in direct jeopardy" (Statement 2.1). This implies that it is morally relevant whether people choose to put themselves in danger.

9   This is a common refrain in the literature on confidentiality in health care. For further discussion around this point linked to specific cases and examples, see Baer (1985) and Fleck (1986).

10   Flaherty (1982) gives an insightful commentary on a similar case.

11   Rose has raised the question of ownership of the records, and this also needs to be considered. However, debate along these lines is moot if, as appears to be the case, the employee had reason to believe that the information would be treated as being confidential.

12   Another document that could be very useful is *Guidelines on Confidentiality of Occupational Health Information in Health Care Facilities* (Ontario Hospital Association, 1990).

13   For a fuller discussion of confidentiality in the context of family situations, see Brody (1988).

14   Mitchell and Smith (1987) discuss a somewhat similar but less complex case.

15   For a review of some of the main legal issues of confidentiality AIDS has raised, see Dickens (1988), especially p. 581.

16   For a critical examination of the idea of the family as client, see Christie and Hoffmaster (1986, especially pp. 68-84).

17   Pre-test counselling would be an appropriate forum in which to raise such matters. However, as the case is described there is no evidence that the couple were given pre-test counselling. If not, they should have been, and the clinic should make provisions for this in the future.

18   Presumably, warning Valerie of the danger would be a way of preventing harm (the expectation being that, knowing the danger, she

would not voluntarily take such a risk). However, it is possible that she would knowingly take such a risk. In this case, warning her would not have succeeded in preventing harm. However, it would at least serve to promote her autonomy, for she would then be taking the risk with her eyes open to the possible consequences.

19   Although it appears that truthfulness and confidentiality would be mutually exclusive in this case, there may be a crafty way out of this double bind that, in letter at least, might satisfy both values: Staff could inform Valerie that the reason the treatment is not going forward concerns information about Alan that is confidential, and that further questions should be directed toward him.

20   The possibility that feelings toward Alan and evaluations of his sexual behaviour may, more or less indirectly, influence nursing staff's opinions on the issue should also be considered.

21   Most accounts link confidentiality both with autonomy and the duty to do no harm (nonmaleficence). For example, the *International Dictionary of Medicine and Biology* defines confidentiality as "the right of a subject to control the disposition of information during the course of a professional relationship, and the reciprocal obligation of the professional to ensure that no harm will befall the subject as a result of disclosure of such information." Fleck (1986) makes a good case for putting the emphasis on autonomy. Brody (1989) is even stronger in rejecting nonmaleficence as the basis for confidentiality in health care.

22   Stephen Toulmin (1981) criticizes the tendency in much ethical theorizing to apply principles and rules indiscriminately across the board, insensitive to differences in context and setting. In this regard, he distinguishes "the ethics of rules and strangers" from "the ethics of discretion and intimacy." His general point is that rules that are appropriate in one setting may not be appropriate in another.

23   Along these lines, Sandy should consider that there are some very questionable motives for sharing such "news" with others. Those who bear such "news" may gain status of one sort or another in the eyes of those with whom it is shared. In part at least, this less than noble motive may shape the practice of nursing staff.

References

American Nurses' Association. ([1976] 1985). *Code for nurses with interpretive statements*. Kansas City: Author.

Baer, O.J. (1985). Protecting your patient's privacy. *Nursing Life, 5* (3), 51-53.

Brody, H. (1988). Confidentiality and family members. In R.B. Edwards & G.C. Graber. *Bioethics* (pp. 81-85). San Diego: Harcourt Brace Jovanovich.

Brody, H. (1989). The physician-patient relationship. In R.M. Veatch (Ed.), *Medical ethics* (pp. 65-91). Boston: Jones & Bartlett.

Canadian Nurses Association. (1991). *Code of ethics for nursing*. Ottawa: Author.

Christie, R.J., & Hoffmaster, C.B. (1986). *Ethical issues in family medicine*. New York: Oxford University Press.

Clark, W.P. (1986). Minority opinion in Tarasoff v. Regents of the University of California. In T.A. Mappes & J.S. Zembaty (Eds.), *Biomedical ethics* (2nd ed., pp. 155-158). New York: McGraw-Hill.

Dickens, B. (1988). Legal rights and duties in the AIDS epidemic. *Science, 239* (4835), 580-586.

Flaherty, M.J. (1982). Case study XIII: Confidentiality of patients' records. In L.L. Curtin & M.J. Flaherty (Eds.), *Nursing ethics: Theories and pragmatics* (pp. 315-320). Bowie, MD: Robert J. Brady.

Fleck, L.M. (1986). Confidentiality: moral obligation or outmoded concept? *Health Progress, 67* (4), 17-20.

Glinsky, J. (1987). The perils of "shop talk." *Nursing Life, 7* (6), 24.

Greenawalt, K. (1978). Privacy. In W.T. Reich (Ed.), *Encyclopedia of bioethics* (Vol. 3, pp. 1356-1363). New York: The Free Press.

International Council of Nurses. ([1973] 1982). *Code for nurses: Ethical concepts applied to nursing*. Geneva: Author.

Krever, H. (1980). *Report of the commission of inquiry into the confidentiality of health information* (3 vols.). Queen's Printer: J.C. Thatcher.

Mitchell, C., & Smith, L. (1987). If it's AIDS, please don't tell. *American Journal of Nursing, 87* (7), 911-914.

Ontario Hospital Association. (1990). *Guidelines on confidentiality of occupational health information in health care facilities*. Toronto: Author.

Ontario Occupational Health Nurses Assocation. (1987). *Guidelines to the occupational health nurse: Confidentiality of health records.* Toronto: Author.

Rachels, J. (1975). Why privacy is important. *Philosophy and Public Affairs, 4* (4), 323-333.

Siegler, M. (1982). Confidentiality in medicine — A decrepit concept. *The New England Journal of Medicine, 307* (24), 1518-1521.

Tobriner, M.O. (1986). Majority opinion in Tarasoff v. Regents of the University of California. In T.A. Mappes & J.S. Zembaty (Eds.), *Biomedical ethics* (2nd ed., pp. 151-155). New York: McGraw-Hill.

Toulmin, S. (1981). The tyranny of principles. *The Hastings Center Report, 11* (6), 31-39.

Veatch, R.M., & Fry, S.T. (1987). *Case studies in nursing ethics.* Philadelphia: J.B. Lippincott.

Wasserstrom, R. (1986). The legal and philosophical foundations of the right to privacy. In T.A. Mappes & J.S. Zembaty (Eds.), *Biomedical ethics* (2nd ed, pp. 140-147). New York: McGraw-Hill.

Westin, A.F. (1968). *Privacy and freedom.* New York: Atheneum.

Winslade, H.J. (1978). Confidentiality. In W.T. Reich (Ed.), *Encyclopedia of bioethics* (Vol. 1, pp. 194-200). New York: The Free Press.

STUDY QUESTIONS: CONFIDENTIALITY

Case 1: Confidentiality in a Nontraditional Therapeutic Setting

1. Would it make any difference if this scenario took place not in a hospital but in a factory?

2. In recent years, health reform has come to be associated with a more business-like approach to health care management. To what extent might it be true that health professionals and business people have different mindsets, the former being oriented around client well-being, the latter around the bottom line of profit? How is "the health care business" different from other businesses?

3. Suppose that, having learned about John's predicament, Evelyn approached him and volunteered to release her health record to management. What ethical issues would this offer raise for John and the Occupational Health Department? Should he approve of her offer? What may be the consequences for Evelyn?

4. Suppose that you are a nurse working in the nuclear industry. Write a draft policy regarding the confidentiality of information available to the health service about employees. Pay particular attention to possible qualifying conditions (if any) under which the health service may make such information available without employee consent.

Case 2: Confidentiality in a Family Context

1. Nursing puts a great deal of emphasis on the family. What arguments can you think of for conceiving the family as a whole as client, rather than individual members of the family? What arguments can you think of against this?

2. In what ways are the issues of confidentiality raised in this case similar to, and in what ways different from, the issues that might arise

when a public health nurse working with a family in their home suspects child abuse?

3. If Alan did agree to share information about his HIV status with his wife, and after counselling he and his wife still wanted to try to have a baby, ought the clinic to continue the treatment?

4. Suppose that Alan decided to tell his wife that he was HIV-positive, but to lie to her about how he became so (e.g., claiming that he had a blood transfusion following a car accident a year before they met). Would clinic staff have an obligation to set the record straight with Valerie?

Case 3: Confidentiality and Seemingly Innocuous Information

1. Should moral principles be universally applied regardless of setting and context (e.g., a small rural community as opposed to a large urban centre)?

2. Does a nurse who discusses clients and events of the workday with her or his spouse breach confidentiality in doing so?

3. Describe a scenario in which *seemingly* innocuous information about a client turns out in fact to be harmful.

4. Discuss the statement: "Nurses shouldn't be too lax about confidentiality, but on the other hand they shouldn't be too legalistic or bureaucratic either."

JUSTICE

*We see people empowered to realize their full health potential
through a safe, non-violent environment, adequate income,
housing, food and education, and a valued role to play in family,
work and the community. We see people having equitable access
to affordable and appropriate health services regardless of geog-
raphy, income, age, gender or cultural background. Finally, we
see everyone working together to achieve better health for all.*

— ONTARIO PREMIER'S COUNCIL ON
  HEALTH STRATEGY

---

*Issues of justice in the allocation of health care resources are
becoming more pressing as decisions made at government and
administrative levels affect the care nurses are able to provide
their clients. Immediate problems of who is to receive what level
and quality of care impinge on fundamental moral values and
principles. Both for their own job satisfaction, and for the good of
their clients, nurses are increasingly called to participate in making ethical decisions about resource allocation and to play a part
in the formation of public policy.*

*Case studies in this chapter examine the availability of care
versus the quality of care when a nursing administrator must
cope with the problems of inadequate staffing as a consequence
of budget reductions; the distribution of burdens and benefits
when a nurse manager is inundated with requests to place a number of students in a unit of a chronic care facility; and the allocation of time and care when a nurse is overburdened with
responsibility for too many critically ill children.*

Justice in the Distribution of Health Resources

The concept of justice has a variety of meanings and applications. In the broadest sense, it has to do with fairness in the determination of what someone or some group is owed, merits, deserves, or is otherwise entitled to. Did the student really merit an A+ on the assignment? Did the drug-dealer deserve a sentence of life-imprisonment? Are people with physical disabilities entitled to special consideration in the hiring process?

Issues of justice in the context of health and health care are more specifically ones of *distributive* justice involving the allocation of resources for health and health care. These issues are most urgent whenever the supply of resources is insufficient to meet the need or demand for them. Choices then must be made between competing resource claims.

In recent years, resource allocation issues have become more prominent, as evidenced by the increased attention given to them in the ethics literature and the popular press. Widespread indignation is reported when a person dies waiting for triple bypass surgery. Some commentators have suggested that alcoholics should be denied liver transplants in favour of those whose livers fail through no "fault" of their own. People living with Acquired Immunodeficiency Syndrome (AIDS) stage demonstrations to protest what they charge is insufficient funding for research and treatment of their disease.

Several factors account for the high profile of health-related justice issues today. Heightened consciousness about personal health along with progress in health care have fuelled consumer expectations and demands. Much more *can* be done to help people. Our improved health care makes it possible for the elderly to become more elderly, the very, very young to become children (and later elderly), and disabled persons to become more fully integrated members of our society. With these added benefits come added costs.

On the supply side, there is a growing concern about health care expenditure, and a growing consensus that limits must be set. The cost of health care, measured on a number of scales, has been rising steadily, although less so in Canada than in the United States.[1] In an effort to control these costs, greater scrutiny is being given to how resources are allocated: "efficiency," "cut-backs," "reallocation," "cost containment," and "rationing," are some of the watchwords of the day.

Health reform — to a great extent fiscally driven — is under way across the country. Changes are taking place very rapidly and nurses are on the front line of these changes. At the bedside and in the community nurses experience first hand the effects of policy decisions concerning the management and delivery of health care. With apprehension, nurses watch the vital signs of the health care system, as measured by quality and availability of care.

By virtue of educational preparation and close experience with clients, nurses have a unique vantage point for evaluating health care. As members of the country's largest health care profession, nurses can and ought to contribute to health care policy and planning decisions.

One of the goals of this chapter is to prepare nurses and nursing students to participate in the policy discussions and debates about health care. If this participation is to be informed and effective, nurses must be familiar with the values and principles of the Canadian health care system. Accordingly, this chapter provides background on the history and evolution of our health care system and on present factors that constrain planning and policy in this area.

Informed and effective participation in health policy discussion and planning also requires some knowledge of the theoretical basis for issues of justice. To this end, the chapter elaborates on the main ethical values and principles pertinent to understanding issues of justice.

Canada's Health Care System

The Canadian health care system, based on universal access regardless of income and social status, is relatively new. To understand the issues and problems we are currently facing, it will be helpful to review briefly the historical context in which the system evolved.

1. Historical Background of the Canada Health Act

The movement toward a comprehensive and universal Canadian health care system began in earnest in the 1930's, during the dire economic conditions of the Depression in the rural communities of Saskatchewan.[2] At the time, adequate health care was available only to the few who could afford to pay. The majority did without or relied on the kindness of neighbours, local government agencies, or charitable organizations.

To meet their needs, individuals and families began to cooperate for the common provision of physician services. From the 1930's to the 1960's, there were similar local initiatives across the country. In addition, many Canadians paid into not-for-profit and for-profit insurance plans to provide for health care.

It was not until 1961 that a provincial health care plan based on universal access was introduced in Saskatchewan. The introduction of the legislation led to a very bitter physician's strike, which ended after sixty difficult days.

At the national level, in 1961 the federal government established a Royal Commission on Health Services, chaired by Justice Emmett Hall, to propose ways to improve health care services across Canada. The recommendations of the Commission's *Report* (the *Hall Report*) are at the core of our current health care system. The philosophical commitments of the *Hall Report* (1964) are evident in the following passage:

> The achievement of the highest possible standards for all our people must become a primary objective of national policy and a cohesive factor contributing to national unity, involving individual and community responsibilities and actions. The objective can best be achieved by a comprehensive, universal Health Service programme for the Canadian people. (p. 11)

In 1966, the federal government introduced a medicare program based on the *Hall Report*'s recommendations. The *Medical Care Act*

(1966) established that all Canadians should have access to necessary health care services.

Still, across the country there were inconsistencies regarding access to health care. Some provinces had extra fees for hospital stays and permitted physicians to supplement the fees they received from the publicly funded health care plan by extra-billing patients for their services.

In response to these inconsistencies, and with the goal of ensuring a national program with universal access, the federal government introduced the *Canada Health Act* (1984), which was supported by all political parties. It proclaims that all Canadians are entitled to services that "are medically necessary for the purpose of maintaining health, preventing disease or diagnosing or treating an injury, illness or disability." The fundamental principles of the *Act* are as follows:

- *Comprehensiveness:* covered services include those provided in hospital and by physicians and surgeons.

- *Universality:* health care services are available to all Canadians, regardless of ability to pay.

- *Accessibility:* Canadians must have access to medically necessary services.

- *Portability:* Canadians must be covered while moving or travelling throughout all parts of the countries, regardless of their home province.

- *Public Administration:* health care services must be administered by a publicly funded agency.

The provisions for the implementation, administration, and enforcement of this *Act* are complex. Although the *Act* falls within federal jurisdiction, the provision of health care is a provincial responsibility. The federal government transfers payments to the provincial governments, who provide health care services in each province or territory.

Failure on the part of provinces to comply with the *Act* (for instance, permitting user fees or extra-billing) may be penalized by a reduction in the federal transfer payments on a dollar for dollar basis. This penalty has proven to be an effective mechanism for ensuring compliance, as evidenced by the strong response of the Ontario government to physician strike action against the prohibition on extra-billing in 1986.

2. The Current Situation

In the past few years, new threats and challenges to the principles upon which our health care system is based have begun to appear. Of particular note are the recent emergence of private clinics in Alberta which charge a "facility fee" to patients for services (e.g., cataract surgery). The provincial government allowed these clinics to operate on these terms against the protest of the federal government that "facility fees" were in effect "user fees" and thus prohibited under the *Canada Health Act*. The Alberta government, ideologically sympathetic to the privatization of health care, rejected the federal government's arguments. Only when the federal government threatened to withdraw funds did Alberta reluctantly agree to take action to prohibit these fees.

However, the power of the federal government has been diminishing in health care. In 1995, the federal government replaced individual transfer payments for health, post-secondary education and social services with a block social transfer payment. This leaves each province to determine how the block payment is to be allocated to each area. Since the total amount of federal transfer payments to the provinces is declining, this could have dire consequences for health care. With reduced financial support from the federal government, there is a reduced incentive for provincial governments to abide by the *Canada Health Act*.

Given the dynamics of health care across the country, commentators worry that the new transfer system could lead to the erosion of national standards in health care and greater discrepancies in health care coverage from province to province. The provinces must cope with increased demands on health care, rising costs, changing demographics, and the effects of a national recession.

In this climate, the provinces are looking very carefully at their health care budgets. There are serious worries about whether the health care system as we know it, based on the principles of the *Canada Health Act*, will or even can survive under these strains and constraints.

Opinion about the viability of the principles of the *Canada Health Act* can be divided into two broad categories. On the one side are those who believe that we can and should preserve our medicare system through comprehensive reform. On the other side are those who think it is not sustainable, and that a different health care system must be established.

Proposals for change on either side of the issue will have profound effects, and it is important to understand the moral issues at stake. For example, increased privatization has been urged on the grounds that the public system cannot possibly meet all needs and demands. Is the development of a second tier of private health care, available only to those with the ability to pay, compatible with the demands of justice (Vail, 1995)?

Some commentators champion user fees as a way of bringing more money into the system and discouraging inappropriate use. Critics raise serious doubts both about the fairness and the effectiveness of such fees (Moorhouse, 1993; Stoddart, Barer, Evans, & Bhatia, 1993).

Issues concerning our health care system will intensify in the coming years. The more that demand exceeds supply, the more pressing are issues of justice. Which people in need of treatment should be given priority? How much money should go to which units and services in the hospital? Ought resources be reallocated from acute care to disease prevention or to health promotion? Ought private, pay-for-service health care to be encouraged, or even tolerated? These are deeply ethical questions, and ethics requires that we make explicit and justify the values, principles, and priorities that guide resource allocation decisions.

Levels of Resource Allocation and Decision-Making

Resource allocation decisions can be grouped into two main kinds: Decisions regarding the allocation of already available resources to or among individuals, and decisions that bear on which services and programs, and of what quality, will be available. The former is the level of micro-allocation. At this level, what is mainly at issue is *access*: Which individuals will receive the limited resource (e.g., treatment, organ, prenatal class) when not all can?

Access to resources is dependent on prior decisions made that determine the *availability* or supply of resources. How much funding or support is allocated to which services and programs? If a given resource (e.g., a liver transplant, home care) is available in supply less than the need or demand for it, individuals will be in competition for the resource, and which of these individuals should have access to it will arise as an issue. The more limited the availability or supply, the more acute are issues of access or micro-allocation. These issues do not arise if the resource in question is available in supply adequate to the demand for it, or indeed if the resource is not available at all.

Decisions about resource availability can be distinguished into meso-allocation decisions and macro-allocation decisions. The former involve the allocation of resources *within* an institution or community. The latter are broader public policy issues and include the allocation of resources *to* an institution or community.[3]

Micro, meso, and macro-allocation decisions, respectively, take place at progressively higher levels of generality. Decisions at a higher level of generality constrain decision-making at a lower level of generality. For example, government macro-allocation decisions about how much money will go to health as against other sectors establish limits that constrain allocation decisions *within* health spending. In turn, decisions at this level, such as how much money will go to hospitals as against community health and other programs, set limits on and constrain decision-making at a lower level, such as *within* a hospital or a neighbourhood health centre. Eventually, we reach the micro-level, at which decision-makers allocate to or among individuals a resource that is limited in supply as a consequence of meso- and macro-allocations made at higher levels of generality.

At all levels, allocating resources is a matter of setting priorities and making trade-offs. Given that not all the demands for limited resources can be met, options must be priorized.

The notion of opportunity costs is crucial for understanding the dynamics of such decision-making. The opportunity cost of deciding for a given option is the lost opportunity of meeting some other demand or realizing some other option.

Suppose it is Friday evening and you have two assignments due Monday morning. Given the time constraints, it is impossible to finish them both. Because your grade in the physiology course is more important to you, you decide to spend the weekend on it and to accept a grade penalty for submitting the anatomy assignment a day late. The opportunity cost of completing the physiology assignment on time is the late penalty for the anatomy assignment.

Dollars spent on health care are dollars not available for other useful services or programs or services, such as creating jobs or daycare spaces. These lost opportunities are opportunity costs. Within health care, dollars spent on acute care are dollars not available to be spent on health promotion and disease prevention. At the front-line of health care, providing resources for one patient may be at the cost of not being able to provide them for some other patient.

At each level of allocation, there are trade-offs and opportunity costs to be considered. The issue concerns how best to make use of the limited resources available to us.

1. Micro-Allocation and Access

Micro-allocation concerns "the distribution of resources such as a treatment, a piece of equipment, a drug or procedure, to an individual in need" (O'Brien, 1983, p. 218). At this most face-to-face level of allocation, practitioners — and physicians especially — have control over the allocation of certain resources to individuals. Who gets access to the resource, and how much of it?

If the supply of resources were unlimited, justice issues would never arise at the micro-level. Resource allocation would be based on what is best for the individual (taking into consideration also the individual's preferences). However, the allocation of a resource to a given individual is always at the expense or cost of foregoing some other opportunity to which the resource might otherwise have been directed. The resources used (money, labour) for a costly diagnostic test or a hip replacement might otherwise be used to produce some other benefit (for some other individual or group of individuals). The benefit of the allocation to the individual, therefore, can always be compared to the benefits foregone by unrealized opportunities. Is a costly diagnostic test (the cost of which could otherwise be directed to other opportunities) morally appropriate when the probability that the condition exists is extremely low?[4] Would it be morally justifiable to deny (or not to offer) a "needed" hip replacement to an elderly person in an advanced stage of terminal cancer?

Health professionals are not accustomed to thinking in terms of opportunity costs, and especially when the opportunities foregone by a resource allocation decision seem abstract as against the concreteness of an individual client in a face-to-face encounter. Even if the benefit of a costly therapy is minimal or uncertain, the opportunities to which this cost might otherwise be directed may seem by comparison to lack reality and urgency. Nevertheless, there are increasing pressures on health professionals to consider opportunity costs in allocating resources to individual clients. Curtin (1980) comments disapprovingly that increasingly "the duty of the health professional is being presented as primarily protecting the welfare of society and only secondarily the welfare of the individual in his/her care" (p. 465).[5]

The issue Curtin identifies is sometimes debated in terms of "gatekeeping." In controlling the "gate" through which individuals gain access to services and programs, does the practitioner have a duty to weigh the good of the individual against the good of others who might otherwise benefit from the opportunity costs foregone?[6] Traditionally, the practitioner-client relationship has relied on the understanding that the practitioner's paramount duty is to the good of the individual client (Pellegrino, 1986). There is reason to be concerned that the client's trust in the practitioner may be eroded if this duty were moderated by consideration for the good of others outside the relationship.

The gate-keeping role appears in a different light when the opportunity costs are on the same plane of concreteness as the allocation option for a given individual. For example, when the supply of a given resource — a transplant, a therapy, or even the practitioner's time — falls short of the need or demand of different individuals seeking access to it, a choice must be made between *identifiable* individuals. In this case opportunity costs are very real: A decision granting access to one individual means that the access of another equally concrete individual will be limited or denied.

A classic scenario for these triage-like decisions is the allocation of the last remaining bed in an intensive care unit. Suppose that the unit has four beds, three of which are occupied. Following a terrible car accident, several people are brought to hospital, two of whom are in critical condition and desperately in need of intensive care. One is the drunk driver of the car who caused the accident, the other a pregnant woman who was sitting in the passenger seat of the car that was struck. The decision about which of the two will get the last bed is at the same time a decision about which one will be denied it.

A number of criteria might be considered for making such selections. Edwards and Graber (1988b, pp. 709-710) group these under five main headings: medical criteria, random selection criteria, constituency criteria, present and or future quality of life criteria, and social worth criteria.[7] More than one type or group of criteria might be weighed together, or arranged serially in order of priority.

Some criteria are more controversial than others. Among the least controversial and most widely used is the likelihood of medical benefit. Social worth criteria are ethically suspect for several reasons, but especially because assigning a higher value to one person's life over that of another offends against notions of equality. Random selection criteria (e.g., first come, first served; a lottery), by contrast, preserve equality, and therefore are favoured by most in the event that other acceptable criteria are insufficient to decide the issue (e.g., Childress, 1983; Rescher, 1988).

One criterion not listed by Edwards and Graber that is generating more and more debate today is personal responsibility for illness. According to this criterion, it is morally appropriate if "persons in need of health services resulting from true, voluntary risks are treated differently from those in need of the same services for other reasons" (Veatch, 1988, p. 599). Smokers, for example, might be given a lower priority than nonsmokers for access to treatment for heart disease based on the rationale that "they brought their sickness upon themselves." In some cases judgments about whether a particular behaviour is the cause of a particular illness, and further about whether the behaviour in question is truly voluntary, are very controversial (Wikler, 1983). Moreover, even if causality and voluntariness could be established beyond a doubt, those who emphasize equality or neediness will object to resource allocations based on such considerations.

2. Resource Availability: Meso-Allocation and Macro-Allocation

Decisions about who should get *access* to an already available resource, and how much of it they should get, are different from decisions about the *availability* and supply of resources. Along these lines, we can distinguish the micro-allocation decision about who should get the last bed in intensive care from some prior decision bearing on how many beds should be available in intensive care in the first place. For example, given its allotted budget, the intensive care unit might previously have decided to allocate its resources to purchase new equipment *instead of* providing additional beds, or against any number of other options. The options considered at this level, in turn, would have been constrained by resource allocation decisions made at higher levels of generality, ascending to the global budget for the hospital. Levels of generality beyond the meso-level of the hospital reach to broader issues of public policy, and eventually to the total government budget for health spending as against other areas. A government decision to reduce health care expenditure by even a small percentage may have effects that eventually trickle down to the micro-level, at which practitioners may find themselves with fewer resources to allocate to individuals.

The ethical basis of meso- and macro-allocation decisions has not always been widely recognized. Some of the principles upon which such decisions are in fact made are ethically suspect. Which group or constituency controlling or demanding resources has the most political clout? Who shouts the loudest or is best able to use the media to amplify their voice? Who is most effective at lobbying decision-makers?

Diseases that catch the public's sympathy fare best in this competitive approach to allocating scarce resources. Less socially acceptable and little understood conditions, and the agencies and charities supporting them, are at a disadvantage. Television appeals for paediatric hospitals are well supported. We have yet to see a telethon for a psychiatric hospital.

Ad hoc approaches to funding fall short of meeting the requirements of justice. In order to ensure a responsible and fair allocation of scarce resources, decision-making should be guided by ethical values and principles. But which ones? Should allocation decisions be guided primarily by concern for individual autonomy, or for equality, or the greatest good for the greatest number? What constitutes a reasonable balance between or among these values? What process should be used to make these choices?

These questions are being energetically debated today. Although there is no consensus about the answers, there is agreement that more scrutiny needs to be given to the allocation practices that have evolved over time. Are we getting good value for our health care dollars? What are the benefits of so-called "high-tech" curative medicine as measured against more care-based approaches, and against health promotion and disease prevention?

The president of a large metropolitan hospital relates a story that puts some of these debates into perspective.[8] In 1983, physicians at the hospital in question started a lung transplant program. Where others before them had failed, they successfully did three such transplants at a cost exceeding $120,000. About the same time, the hospital also started a chiropody clinic and training program, which treats about two thousand people a year. As a result of treatment, thousands of people, most of them elderly, can function at home, and hence need less institutional care. The budget for twenty thousand visits is equivalent to the cost of the three transplants.

3. Levels of Decision-Making

Each level of allocation involves different decision-makers. At the level of micro-allocation, decision-making is mainly the prerogative of physicians, although other health professionals, including nurses, may have control over or input into the control of some resource allocation decisions. At the meso-level, allocation decisions are made by trustees and administrators working in collaboration with health professionals. At the macro-level, decisions are made by political authorities or their designates, with input being sought from health professionals and the public.

At every level, decision-making is coming under increased public scrutiny and decision-makers are expected to be more accountable. The difficult questions that must be tackled are not for these decision-makers alone. In a democracy, the authority to make these decisions is ultimately rooted in the will of the people, and the questions therefore are public questions involving all.

Today, there is increasing dissatisfaction with the existing mechanisms by means of which decisions about resource allocation and health care delivery are made. A major criticism is that these mechanisms do not adequately incorporate the community in decision-making. In this vein, the Ontario Premier's Council on Health Strategy (1991a) supports what it calls the "devolution" of decision-making authority from central planners to more local decision-making bodies:

Society is increasingly questioning the validity of a system where decisions intended to be in the best interests of all are made by an elite few.... How can those who have not had the opportunity to contribute to decisions affecting their lives, particularly the most vulnerable members of society, be empowered to do so? What mechanisms facilitate participation in decision-making? What skills, knowledge and information do people require to participate effectively and responsibly? (p. 10)

In the years ahead, it is likely that the trend to "devolve" authority and responsibility for decision-making to more local bodies will continue in an effort to involve the public, and issues of justice will become even more public.

Principles of Justice[9]

Decision-making at every level of allocation involves setting priorities and making trade-offs. How should we trade-off health care against education, a costly magnetic resonance imaging machine against other demands for funds within the hospital, one patient in line for a treatment available in short supply against another patient?

In examining such trade-offs, two lines of moral questioning are particularly relevant: "What criteria ought to be used to decide what constitutes a fair *outcome* in the distribution of health care resources?"; and "By means of what *process* ought allocation decisions to be made?"

Both are commonly referred to as questions of justice. The former concerns what are called *substantive* or *material principles of justice*, the latter *procedural* or *process principles of justice*. For example, a "neediest first" policy for prioritizing candidates for transplantation is based on the principle that health services ought to be apportioned according to need. This principle is substantive because it specifies a criterion for determining what a just outcome or pattern of distribution would be.

On the other hand, creating a committee with community representatives to develop prioritization policy is based on a procedural or process principle, namely, that decision-making should represent the values of those with a stake in the outcome. This principle does not say what the outcome of the decision should be, but rather concerns the process by means of which the decision should be made.

In either case, the issue of justice turns on "fairness." What constitutes a *fair distribution or outcome* of resource allocation? What constitutes a *fair process* for making decisions? With respect to either question, people differ in their intuitions about what is fair, or judge fairness in light of different values.

In what follows, the main moral values and principles relevant to resource allocation are organized under the general headings of substantive and procedural justice. It is important to realize that these values and principles do not have the precision that one rightfully expects in scientific enquiry. Because moral principles are general and abstract, their application to a given issue is usually open to debate. Distinctions among them are often imprecise. Principles shade into one another and overlap. Even the distinction between substantive and procedural principles is confounded because issues of substance and process tend to be intertwined.

1. Substantive Principles of Justice

A substantive principle of justice specifies a distributive criterion for resource allocation decisions and indicates what a just outcome would be. It helps complete the sentence "A fair distribution of resources would be one in which...." The main such principles are listed below:

a. Principle of Need

This principle is informed by the belief that the condition of being in need imposes on others an obligation to help meet this need. Health needs are special because sickness and disability are major impediments to happiness and flourishing in human society, and are distributed unevenly in the natural lottery. A just society is one that is compassionate and humane, and a critical measure of this is how well it meets "basic" or "essential" health needs. Accordingly, resources ought to be allocated proportionate with health needs. As needs differ, so too should the resources allocated. When not all needs can be met, the greatest and most urgent needs should be given priority.

b. Principle of Equality

Intuitions about equality in health care are rooted in solidarity, a sense of being together with everyone else in the same boat and sharing a common humanity. Equality has several meanings, including equality of access, equality of shares, and equality of health status. Most meanings are closely associated with the notion of need. Thus some commentators distinguish horizontal equality (equal resources for equal needs) and vertical equality (unequal resources for unequal needs). It may be justifiable to allocate resources unequally insofar as people have unequal needs and therefore may require more than an equal share of resources to achieve a health status approaching equality with that of others in society. The injunction "treat like cases alike" permits differential treatment based on need while forbidding discrimination based on factors such as sex, race, and religion.

c. Principle of Utility

Those who champion utility argue that health care resources ought to be allocated so as to maximize utility or benefit. In utilitarianism, this imperative is expressed in the phrase "Do what will yield the greatest good for the greatest number." Decision-making should be guided by the objective of maximizing benefit, or producing the greatest amount of net utility possible. When two or more allocation options are in competition, we should choose the one with the lowest ratio of cost to benefit, or the greatest "bang for buck".

d. Principle of Liberty

Liberty pertains to the right of individuals to make choices in matters of their own good and with respect to their own business, without interference from others. One such right, which is claimed by libertarians, is the right to dispose of one's personal resources as one sees fit. A just distribution of health care resources is one that is maximally compatible with this right. Libertarians object to the exercise of state power whereby money is taken from some people to subsidize health care for others. Health resources, they believe, ought rather to be allocated in accordance with what people are willing and able to pay for them. Therefore, the ideal system for allocating these resources is a free market in which supply is adjusted to consumer demand.

Not all appeals to liberty in resource allocation are expressly libertarian, or expressly concerned with property rights. For example, the principle of liberty also relates to the notion of autonomy and encompasses the freedom to make treatment choices based on adequate information and to select the caregivers who will administer to one's health needs. Merit or desert as a basis for resource allocation also supposes a certain notion of freedom or liberty. Basing allocation decisions on this latter criterion disfavours individuals or groups thought to be responsible for being in a condition of need in the first place. For example, health services directed to needs resulting from supposedly voluntary behaviour (e.g., tobacco smoking), or individuals or groups presenting with such health needs, would be given a low priority.

e. Principle of Restitution

According to this principle, individuals or groups disadvantaged as a consequence of injustice done them in the past deserve preferential consideration. On these grounds, aboriginal people may be entitled to a proportionately greater share of health resources because they have been victimized by unjust practices that have contributed to their situation of being in need. On grounds of restitution, the Canadian government offered compensation packages to persons who unknowingly received blood products carrying the HIV virus.

Two main problems attend the application of these principles to particular issues and decisions. The first is that, because they are so general, applying them requires interpretation involving sometimes complex conceptual and empirical issues. Even among those who subscribe to the same principle there may be considerable disagreement about its application in practice. For example, it is one thing to espouse that everyone should have equal access to a "decent minimum of health care," and another to specify exactly what should be included in such a package. How should we distinguish between meeting essential and non-essential needs? How do we define "medically necessary" services?

The second problem is that because these principles express different and opposing intuitions about justice, they are sometimes incompatible in the guidance they provide for deciding particular issues. How they should be balanced when in conflict turns on such things as whether one believes that individuals have a right to health care and how one conceives the sort of good that health care is.

In this regard, it is important to note that different principles receive greater weight and emphasis in different social arenas, or with respect to different kinds of goods to be distributed. Thus merit is generally accepted as fair for distributing grades to students, means or entitlement for distributing most consumer goods, and equality for distributing opportunity for primary education. A deep values cleavage divides those who view health care as a commodity like other consumer goods and those who view it is as a public good.

2. Procedural Principles of Justice

Procedural justice concerns the *process* by means of which decisions are made. If substantive principles answer such questions as "According to what criteria should the outcome of resource allocation be determined?" and "What services should be publicly funded?," procedural principles answer such questions as "Who has the rightful authority to make or influence these decisions?;" "Which individuals or groups need to be consulted or considered in decision-making?;" and "What is a fair process for making decisions?" They help complete the sentence "A fair process for making resource allocation decisions in health care is one in which...." Three main procedural principles are outlined below:

a. Principle of Explicitness or Publicity

According to this principle, the criteria for allocation decisions and the processes by which they are reached must be explicit and open to public scrutiny. The public has a right to know how decision-makers reach their decisions and on what grounds.

b. Principle of Accountability

According to this principle, those entrusted to make allocation decisions must be accountable — and capable of being held accountable — for the decisions that they make. This presupposes that the grounds for their decisions have been made explicit. Decision-makers must be able to give defensible reasons supporting decisions taken. Procedures must be in place to ensure that their decisions are consistent with whatever mandate they have been given that authorizes their decisions.

c. Principle of Autonomy

According to this principle, people are entitled to input or representation in decision-making that directly affects them or in which they have a stake, and the more so the greater their stake. In a publicly funded system such as ours, the public is the ultimate source of authority, and therefore decisions ought to express the will of the public, however this is determined. At the level of macro-allocation, considerations of autonomy inform current movements toward "devolution" or "decentralization" in resource allocation decision-making. At the micro-level, the doctrine of informed consent is rooted in the principle of autonomy.

Procedural principles are more complementary than substantive principles. Indeed, they are rooted in a common value — the quintessential democratic value — namely the right of stakeholders to have voice or representation in decision-making that concerns them.

The commitment to process values poses considerable difficulties. Some of these concern the practicalities of realizing process values. How should we determine which stakeholders should be involved in decision-making? Exactly what form should this involvement take? Does having one or two designated public representatives on a decision-making body mean that the process is participatory? How should they be selected? Given that the people and organizations who tend to be most effective in consultative processes are articulate and financially well-supported, how can we can ensure that the voices of vulnerable and disadvantaged persons and groups are heard? Where public opinion is sought, what influence should it have on decision-making?

Other difficulties and questions penetrate deeper. What is the value of this value? What, after all, is the point of greater public involvement in resource allocation decision-making? Is it valued for its own sake, or because it is expected that such involvement will lead to better decisions? If the latter, is this a reasonable expectation? Is the public more likely than are experts to make allocation decisions based on rational considerations? Is the public sufficiently informed and qualified to work through the medical, economic, and scientific issues on which many allocation issues turn? What are the costs and benefits of more participatory decision-making? Do gains in participation mean losses in efficiency?

Various mechanisms are being tried to realize process principles for health care decision-making. In various Canadian jurisdictions, efforts are being made to "decentralize" or "devolve" decision-making away from central planners and closer to the ultimate users of health care. Different ways of insuring greater stakeholder participation include public opinion polling, referendums, focus groups, town hall meetings, and the appointment of community representatives on decision-making bodies.

3. Integrating Substance and Process

In the context of substantive justice, fairness has to do with outcomes. To say that a given allocation is fair means that it is consistent with or follows from a preferred substantive principle of justice. From the standpoint of substantive norms, the evaluative question has the form "Is the outcome of this decision — i.e., the distribution of resources that will follow from it — fair with respect to substantive values such as equality, need, and benefit?" Does it distribute benefits more or less equally? Is it superior to other options with respect to meeting needs? Will it yield more benefit for the cost than other alternatives? The main challenge is that several sometimes competing values need to be considered, interpreted, and balanced by decision-makers.

In the context of procedural justice, fairness has to do with process. To say that a given allocation is fair in this sense means that it has been decided by a process consistent with procedural principles of justice. From the standpoint of procedural norms, the evaluative question has the form "Has the decision been reached through a process that is fair?" Was the decision-making open to public scrutiny? Can the decision-makers articulate the reasons for deciding as they did? Were they sufficiently representative of the stakeholders of the decision, and were stakeholders given appropriate influence over the decision? The main challenge posed by these procedural values concerns how best to translate principle into practice.

Both lines of questioning are clearly important. Resource allocation, if it is to be just in a comprehensive way, must integrate considerations of both substantive and procedural justice.

Fundamental Orientations to Issues of Justice

Most people's beliefs about health care cannot be compartmentalized as falling exclusively under any single principle identified in the previous section. Even so, the views individuals and even societies have with regard to justice can be distinguished according to which principles they tend to emphasize.

Along these lines, it is helpful to distinguish three main justice orientations or theories of justice: libertarianism, egalitarianism, and utilitarianism (Beauchamp & Childress, 1989, pp. 264-275).

1. Libertarianism

Libertarians value *individual freedom* or *liberty* above all else. Issues, such as which services should be made available and accessible to which individuals, should be decided mainly with reference to this value. Libertarians favour a free market approach to resource allocation because they believe that this approach is most compatible with individual freedom. A free market system distributes health care resources in accordance with what consumers are willing and able to pay. Libertarians tend to view allocation systems wherein some people are required to subsidize expenditure for the health needs of others as unjustifiable intrusions on freedom.

2. Egalitarianism

Equality is the main value that guides decision-making for those with an egalitarian orientation in matters of justice. Equality, however, can be interpreted in a number of different ways. For example, equality of *opportunity* is quite different from equality of *outcome*. With reference to health, Gorovitz (1988, p. 570) distinguishes four main senses of equality: equality in the amount of money spent on each individual, equality in individual health status, equality in the maximum to which each person is benefited, and equality in the treatment of similar cases. Each sense of equality furnishes a different standard for making resource allocation decisions.

Some egalitarians put special emphasis on the fact that people have unequal needs. They would be willing to give more than an equal share of resources to those in our society who are sickest because generally they have greater needs. Along these lines, O'Connell (1988) argues that the poor deserve preferential consideration in allocation decisions because their health needs tend to be greater.

3. Utilitarianism

The main value that guides utilitarian decision-making in matters of resource allocation is *beneficence*. However, for the utilitarian it is not so much the *good of the individual* that is the focus of concern (as was the paradigm case in the chapter on beneficence) as it is the aggregate *good of society* as a whole. What allocations or distributions will produce the greatest amount of good or benefit for the greatest number of people? The answer to this question requires a comparative cost-benefit analysis of the various options. The resource allocation likely to produce the most overall benefit would be favoured.

Cost-benefit comparisons — and some more so than others — are bound to be controversial when human lives and health are at stake. Even so, such calculations and comparisons are to some extent unavoidable in decisions about the allocation of resources.

As stated, these orientations represent extremes of emphasis. Most people find the values expressed in more than one orientation compelling and would make allocation decisions weighing these values against one another. These orientations may be complementary with respect to a given allocation decision, but often they will be in conflict. For example, allocating resources on the basis of the ability to pay is bound to result in an unequal distribution of resources; an allocation that best realizes equality may not produce the most overall benefit.

These orientations also differentiate the decision-making style of groups or collectives. In Canadian society, as Williams (1989) points out, "the egalitarian approach to health care has prevailed until now" (p. 10).[10] The American health care system is much more oriented around libertarian values than the Canadian system.[11]

Justice and the Scope of Health and Health Care

Ethical enquiries into allocation issues must contend with such difficult things as the comparative analysis of costs and benefits; with concepts such as benefit and health that are ambiguous and subject to different interpretations; and with values and principles about which there is no clear social consensus. Some of the major issues being debated today, such as how much money should go to cure as against health promotion and disease prevention, or whether there is a right to health care, are deeply dependent on how one conceives the nature and scope of health and health care.

1. Health Care and Health Status

Until recently, the ethics literature on distributive justice focused mainly on the distribution of *health care*. Health care has typically been interpreted as including mainly those services and programs directed to the care and cure of people who are "sick." In this sense, *health care* could more aptly be called *sickness care*. Questions of distributive justice framed within these parameters have mainly to do with what resources should be available for people who are sick, and which sick people should get access to those resources when not all can.

Health care, thus understood, is only one of a number of variables that effect *health status*, and indeed may not be the most important one. Other important variables include such things as income, education, life-style, and environment.[12] Health status is not equal throughout our society, as anyone who has worked in an inner city slum or with

Native people in the North could attest.[13] Poor people, in particular, "suffer from a greater incidence and prevalence of virtually all kinds of medical complications, diseases and health risks" (Manga, 1987a, p. 643).

If we are concerned about health status as a problem, health care must be seen as only a part of the solution, and a narrowing one at that. Even the most just distribution of *health care* resources would not equalize the considerable differences in *health status* throughout our society.[14] In order to address basic inequalities in health status, and indeed maximize health benefits, our society has to address the root causes of this inequality. These include factors beyond the scope of health care narrowly conceived, such as income, housing, and the environment. It is becoming increasingly apparent that a comprehensive and effective health policy requires the coordination of a number of sectors of public policy towards the objective of achieving health (e.g., see the Premier's Council on Health Strategy, 1991b).

2. Health Promotion, Disease Prevention, and Cure of the Sick

A growing number of commentators are calling for more societal resources to be allocated to programs and services aimed at improving and equalizing health status.[15] Given its long-standing emphasis on health promotion and disease prevention, nursing has taken a leadership role in these matters. Because resources are limited, however, increasing the amount of monies allocated for illness prevention and health promotion would at the same time mean *decreasing* monies currently directed elsewhere. Some commentators have argued that, since sickness care currently consumes such a great amount of resources, it would be morally appropriate to reallocate resources away from sickness care and into health promotion and disease prevention.[16]

In order to decide whether, and to what extent, such reallocation would be morally appropriate, it is necessary to compare specific options in light of guiding values. How much overall benefit would be produced from X dollars allocated to a "Blue Ribbon Baby" prenatal program as against a lung transplant program, or a chiropody clinic?

Which among the various options would best improve and equalize health status throughout our society? How would the needy fare under each option? How do the various options compare with respect to considerations of freedom?

An option that scores well in terms of one value may not score as well in terms of another. It may be that health promotion and disease prevention programs yield more "bang for buck" than do some or many sickness care programs. The Premier's Council on Health Strategy (1990), for example, advanced that "many health promotion and disease prevention programs are likely to prove more efficient and cost-effective in the long term" than "additional dollars spent on curative care" (p. 4).

However, such comparisons are controversial.[17] Part of the difficulty of comparing sickness care options with health promotion and disease prevention options is that the benefits that would accrue from each are not on the same level of concreteness. The benefits of resources allocated to health promotion and illness prevention may not be immediately realized, and are never amenable to precise measurement. A neighbourhood health centre may indeed help many families in the raising of healthy children, but this benefit may seem less important and urgent than the benefit of a costly transplant for a particular person presenting in the flesh with heart or lung disease.

3. The Right to Health and Health Care

Issues of justice in the health context are often couched in the language of rights. To say that someone or some group has a right to some resource is a shorthand way of saying how one thinks the resource ought to be allocated.

The language of rights, although powerful and rhetorically appealing, is often used without analytic clarity or precision.[18] Questions may arise about the grounds for a claimed right, and very different theories, such as natural law theory or contract theory, will provide different answers. Important distinctions need to be made between the different kinds of rights, such as positive rights, which impose a duty on someone else to provide for their fulfillment, and negative rights, which require only that others not stand in the way of my doing what I wish to do.

In the health context, it is especially important to be clear about what the claimed right is supposed to be a *right to* (or from). Some people, for example, speak not only about a *right to health care* but more sweepingly about a *right to health*. A right to the latter would be much broader and all-encompassing than a right to health care. Presumably, it would place a corresponding obligation on others, and upon government in particular, to provide services and programs (health care being only one among others) that will impact beneficially on health status.

Depending on how broadly one understands health, the factors impacting on health are numerous, and the scope of a right to health is therefore virtually limitless. The definition of health that has received the most attention in discussions about health rights is the well-known World Health Organization (WHO) definition that health is "a state of complete physical, mental, and social well-being and not merely the absence of disease or infirmity" (Callahan, 1983, p. 528). Several commentators have criticized this definition as being too unwieldy for the purposes of discussing health rights (e.g., Curtin, 1980; Callahan, 1983). Says Callahan:

> Our society cannot continue to work with a concept of "health" that is infinite in its scope, and, at the same time, try to carry on a sensible discussion of the "right to health" or the "right to health care." A narrow, limited concept of "health" would make it possible to have a rational discussion of "rights": a vague and woolly one does not. (p. 529)

For whatever its merits, the WHO definition is so broad that it is difficult to specify limits as to what a right to health or health care based on it would entail.

Callahan's critique can itself be criticized, and a broad conception of health and health rights defended. In 1984, the WHO elaborated upon their earlier definition of health. Their new definition, which follows, has been widely endorsed and adopted:[19]

[Health is] the extent to which an individual or group is able, on the one hand, to realize aspirations and satisfy needs; and on the other hand, to change or cope with the environment. Health is therefore seen as a resource for everyday life, not the objective of living; it is a positive concept emphasizing social and personal resources, as well as physical capacity.

Although this definition is also broad, it is more precise than the WHO's earlier definition, and therefore better suited for use in the context of public policy discussions. However, even if it is granted that broad definitions of health are inappropriate for the purpose of discussing health rights, this does not argue against such definitions of health *per se*.[20]

A *right to health care* would be much narrower in scope than a *right to health*, but even thus restricted, difficult issues arise. Health care comes in a number of different models, so to speak. Does a right to health care mean that everyone is entitled to a "Cadillac," or would it be enough if everyone were guaranteed at least a basic "Volkswagen"? Does health care include cosmetic surgery? Does it include services directly concerned with the development of health, or only those having to do with the prevention, diagnosis, and treatment of illness? Does a right to health care obligate the government to make quadruple bypass surgery available and accessible to everyone who might need it, regardless of the costs?

Along these lines, Buchanan (1984) distinguishes the right to a "decent minimum" of health care from a "strong equal access principle," which would guarantee everyone "a right to the best health-care services available" (p. 58). Undoubtedly, Canadians feel entitled to at least a decent minimum of health care, but what we can afford beyond that — what opportunity costs we are willing to forego — is a matter of some debate.[21] Nurses have an important role to play in this debate.

An Expanding Role for Nursing

Nurses have reason to be proud about the contribution they have made to the Canadian health care system and about the difference they have made in the quality of life of Canadians.

At the turn of the century, nurses took a major role in providing health care. They worked in the community to prevent and halt the spread of communicable diseases. Many health problems associated with poor living and working conditions were ameliorated by nurses providing care in communities and working for social reforms. Nurses worked with colleagues in public health toward the introduction of public health measures including clean water, garbage collection, public sanitation, and regulations regarding working and living conditions.

As new and successful medicines and treatments began to proliferate in the 1920's, the need grew for nurses and physicians to work in hospitals. For the next sixty years, the majority of nurses were employed in hospitals.

In the 1990's, the emphasis on hospital care is being re-evaluated. Nurses have supported the emphasis on wellness and the philosophy that more health care should be provided in the community.

However, the promises of restructuring and reform cannot be realized if funds are not transferred to the community. The needed services may be reduced too severely and perhaps even endanger the lives of patients returning home quicker and sicker to communities lacking needed support services.

Closure of beds, reduction or termination of hospital-based programs, and even hospital closures can be justified in some cases. This will mean lay-offs and redundancies for hospital-based nurses. What consequences will these changes have for the quality of life in the workplace for those nurses who remain, and for the quality of care of their clients? And what of those nurses who are laid off? Will they be employed in the community? They may be needed there, but will there be sufficient funding to employ the surplus of nurses?

Looking at the past hundred years, Canadian nurses have moved from working in a system based on the ethic of charity to one based on the ethic of justice. According to the justice ethic, persons are entitled to health care because of their needs and should not have to rely on the generosity of nurses, physicians, philanthropists, charitable organizations and communities for access to health care.

The justice ethic allows the person in need to maintain dignity and expresses a solidarity between the care provider, community, and person in need. It also has immense social benefits in terms of social stability, improved health, control of communicable diseases, and economic growth. For these reasons, nurses have traditionally favoured universal access to health care.

At the end of the century, nurses are concerned about how and even whether the justice approach can be maintained in the current economic climate. Reduced resources have affected nursing practice and given rise to ethical problems, worries, and dilemmas. Allocation decisions will have a direct bearing on the type and quality of care nurses can provide and on the health and quality of life of those they serve.

Issues of justice once seemed quite removed from the average nurse's concern for and involvement with direct client care. As Silva (1984) reports, "the topic of distributive justice as a moral responsibility" received scant attention in the nursing literature (p. 11). Nurses did not play a major role in discussions about allocation of scarce resources.

Times have changed. Before the recession and restructuring of the health care system, a shortage of nurses and not a shortage of beds, supplies and programs was the major issue. Today it is painfully obvious to nurses that issues of justice cannot be separated from concern for and involvement with direct client care. Nurses sometimes find themselves coping at the micro level with the adverse consequences of policy decisions over which they have had little control.

A decade ago, Flaherty issued a clarion call to nurses "to go beyond direct patient care to consider and act upon factors associated with the nature and shape of the health care system" (p. 105). This message is even more urgent today. The broader "factors" Flaherty speaks of ultimately bear on nurses' own well-being and job satisfaction and on their ability to provide quality care. Those who practice nursing in these times know first hand that allocation decisions at the macro- and meso-levels influence patient care and nursing practice.

At all levels of resource allocation, nurses have an obligation to become more involved.[22] At the micro-level, the development of genuinely open and participatory health teams will facilitate this. At the meso-level, nurses can express their concerns about justice by becoming more administratively and politically involved in the affairs of the institutions in which they work. For example, nurses can sit on constitutional committees, including budget and planning committees. At the broader macro-level, nurses, as informed and concerned health professionals and citizens, can make a valuable contribution to the process of forming public policy.[23]

If, as seems likely in Canada, the emphasis of health policy continues to shift from sickness care to health promotion and disease prevention, the involvement of nurses in decision-making will be especially valuable, since their training and orientation gives nurses an ideal vantage point from which to view the issues.

Case 1: Availability of Care Versus Quality of Care

That a health service is available and accessible to individuals does not necessarily mean that it will be a quality service. One of the most important factors bearing on the quality of a service is the ratio of health professionals to clients. Beyond a certain critical ratio — which may be very difficult to determine with any precision — the quality of care will suffer.

Downsizing and restructuring in various health care institutions may place increased strains on nurses with regard to their ability to deliver quality care. As a consequence of budget cuts and lay-offs, working conditions for nurses are sometimes such that their ability to provide safe, quality care is seriously compromised.

When, for whatever reasons, nursing resources are inadequate or scarce relative to demands on a service, a trade-off will have to be made between access to the service, on the one hand, and the quality of the service, on the other. If the service admits clients in numbers exceeding the critical ratio, it will preserve access, but sacrifice quality. If the service limits access to keep within the critical ratio, it will preserve quality, but at the expense of access.

Faced with such a choice, the interests, needs, and limits of nurses working in the service must also be considered. Nurses rightly take pride in their ability to deliver quality care. As a service reaches the critical ratio, nurses will endeavour to maintain the quality of care at the same level. Under such circumstances, the only way to do this will be to work harder. This will create stress and job dissatisfaction, which may further jeopardize the quality of care.

The following case illustrates the ethical challenges related to supply and demand:

Shirley Conrad is the Vice-President of Nursing in an urban teaching hospital. Last year, the hospital budget was reduced by five per cent. Shirley worked hard with nursing managers in the various units and with other administrators to find creative solutions to the hospital's budget problem. Lay-offs were thus avoid-

ed. However, the price for this limited victory was an agreement that nursing staff positions lost due to attrition and early retirement would not be filled.

The number of positions thus lost proved to be greater than anyone had anticipated. In the months that followed Shirley heard many complaints from nursing staff about their inability to give quality care, and at times, safe care. The medical staff were concerned because the loss of nurses directly affected their ability to practise medicine. The administration and the Board of Trustees was concerned about whether the hospital's responsibility to the public was being compromised.

All parties involved recognize that the hospital must be responsive to the public need. However, given the loss of nursing positions and the increased demands on those nurses left behind, most nurses are advocating that beds be closed. This would mean limiting the numbers of clients admitted in order to ensure safety and quality care. All of the interested parties are looking to the Vice-President of Nursing, who must recommend either closing beds or leaving them open and risk compromising the quality and safety of care.

Commentary

Shirley is faced with a trade-off between access to an available service and diminished quality of care available within that service. If beds are closed, she and the nursing staff can take comfort in knowing that the care being provided is both safe and of an acceptable quality. However, clients who need care may not get it, physicians will be limited in their practice, and the hospital may be accused of not meeting the community's needs.

Should Shirley recommend that beds be closed and thus fail to meet the needs of some clients whose access would be impeded as a consequence? Or should she opt for the status quo, in which nurses are overworked and care is compromised? In choosing between these two options, she will have to weigh in the balance the needs and interests of clients, nursing staff, medical staff, and the hospital.

In determining what would be best for clients, it is necessary to distinguish between the good of those who are or will be admitted to the service and the good of others waiting in line. How can the burdens and benefits to these two constituencies be compared?

Put bluntly, the more people who are given access, the poorer the quality of care. The poorer the quality of care, the smaller the benefit to clients in the service. A little for everybody may mean not enough for anybody. Indeed, beyond a certain point, low quality care crosses over into unsafe care, and admission to the hospital may no longer be a benefit at all. On the other hand, although limiting access to ensure quality care will undoubtedly be a benefit for those admitted, those waiting in what will now be a longer line-up may not receive any benefit at all. What harms and adverse consequences might they suffer as a consequence of diminished access? How do the benefits of quality care for some and no benefit for others weigh against the benefits of watered down quality of care for many?

Such weighing of benefits is especially difficult when the resources being allocated are people, whose interests and concerns must also be taken into account in the decision-making process. As Vice-President of Nursing, Shirley is obliged to represent the needs and interests of the nursing staff. They have expressed their wishes on the matter, and what they ask for is not unreasonable. They are working under less than ideal conditions, and their job satisfaction is suffering. As a result of being hurried, they are more likely to make mistakes, which could have very grave consequences.

Furthermore, the present situation is one in which the nursing staff will continually be faced with difficult micro-allocation decisions about how best to distribute their scarce time between the clients in the service. These decisions will lead to even greater stress.

Such concerns about the nursing staff are important in their own right, but they also have a bearing on the good of present and future clients admitted to the service. Under the existing circumstances, the safety and quality of the care available is being diminished, and it is likely to diminish further if the situation continues or worsens. It is one thing to deal with short-term emergency situations, in which nurses can be expected to give a little extra, and another to deal with a situation tantamount to a permanent emergency.

As concerns the point of view of the hospital and other practitioners, the duty to respond to the health needs of the community is very important. However, in light of the considerations mentioned above, it may be that the best way to fulfil this duty would be to close beds. No doubt this would be an unfortunate solution, but it may be the best among unattractive options. Would the hospital be realizing its mandate by giving low quality or even unsafe care? Access is certainly important, and the closing of beds might even draw negative media attention. So too would an accident or mistake made more likely if nursing staff are overworked.

The hospital is understandably concerned about its reputation and image if it closes beds. This is the stuff of which headlines are made. Yet, would it be better to pretend that the status quo is working well, and that under the circumstances the goals of open access and quality care can both be realized?

The community would like high quality care accessible to all, and a case can be made that they have a right to it. If circumstances are such that this is not possible, should the community be shielded from the reality? Would it not be better to put the matter squarely before the community and invite more general discussion about the justice issue?

The reality is that, for this and other hospitals, budget reduction is a major problem. This problem is a function of broader macro-allocation decisions within health spending. The community has a role to play in such decision-making and cannot exercise its rights and responsibilities if the truth of the situation is kept from them.

The burden of the difficult decision at hand is not for the Vice-President of Nursing alone to bear. Given the far-ranging consequences of this decision, it would be appropriate to bring together the various parties involved (or their representatives) to discuss the issue. The factors that created this problem in the first place should also be addressed.

Case 2: Burdens and Benefits of Teaching Placements

One of the main factors bearing on the quality of health care is the education of health professionals. If this training is to prepare future practitioners to deal competently with the often challenging situations in which they will later find themselves, students must try out and practise in actual clinical situations what they have learned in the classroom. Some clinical situations will be more instructive and beneficial to students than others. The teacher or clinical supervisor, therefore, will naturally endeavour to assign students to clinical settings from which they will derive the most benefit.

At the same time, however, the clinical supervisor is obliged to consider the good of the institutions in which students are placed, and even more importantly the good of the clients with whom they will come in contact. The assignment of practitioners-in-training, depending on a number of variables, may be either a burden or a benefit.

Issues of justice arise in the course of student assignments insofar as the goal of educating students for the benefit of future clients must be weighed alongside the burdens and benefits of allocating them to institutions and clients. A balance must be struck between what would be a "fair" assignment for students (e.g., one which will facilitate their learning and develop their competence) and what would be a "fair" assignment to clients and institutions. The following case illustrates this problem:

Jason Green is a faculty member at a university school of nursing. His students are in the first year of a four year program. Their clinical experience focuses on the provision of basic nursing care. The agency that has agreed to provide this experience is a long term care facility with a mixture of rehabilitation and chronic care clients. Three schools of nursing, one school of occupational therapy, and one school of social work use this facility for teaching.

Mabel Brown is the Nurse Manager of unit A, which is currently operating at a maximum capacity of twenty chronic care beds, and is the largest and busiest in the agency. Following an energetic recruitment drive, the unit is relatively well-staffed, and Mabel is proud of the quality of care that is being provided.

Because the variety of client problems is so great in Unit A, it is much sought after by various clinical supervisors to give their students the most rounded experience possible. Several clinical supervisors from different programs have approached Mabel about placing students in her unit. The school of social work would like to place four students, and Jason Green has asked to place seven nursing students. Combined with other requests, this would add up to fifteen students. Mabel is concerned that having this many students working in the unit may lead to fragmented care for her clients. She is also concerned that it may create difficulties for her staff, some of whom have previously complained about the number of students working in the unit.

Commentary

Depending on the circumstances, practitioners-in-training can be more or less of a burden or a blessing for institutions and clients. In this case, the "over-supply" of students is perceived as being more of a burden than a benefit. The main conflict that arises is between the benefits of student education as against the corresponding burden on the institution and its clients.

The benefits of clinical training *for students* are indisputable. On this side of the issue, the main objective will be to seek out clinical settings that will best facilitate the development of well-rounded and competent practitioners. This is in the interest not only of the individual students, but also of society as a whole. From the perspective of the students, there will be concern for a just distribution of beneficial learning experiences *between* or *among* students. For example, it would be unfair for Jason to assign one student to several clinically interesting cases, and another student to cases that would provide little opportunity for learning and growth.

On the other side of the issue, the good of the institutions in which the students will be placed and the clients they will serve must be considered. Beneficence (or more precisely, non-maleficence) requires that any burdens that might arise out of such placements should be minimized, if not eliminated. With regard to the good of the institution and its staff, this will mean taking steps to ensure that students do not disrupt the smooth functioning of the unit to which they are assigned. To this end, it is important that staff who will be working with students be involved in the assignment process, and that students understand what is expected of them.

In most cases, it should be possible to develop a working relationship in which students are perceived by the staff as a benefit and not a burden (indeed, this is probably the norm). In any event, it can be argued that nursing staff, in virtue of their professional role, have a duty to participate in the education of future practitioners.

Concerns about the good of the clients may be more difficult to address. Mabel Brown is right to be concerned about the possibility of "fragmented care" if the number of students is too great. Clients (and their families) are entitled to the best care possible, and do not want to be treated as "test cases" or "guinea pigs." To some extent, these concerns can be addressed by cautionary measures, such as ensuring that students are closely supervised and not given responsibilities beyond their competence.

Nevertheless, even under ideal arrangements, student placements may involve some compromise with the goal of quality care. For some clients, simply being interviewed (let alone being touched, probed, and examined) is in itself a burden, and all the more so when this is not strictly necessary for therapeutic purposes. In some cases, the potential burden of student care will be even more serious. For every practice or skill acquired, there must be a first time: the first time one changes a dressing, draws blood, inserts an intravenous, and so on. With reason, most clients would prefer not to be a student's (albeit necessary) "first time" experience.

To the extent that student assignments, however carefully planned and supervised, do constitute a burden for clients, there is an issue as to how the benefits of education should be weighed against these burdens.

This issue is very similar to one raised by research and experimentation, in which the goals of learning may also conflict with the goals of the client's care. In the research context, it is agreed that some harms or burdens are so great that they cannot be justified *regardless of the benefits*.

If the burdens of student assignments (all efforts having been made to minimize or eliminate these burdens) are indeed acceptable as against the benefits, further considerations arise about justice in the distribution of these burdens. Respect for autonomy also comes into play in the selection of individual clients to bear these burdens. A strong case can be made that the consent of clients is required if they are to be part of a student's learning experience.

Broader issues arise regarding justice in the distribution of burdens among *population groups*. Edwards and Graber (1988a, pp. 186-187), addressing themselves to the research context, discuss various considerations of fairness that are relevant to this matter. Why has this particular population group been selected? Are the chronically ill and the elderly disproportionately assigned the burden of student assignments, perhaps reflecting some broader pattern of discrimination within the health system?

The various questions and issues that arise in this case should be explored and decided with input from the various parties involved. It may be that steps can be taken to address Mabel Brown's concerns for her staff and the good of her clients. Perhaps a compromise solution can be worked out limiting the number of student assignments in the unit. This may be an opportunity for students, staff, and faculty to reflect more deeply on the values of the health system in which they work.

Case 3: Distributing Nursing Time and Care

For the most part, nurses do not have much control over the allocation of resources at the micro-level. However, one resource individual nurses do have some control over is their own time and nursing care. Under present circumstances, this is becoming one of the scarcest resources in the health system.

Mitchell (1987) recounts a personal experience involving an elderly man dying of mouth and throat cancer. In the course of hurriedly feeding him, the man choked to death. The risk of choking is great for such clients, and Mitchell notes that the man might very well have come to the same end even if she had devoted more time to feeding him. However, even if allotting more time to such clients would reduce the risk of harm, this would still have to be weighed against other demands on the nurse's time. Mitchell asks:

> But what about all the other patients: their dinners, their six o'clock meds, their need for the nurse's time and attention? The nurse does not have the luxury of devoting herself to a single patient.... Moral obligations of justice impose themselves as well. (p. 294)

Indeed, "moral obligations of justice impose themselves" whenever there is not enough of a resource to go around. In such situations, difficult decisions must be made between the competing needs and demands of various individuals, as the following case illustrates:

> *Veronica Robertson has been working in the paediatric intensive care unit of a community hospital since her graduation from a local college four years ago. The unit is usually staffed by two nurses, but on this particular shift her colleague has gone home ill, and there are no critical care nurses available for relief. The unit is presently at maximum capacity with three children:*

Sally, a profoundly retarded infant of three months awaiting transfer to a specialty hospital for cardiac surgery;

John, a three year old trauma victim admitted the previous day, on a ventilator and requiring constant care; he is not expected to survive;

Ansari, a five year old, who is post-surgery, ready for the step-down unit as soon as a bed becomes available. He is extremely anxious about leaving the protective environment of the unit.

Even with two nurses, it would be task enough to attend to the needs of these three children. Left to herself, Veronica is anguished by the question of how she should distribute her limited time and care among them.

Commentary

"The chief criteria for allocating a nurse's time," Mitchell (1987) argues, "are consideration of each patient's needs along with his capacity to benefit from her attention, with the qualification that every patient in her care receive at least some of her attention" (pp. 295-296). Three distinct criteria can be distinguished here: Need, likelihood of benefit, and equality. Organizing her options in terms of these three criteria will help Veronica to achieve clarity about the choice she must make.

If the constraints on this situation are indeed as described in the case, Veronica has essentially two options. One option would be to divide her time and care evenly among the three children. This option, however, is incompatible with considerations of need and benefit, and indeed may not even be promotive of equality. The three children, after all, have unequal needs, and allocating them equal shares of her time may not be fair.

A second option, and one more consistent with standard nursing practice, would be to prioritize the three children in terms of need and the prospect of benefit, and to distribute her time with each accordingly. In essence, this would amount to choosing between the three children.

John is clearly the sickest of the children, and therefore needs the greatest amount of attention. Although he would likely benefit the most in the short term, unfortunately in the long term it would probably not make much difference. Ansari, who is on the road to recovery, requires very little truly "critical care" but could benefit from support and attention because he is so anxious. Veronica's attention to Ansari would likely have little short-term gain, but could make a difference to him in the long run. Sally's needs are likely to be great, but what benefits can be expected down the road, and what "quality of life" can she expect?

The tragic thing about such a decision is that to decide in favour of one child is at the same time to decide against another. Whatever comfort and satisfaction Veronica may take from being able to help and care for the child to whom she devotes the lion's share of her time will be spoiled by the painful knowledge that this will be at the expense of one or both of the other children. The situation is a "zero-sum" game in which one person can win only at the expense of someone else losing. Who will be the loser in this decision?

If Veronica devotes the least amount of time to John, it may be that he will die sooner than he otherwise would if given more needed care. Even if unable to provide him lasting benefit, she could at the very least make his dying easier, and provide added comfort to his family. Ansari's life is not in imminent danger, but in neglecting his need in favour of the others she may be contributing to his poor adjustment to hospitalization. Sally's long-term prognosis may not be very good regardless of how much time Veronica gives her, but she is certainly very sick and would benefit from more attention. If Veronica decides to give Sally the lowest priority, will she be making a "quality of life" judgement and communicating to Sally's family the message that Sally's life is less valuable than that of the other children?

Given these limited and less than ideal options, the choice to be made is a painful one. However, it is difficult to imagine that Veronica would be limited to these options. One wonders if other options have been fully explored. Would it not be possible to transfer one or more of the children to another critical care unit? Ansari, in particular, seems an ideal candidate to be transferred. Indeed, the kind of emotional support he needs could be provided by people with less training than Veronica, or even a parent or a volunteer. Alternatively, would it not be possible to second one or more staff nurses who, even without special training, could provide basic nursing care under Veronica's supervision? At the very least, Veronica should receive advice and emotional support from supervisors and colleagues. Are there any hospital policies or guidelines that might give some guidance (and comfort) on this matter?

The case, however, raises issues that go beyond Veronica's immediate problem. The fact that a hospital admits a child to an intensive care unit, some might argue, itself constitutes an agreement to provide the child a standard of care. Hospitals are obliged to take whatever steps are necessary to ensure that nurses or other health professionals are not forced into situations, like the one in which Veronica finds herself, of unilaterally renegotiating the standard of care. How typical and common is the situation in which Veronica finds herself? Why, apparently, are there no provisions for back-up resources to be brought in for such emergency situations? What prior decisions contributed to this crisis in the first place, and what future decisions will minimize the possibility of such crises, or at the very least provide greater support and guidance for decision-making? To what extent is the policy of performing expensive and resource intensive surgery on children who are going to be disabled for life a factor contributing to these sorts of situations? How ought considerations of "quality of life" and "opportunity costs" to enter into these treatment (or nontreatment) decisions? Could a better administrative system be devised for dealing with children awaiting internal or external transfer?

For the well-being of the nursing staff and the good of the children served by the unit, Veronica will later be obliged to see that these issues are raised and dealt with in a thorough manner. Nursing rounds, ethics rounds, or a health team meeting in the unit would be appropriate forums for venting these issues. Hopefully, the next time this situation arises (if indeed steps cannot be taken to ensure that there is no "next time") the nurse will benefit as a result of lessons learned from Veronica's experience.

Conclusion

Issues of justice will become more acute as our society comes to terms with the problems of limited resources for health and health care. For the good of all concerned, it is imperative that processes at the macro-, meso-, and micro-levels be put into place to enhance and facilitate just decision-making in these areas. At every level, nurses should seek to become more involved because they are players whose interests, expertise, and concern are necessary for just solutions. A clinician quoted in Jameton (1984) captures the feelings of many nurses about these matters:

> You know, sometimes I feel like this. There I am standing by the shore of a swiftly flowing river and I hear the cry of a drowning man. So I jump into the river, put my arms toward him, pull him to shore and apply artificial respiration. Just when he begins to breathe, there is another cry for help. So I jump into the river, reach him, pull him to shore, apply artificial respiration, and then just as he begins to breathe, there is another cry for help. So back in the river again, reaching, pulling, applying, breathing and then another yell. Again and again, without end, goes the sequence. You know, I am so busy jumping in, pulling them to shore, applying artificial respiration, that I have *no* time to see who the hell is upstream pushing them all in. (p. 261)

Increasingly, it is becoming obvious that justice requires nurses to make the time to walk upstream — against the current — and educate people about the dangers by the river ... or teach them to become better swimmers.

Notes

1   Higher public demand and expectations, expensive new technologies and pharmaceuticals, and rising labour costs are the main factors driving health care costs. For a discussion of these issues comparing the Canadian and American systems, see Evans (1985).

2   A more comprehensive history of medicare in Canada can be found in Roy, Williams, and Dickens (1994, pp. 87-98).

3   Buchanan (1989, pp. 294-295) points out that terms like "micro-allocation" and "macro-allocation" are too imprecise to capture decision-making in these matters. Even so, they do serve a useful purpose and therefore are employed throughout this chapter.

4   In the contemporary climate of cost-consciousness, there is much discussion of "waste" in the health care system in the form of "useless" tests and therapies. Everyone will agree that, to whatever extent such waste takes place, it ought to be eliminated (and costs thereby contained). The issue under discussion here, however, concerns tests and therapies that hold out at least some promise of benefit to the individual, and which, if this benefit alone were the only consideration, would be deemed appropriate.

5   Expressing this as a conflict between the duty to the individual as against the duty to society is very misleading. The "duty to society" is more properly described as a duty to other individuals who may have a claim to the opportunity costs foregone.

6   Those who control the gates by means of which consumers are granted access to health care resources wield considerable power. This power resides mainly with physicians. In the coming years, there is likely to be increased debate about the power physicians have relative to other professional groups (e.g., midwives, public health nurses) *vis-à-vis* consumer access to and the distribution of health care resources. The nature of the health system (e.g., highly socialized, free market) is also extremely relevant to gate-keeping issues.

7   Gorovitz (1988, p. 573) and Curtin (1984, p. 8) each list five slightly different principles for decision-making in these contexts. Some

authors advocate a decision method that combines various criteria in order of priority. Rescher (1988) is probably the best known advocate of this approach. The most comprehensive and thorough overview of these issues to date is given by Kilner (1990).

8   W. Vickery Stoughton, President, Toronto General Hospital, reported in Williams (1987, p. 11).

9   The analysis in this section has been adapted from Yeo (1993).

10   Manga (1987b) gives a concise overview of the values dimension of the Canadian health care system:

> Medicare in Canada embodies a highly egalitarian conception of distributive justice. The right of access to health services is associated with important societal values such as equality of opportunity, dignity of persons, equal worth of persons and the exercise of autonomy and informed choice. To the extent that any allocation of resources "disfavours" some group's or individual's needs there is prima facie question of whether such unmet needs are just and consistent with the above societal values. (p. 2)

The following passage also gives a good insight into the guiding values of the Canadian system:

> The Government of Canada believes that a civilized and wealthy nation such as ours should not make the sick bear the financial burden of health care. Everyone benefits from the security and peace of mind that comes with having prepaid health insurance. The misfortune of illness . . . is burden enough: The cost of the care should be borne by society as a whole. (Government of Canada, 1983, p. 7)

For background on the Canadian health system, see Manga (1987a), Taylor (1987, 1992), Torrance (1987), Williams (1987), and Baumgart (1988).

11   For a succinct comparison of the value orientations of the two systems, see Storch (1988, pp. 264-265).

12   For a more detailed discussion of these other variables, see Manga (1987a) and the Premier's Council on Health Strategy (1991b).

13   Whether such inequality of health status is in itself unjust is a debatable point, which depends on one's fundamental orientation in matters of justice. Libertarians will view the matter quite differently from egalitarians and utilitarians.

14   Further to this point, Manga (1987a) writes:

> Most health policy planners in the past naively assumed that hospital and medical-care service were a "good thing" and the more the better. However, it is now quite apparent that if we wish to equalize health, equalizing access to hospitals and medical service is clearly insufficient. Other strategies and tactics are needed to supplement a policy of equal access to health-care services. (p. 645)

The Premier's Council on Health Strategy (1991c) makes the same point:

> Adding more money to an already sizable health care budget will not necessarily improve the health status of Ontario's citizens. A more strategic approach to determining needs and establishing priorities is needed.(p. 2)

The extent to which equal distribution of health care would remove inequalities in health status is debatable. Illich (1976) takes the very extreme view that health care, rather than being a good, is in fact inversely correlated with health status.

15   Childress (1988) is one among many philosophers advocating that increased efforts be directed toward health promotion and disease prevention. In Ontario, the first of the five main goals adopted by the Premier's Council on Health Strategy (1990) is to "shift the emphasis to health promotion and disease prevention" (p. 4). This was advanced as a goal worthy of guiding public policy in Canada as early as the Lalonde Report (1974), and by numerous other reports

that followed thereafter. A number of signs indicate that in coming years this goal will be sought after with greater political commitment than it has been in the past.

16 Spasoff et al. (1987), for example, argue as follows:

> Reallocation is ... the more powerful approach, and is inevitable if realignment of efforts to promote health is to occur. Reductions in our current high rates of institutionalization (both acute and chronic) could free up considerable amounts of resources to be applied to achieving health goals. We must put into place a policy to reallocate resources in conscious efforts to support health. (p. 96)

17 Curtin (1980) makes the point clearly:

> If the amount of funds for prevention significantly decreased the amount allocated for treatment and rehabilitation, grave injustices may occur. Although we know that such a course of action undoubtedly will save more lives in the future, there is legitimate concern about the public ethos that may result from adopting policies designed to save future statistical lives if current actual lives are neglected. (p. 463)

18 For a concise and helpful elucidation of some of the issues involving the language of rights, see Thomas and Waluchow (1990, pp. 30-35).

19 The definition that follows is cited in Spasoff et al. (1987, p. 1).

20 Broader definitions of health tend to be favoured in nursing. In Canada, the views of nurse theorist Moyra Allen, who views health in terms of learning and coping, have been very influential (Kravitz & Frey, 1989).

21 The right to health care is not included in *Canadian Charter of Rights and Freedoms*. Neither is it enshrined in the *Canada Health Act*, which is designed to ensure that all Canadians have access to medically necessary health services but refrains from using the language of rights. However, Storch (1988) points out that although technically there is no legal right to health care in Canada, the *Medical Care Act* of 1966, which preceded the *Canada Health Act* of

1984, "outlined a set of criteria which, in principle and in operational reality, did establish health care as a 'right'"(p. 264).

22   Murphy (1986, p. 68) lists a number of more specific ways by which nurses may express concern for justice in their practice, including assessing and comparing the costs of existing interventions, measuring the clinical effects of policy changes, and lobbying on behalf of medically indigent clients.

23   Flaherty (1985) says that the responsible nurse is someone "who influences and promotes change in health care policies in national, provincial and local domains and has input to policy decisions" (p. 110). This is only to restate the position of the profession as stated in various codes of ethics. For example:

> The nurse shares with other citizens the responsibility for initiating and supporting action to meet the health and social needs of the public. (International Council of Nurses, [1973] 1982)

> For the benefit of the individual client and the public at large, nursing's goals and commitments need adequate representation. Nurses should ensure this representation by active participation in decision-making in institutional and political arenas to assure a just distribution of health care and nursing resources. (American Nurses' Association, [1976] 1985, Statement 11.2)

Aroskar (1984) grounds this duty to participate in public policy in client advocacy:

> As the largest group of health care professionals and as client advocates, nurses are and should be part of public and political dialogues and decision-making about resource allocation in health care. (p. 5)

References

Aroskar, M. (1984). Ethics are important in allocating health resources. *American Nurse, 16* (1), 5, 20.

American Nurses' Association. ([1976] 1985). *Code for nurses with interpretive statements.* Kansas City: Author.

Baumgart, A.J. (1988). Evolution of the Canadian health care system. In A.J. Baumgart & J. Larsen (Eds.), *Canadian nursing faces the future: Development and change* (pp. 19-37). St. Louis: C.V. Mosby.

Beauchamp, T.L., & Childress, J.F. (1989). *Principles of biomedical ethics* (3rd ed.). New York: Oxford University Press.

Buchanan, A.E. (1984). The right to a decent minimum of health care. *Philosophy and Public Affairs, 13* (1), 55-78.

Buchanan, A.E. (1989). Health-care delivery and resource allocation. In R.M. Veatch (Ed.), *Medical ethics* (pp. 291-327). Boston: Jones & Bartlett.

Callahan, D. (1983). Health and society: Some ethical imperatives. In S. Gorovitz, R. Macklin, A.L. Jameton, J.M. O'Connor, & S. Sherwin (Eds.), *Moral problems in medicine* (2nd ed., pp. 527-535). Englewood Cliffs, NJ: Prentice-Hall.

Childress, J.F. (1983). Who shall live when not all can live? In S. Gorovitz, R. Macklin, A.L. Jameton, J.M. O'Connor, & S. Sherwin (Eds.), *Moral problems in medicine* (2nd ed., pp. 640-649). Englewood Cliffs, NJ: Prentice-Hall.

Childress, J.F. (1988). Priorities in the allocation of scarce resources. In R.B. Edwards & G.C. Graber (Eds.), *Bioethics* (pp. 715-723). San Diego: Harcourt Brace Jovanovich.

Curtin, L.L. (1980). Is there a right to health care? *American Journal of Nursing, 80* (3), 462-465.

Curtin, L.L. (1984). Ethics and economics in the eighties. *Nursing Management, 15* (6), 7-9.

Edwards, R.B., & Graber, G.C. (1988a). Introduction: Medical experimentation. In R.B. Edwards & G.C. Graber (Eds.), *Bioethics* (pp. 179-188). San Diego: Harcourt Brace Jovanovich.

Edwards, R.B., & Graber, G.C. (1988b). Introduction: Allocation of scarce or expensive medical resources. In R.B. Edwards & G.C. Graber (Eds.),

Bioethics (pp. 699-715). San Diego: Harcourt Brace Jovanovich.

Evans, R.G. (1985). Illusions of necessity: Evading responsibility for choice in health care. *Journal of Health Politics, Policy, and Law, 10* (3), 439-467.

Flaherty, M.J. (1985). Ethical issues. In M. Stewart, J. Innes, S. Searl, & C. Smillie (Eds.), *Community health nursing in Canada* (pp. 97-113). Toronto: Gage.

Gorovitz, S. (1988). Equity, efficiency, and the distribution of health care. In T.A. Mappes & J.S. Zembaty (Eds.), *Biomedical ethics* (2nd ed., pp. 558-579). New York: McGraw-Hill.

Government of Canada. (1983). *Preserving universal medicare: A government of Canada position paper.* Ottawa: Ministry of Supply and Services.

Illich, I. (1976). *Medical nemesis: The expropriation of health.* New York: Pantheon.

International Council of Nurses. (1982). *Code for nurses: Ethical concepts applied to nursing.* Geneva: Author. (Originally published 1973)

Jameton, A.L. (1984). *Nursing practice: The ethical issues.* Englewood Cliffs, NJ: Prentice-Hall.

Kilner, J.F. (1990). *Who lives? Who dies?: Ethical criteria in patient selection.* New Haven, CT: Yale University Press.

Lalonde, M. (1974). *A new perspective on the health of Canadians: A working document.* Ottawa: Information Canada.

Manga, P. (1987a). Equality of access and inequalities in health status: Policy implications of a paradox. In D. Coburn, C. D'Arcy, G.M. Torrance, & P. New (Eds.), *Health and Canadian society* (2nd ed., pp. 637-648). Markham, ON: Fitzhenry & Whiteside.

Manga, P. (1987b). Guest editorial: Health economics and ethics. *Synapse, 3* (2), 2-3.

Mitchell, C. (1987). Steadying the hand that feeds. *American Journal of Nursing, 87* (3), 293-295.

Moorhouse, A. (1993). User fees: Fair cost containment or attack on the sick? *Canadian Nurse, 89* (5), 21-24.

Murphy, E.K. (1986). Health care: Right or privilege? *Nursing Economics, 4* (2), 66-68.

O'Brien, L. (1983). Allocation of a scarce resource: The bone marrow transplant case. In C. Murphy & H. Hunter (Eds.), *Ethical problems in the nurse-patient relationship* (pp. 217-232). Boston: Allyn & Bacon.

O'Connell, L.J. (1988). The preferential option for the poor and health care in the United States. In J.F. Monagle & D.C. Thomasma (Eds.), *Medical ethics: A guide for health professionals* (pp. 306-313). Rockville, MA: Aspen.

Pellegrino, E.D. (1986). Rationing health care: The ethics of medical gatekeeping. *The Journal of Contemporary Health Law and Policy, 2*, 23-45.

Premier's Council on Health Strategy [Ontario]. (1990). *A vision of health: Health goals for Ontario* (Revised). Toronto: Author.

Premier's Council on Health Strategy [Ontario, Integration and Coordination Committee]. (1991a). *Local decision making for health and social services.* Toronto: Author.

Premier's Council on Health Strategy [Ontario, Healthy Public Policy Committee]. (1991b). *Nurturing health: A framework on the determinants of health.* Toronto: Author.

Premier's Council on Health Strategy [Ontario, Health Goals Committee]. (1991c). *Towards Health Outcomes: Goals 2 and 4.* Toronto: Author.

Rescher, N.P. (1988). The allocation of exotic medical lifesaving therapy. In T.A. Mappes & J.S. Zembaty (Eds.), *Biomedical ethics* (2nd ed., pp. 601-611). New York: McGraw-Hill.

Roy, D.J., J.R. Williams &, Dickens, B.M. (1994). *Bioethics in Canada.* ON: Prentice-Hall.

Royal Commission on Health Services [Hall Report]. (1964). *Report of the royal commission on health servies* (Vol.1). Ottawa: Queen's Printer.

Silva, M.C. (1984). Ethics, scarce resources, and the nurse executive. *Nursing Economics, 2* (1), 11-18.

Spasoff, R.A., Cole, P., Dale, F., Korn, D., Manga, P., Marshall, V., Picherack, F., Shosenberg, N., & Zon, L. (1987). *Health for all Ontario: Report on the panel on health goals for Ontario.* Toronto: Author.

Stoddart, G., M. Barer, R. Evans &, V. Bhatia. ((1993). *Why not user charges?* The real issues. The Premier's Council on Health, Well-being and Social Justice. ON: Queen's Printer.

Storch, J.L. (1988). Major substantive ethical issues facing Canadian health care policymakers and implementers. *The Journal of Health Administration Education, 6* (2), 263-271.

Taylor, M.G. (1987). The Canadian health-care system: After medicare. In D. Coburn, C. D'Arcy, G.M. Torrance, & P. New (Eds.), *Health and Canadian society* (2nd ed., pp. 73-101). Markham, ON: Fitzhenry & Whiteside.

Taylor, M.G. (1992). Another look at Canada's health care system. *Policy Options*, 13 (4), 31-36.

Thomas, J.E., & Waluchow, W.J. (1990). *Well and good: Case studies in biomedical ethics* (2nd ed.). Peterborough, ON: Broadview Press.

Torrance, G.M. (1987). Socio-historical overview: The development of the Canadian health system. In D. Coburn, C. D'Arcy, G.M. Torrance, & P. New (Eds.), *Health and Canadian society* (2nd ed., pp. 6-32). Markham, ON: Fitzhenry & Whiteside.

Vail, S. (1995). Is privatization the answer? *Canadian Nurse, 91* (9), 59-60.

Veatch, R.M. (1988). Voluntary risks to health: The ethical issues. In T.A. Mappes & J.S. Zembaty (Eds), *Biomedical ethics* (2nd ed., pp. 593-601). New York: McGraw-Hill.

Wikler, D.I. (1983). Persuasion and coercion. In S. Gorovitz, R. Macklin, A.L. Jameton, J.M. O'Connor, & S. Sherwin (Eds.), *Moral problems in medicine* (2nd ed., pp. 587-602). Englewood Cliffs, NJ: Prentice-Hall.

Williams, J.R. (1987). Health economics and ethics. *Synapse, 3* (2), 9-14.

Williams, J.R. (1989). Allocation of health care resources. *Synapse, 5* (3), 10-13.

Yeo, M. (1993). *Ethics and economics in health care resource allocation* (Working Paper No. 93-07). Ottawa: Queen's/University of Ottawa Economic Projects.

STUDY QUESTIONS: JUSTICE

Case 1: Availability of Care Versus Quality of Care

1. Discuss the statement: "Stress is a fact of life for nurses working in a number of situations. Nurses who can't handle the stress should reassess why they went into nursing in the first place."

2. What involvement should the community have in shaping hospital policies? What mechanisms can you identify or suggest for facilitating such involvement?

3. Discuss ways in which an institution's concern for public relations might interfere with its duties to clients and to the community.

4. From the standpoint of an individual nurse who is overworked, how would you balance personal interests against concern for the good of present and future clients?

Case 2: Burdens and Benefits of Teaching Placements

1. What input should student nurses have concerning their placement into agencies and institutions?

2. Discuss ways in which student nurses may be a benefit rather than a burden for clients.

3. What issues of justice may arise for student nurses in the context of their clinical assignments? What issues may arise for faculty?

4. What information are clients entitled to when student nurses are involved in their care?

Case 3: Distributing Nursing Time and Care

1. Some nurses working in neonatal intensive care units have mixed feelings about the surgical and technological innovations that make it possible to "rescue" infants who would otherwise die. Discuss this issue with reference to both "quality-of-life" considerations and considerations of justice.

2. In the course of caring for children, nurses understandably develop more positive relationships with some children and their families than with others. To what extent might and should this influence the nurse's allocation of his or her time between various children?

3. What bearing, if any, should the fact that Sally is "profoundly retarded" have on the decision about how much care she should receive relative to the others?

4. Allocation decisions of the kind with which Veronica is faced are extremely painful, and are bound to be emotionally charged. To what extent is emotion an obstacle to such ethical decision-making, and to what extent might it be a pre-condition for it?

INTEGRITY

A philosophy of life which involves no sacrifice turns out in the end to be merely an excuse for being the sort of person one is.

—T.S. ELIOT

Integrity is the fundamental value underlying ethical behaviour. Sometimes the nurse's values conflict with respect for a client's autonomy; with the rules, policies, and expectations of the institution; or with the views and wishes of colleagues. Balancing such multiple obligations may result in "moral distress," as the tension between ethical ideals and experienced reality challenges the nurse's moral autonomy. However, as important as it is for nurses to maintain their individual and professional integrity, it is also necessary to work with others in a spirit of cooperation and collaboration in order to serve the best interests of the client.

Case studies in this chapter include the conflict of individual conscience and institutional policy for a nurse who is expected to participate in abortions; the challenge to a nurse who disagrees with the health team about whether a suicidal client should be discharged; and the problem faced by a nurse who must decide how to proceed upon discovering a colleague's incompetence.

MICHAEL YEO AND ANN FORD   267

Integrity Defined

Integrity has a unique place among the values that guide nursing practice. Mitchell (1982) points out that whereas these other values have to do with what is owed to clients, integrity "directs attention to the moral agency of the health professional" (p. 163). It is thus more fundamental than the values discussed in the previous chapters. Any issue involving these values, pushed to a limit, also can become an issue of integrity.

Integrity is extremely rich in meaning, and therefore very difficult to define. Nevertheless, four constituent features of the concept can be distinguished: (1) moral autonomy; (2) fidelity to promise; (3) steadfastness; and (4) wholeness.[1]

1. Moral Autonomy[2]

Becoming a moral agent involves an ongoing passage from subjection to the moral authority of others to authorship of one's own moral life. As we enter adulthood and begin to reflect on who we are, we find that already we have been instilled with various moral beliefs, values, and principles. So long as we blindly adhere to these without having given them critical examination, we remain under the authority of the influences (e.g., family, church, friends) that have shaped our moral lives.

As we question what we have inherited and the external authorities to which we are subject, we reject some things and accept and deepen others. We shape our own moral code, or make the code we have inherited more fully our own by assuming responsibility for it. In doing so, we become more fully autonomous, directing our own moral life rather than being guided by others. Our sense of integrity develops as we assume greater control over and accountability for our moral lives.

2. Fidelity to Promise

Moral agency is partially bound up with our willingness to promise, and to hold ourselves to promises made. Moral agents are expected to be true to their word — to make promises and stick by them. Someone whose word means nothing, who cannot be counted on to keep a promise, lacks integrity.

The moral values and principles to which we commit ourselves are implicit promises. We project ourselves into the future as the sort of person whose actions will be guided by that to which we now promise ourselves. More or less explicitly, we promise others who know us that we can be counted on to act consistently with the moral values and principles we now profess. To be sure, many factors and forces will mould us into the people we eventually become, but moral agency requires that we at least assume the task of shaping our lives in faithfulness to promises made.

3. Steadfastness

Being true to our moral code or promises is sometimes difficult. Sometimes we have to work hard at it. There may be powerful forces constraining what we can and cannot do. Temptations or fears may militate against doing what we believe to be right and good. Sometimes doing what is right carries a price or involves a sacrifice. Steadfastness has to do with standing fast and speaking up for what is right. People of integrity have a certain incorruptibility, an unwillingness to yield their principles and values even when the pressures to do so are great.

4. Wholeness

A human life is multidimensional. We exist in many different relationships, roles, and settings. The task of becoming whole requires us to integrate the various parts of our lives under the guidance of the values and principles to which we have promised ourselves. People who aspire to wholeness endeavour to achieve consistency and continuity across the various dimensions of their lives.

The opposite of wholeness is a kind of self-dividedness or moral "schizophrenia." Such division might exist between our professed ideals and our actual practices, hypocrisy being an extreme instance.

Such division might also exist between the different roles or relationships in which we exist. Some people are very different at work than they are at home, or with one group of people than with another. Such differences are appropriate to a point, but at the extremes may amount to a betrayal in one role of values promised in another. Integrity, by contrast, requires that we *integrate* our ideals into our lives. We endeavour to *realize* our values and principles in and throughout our practices. We assume it as a task to make *real* the ideals to which we are promised.

Personal and Professional Integrity

The analysis of personal integrity given above can also be applied to groups: A business, an institution, and, for our purposes, a profession. For part of its history, nursing did not satisfy the conditions of moral agency, and was not in a position to make its own promises. An early textbook in nursing ethics illustrates the point eloquently: "Implicit, unquestioning obedience is one of the first lessons a probationer must learn, for this is a quality that will be expected from her in her professional capacity for all future time" (Robb, 1900, p. 57). Such "unquestioning obedience" is inconsistent with moral autonomy. A profession whose members are bound by blind obedience is not much of a profession at all.[3]

The history of nursing has been in part a struggle for moral autonomy.[4] A decisive moment in this struggle occurred when nurses, against considerable resistance, committed themselves to a code of ethics. A code of ethics is a "professional promise" to clients and to the public in general. It publicizes the values and principles for which nurses will stand accountable. In essence, a code professes that for which nursing stands, and says that nurses will be responsible for the exercise of independent judgement.

One who enters a profession assumes a duty to stand up for and act in accordance with the values of that profession. The values for which nursing stands, as is generally true of other professions, are unlikely to conflict with personal values. Benefiting others, being respectful of autonomy, being truthful, preserving confidentiality, being just: who could argue with such ideals? However, the scope of various professions includes practices that, while sanctioned by a code of ethics, may nevertheless be inconsistent with personal values. Soldiers, under certain conditions, are expected to kill people. Lawyers may be expected to defend people whom they find morally repugnant. In some instances, and for some people, questions of conscience will arise in the execution of their duties as professionals.

In nursing, such questions are most likely to arise in matters of life and death. Abortion, for example, is accepted by the nursing profession as a legitimate health service. Many nurses, however, are personally opposed to abortion. A nurse who believes that abortion is morally wrong is likely to feel that assisting in abortions would mean a loss of personal integrity.

Like most professions, nursing recognizes that some of its members will have moral objections to some of the practices it endorses. The profession is respectful of personal conscience. For example, the *Code of Ethics for Nursing* of the Canadian Nurses Association (CNA, 1991), as a limitation to the duty to provide care, states that "a nurse is not ethically obliged to provide requested care when compliance would involve a violation of her or his moral beliefs" (Value V, Limitation). Even so, it is incumbent upon nurses to avoid situations in which such issues of conscience will arise. The CNA goes on to qualify the point made above by adding that "nurses who have or are likely to encounter such situations are morally obligated to seek to arrange conditions of employment so that the care of clients is not jeopardized" (Value V, Limitation).

Reconciling the personal and the professional may pose other, less dramatic issues than ones of conscience. There is a difference between mouthing the ethical ideals of one's profession and making them real in one's daily practice. Ethical ideals indicate a task. Some effort will be required to shape oneself in accordance with these ideals and to pursue them with commitment. For example, respect for autonomy may not come naturally, or maintaining a caring manner may be difficult when dealing with a client one personally dislikes.

Professional integrity also requires the nurse to promote and stand up for the values of the profession. The American Nurses' Association ([1976] 1985), for example, commits the nurse to "maintain the integrity of the profession" (Statement 10.1). Among other things, this means being aware that one's practice and that of others reflects on the image and reputation of the profession. Thus, one is obliged to keep within the bounds of one's competence, and to intervene when one suspects unprofessional or incompetent conduct in colleagues. To be sure, the commitment to the good of the client requires this much, but it also requires one to uphold the integrity of the profession.

Integrity and Multiple Obligations

Although maintaining integrity can be a challenge for people in any profession, it is particularly so for nurses. Nursing has a history of subordination in health care settings, and especially in hospitals where nurses have often lacked the power to define their activity in the workplace.[5]

Closely related to this lack of moral autonomy is what Storch (1988) calls "multiple obligations." The professional obligations of nurses extend to clients, families, physicians, colleagues, and employing institutions. Sometimes these obligations may be in conflict, and the nurse will have to decide which should prevail in the situation. "The problem of ordering these multiple obligations," Storch points out, "is at the root of many ethical dilemmas for nurses in health care" (p. 213).

Such dilemmas may arise when the nurse is expected, or even obligated, to do something inconsistent with personal or professional values. Integrity may be at issue in any of four intersecting relationships: (1) with clients; (2) with the institution in which one practises; (3) with other health professionals; and (4) with the community.

1. Integrity and the Nurse-Client Relationship

In some cases, the nurse may experience conflict between respect for the client's autonomy and her or his own moral autonomy. This may happen when the client wishes something that the nurse believes is contrary to her or his professional judgement or that is otherwise inappropriate. A client who requires and asks for assistance to smoke may put the nurse in such a situation. More generally, integrity may arise as an issue whenever the client puts the nurse in a situation of dividedness with respect to values. For example, a client diagnosed with cancer may request that this information be withheld from a spouse. If the nurse feels strongly that the spouse, with whom she or he may also have developed a relationship (albeit, informal) over time, has a right to know and should be told, it may be difficult for the nurse to maintain wholeness in the situation.

More extreme situations may directly raise questions of conscience when respecting the client's wishes would mean being complicit in something the nurse believes to be morally wrong, or even illegal. For example, the nurse attending someone who has refused life-saving treatment may feel that this is inconsistent with what she or he stands for to the point of violating conscience. A similar situation might arise in connection with abortion.

Nurses, both as private persons and professionals, also have certain rights. Curtin (1982c) points out that, while the patient/client is at the centre of the nurse's moral concern, "the patient has no more right to coerce the professional than the professional has to coerce the patient" (p. 91). Respect for the autonomy of clients should not be at the expense of the moral autonomy of nurses.[6] Along these lines, Tunna and Conner (1993) have advocated a "covenantal relationship" for nursing, in which "nurses could not be deprived of, nor could they escape from, their freedom to be moral" (p. 26).

2. Integrity and the Nurse-Institution Relationship

Most nurses are employed in health care institutions and do not contract directly with clients. Theis (1986) points out that as "employees of health care institutions," nurses are "obliged to abide by institutional policies, rules, and expectations," and are "thus accountable not only to their patients but also to their employers" (p. 1223).

Integrity may arise as an issue whenever a nurse is expected or obligated to do something by virtue of her or his employee status that is inconsistent with personal or professional values. For example, institutional policies or practices may require a nurse to act inconsistently with the professional promise to promote the autonomy and well-being of the client. Client care may be jeopardized by unsafe practices, or by cost-cutting measures. "When a patient's needs compete with those of the employers," Carnerie (1989) writes, "nurses are trapped on the dangerous ground in the middle" (p. 20). Problems of this sort sometimes come to a head in terms of assignment refusal. Examples here include such things as refusing additional assignments because the workload is already too heavy and clients will be endangered, or because the assignment is beyond one's professional competence.

Questions of professional integrity may also arise in contexts other than when the commitment to the client is directly at stake. Conflict between nurse and institution may also threaten the integrity of the profession itself, or the nurse's integrity as a professional. The employing institution may treat nurses as being less than professionals, or fail to respect their autonomy. Nurses may lack input into policy-making and control over the conditions of their work. In some institutions, nurses may be expected to do things not befitting the dignity of the profession.[7]

3. Integrity and the Nurse-Colleague Relationship

Issues similar to those described above may arise in relationships with colleagues. The classic example involves a conflict between the nurse's obligations to a physician and to a client.[8] Having these conflicting obligations may put the nurse in a double bind. Johnstone (1988) points out that "nurses are expected to obey doctor's orders, on the one hand, and yet are held independently accountable on the other" (p. 155). How should nurses proceed when these obligations conflict?

A number of considerations may bear on the resolution of such an issue, but ultimately the question reduces itself to how much weight should be assigned to each obligation relative to the other. On this question, there has been a major shift in the professed values and principles of nursing. Owing to a wide variety of factors, the earlier belief that the nurse's primary loyalty is to the physician has been superseded by the current belief that the nurse's primary obligation is to the client.

Today, this belief is enshrined in various statements by the profession. For example, the International Council of Nurses ([1973] 1982) proclaims that "the nurse's *primary* [italics added] responsibility is to those people who require nursing care." Likewise, the American Nurses' Association ([1976] 1985) *Code for Nurses with Interpretive Statements* makes it explicit that "the nurse's *primary* [italics added] commitment is to the health, welfare, and safety of the client" (Statement 3.1). It further goes on to say that "neither physician's orders nor the employing agency's policies relieve the nurse of accountability for actions taken and judgments made" (Statement 4.3).

However, as Yarling and McElmurry (1986) point out, the present "ideology of nursing" which emphasizes "nursing commitment to patients, and autonomy in the exercise of that commitment, is a very recent development in the history of nursing" (p. 67). Nursing has come a long way from the days when unquestioning obedience was a virtue, but nurses still must contend with the realities shaped by this legacy.

4. Integrity and the Nurse-Community Relationship

Although the majority of nurses are employed in institutions, in recent years there has been a shift to community-based care. The community may become the dominant employment setting for nurses in the future.

The practice environment in the community is much less controlled than it is in institutions. Rules and norms governing professional behaviour are not as settled and codified. Nurses in the community have much greater latitude for the exercise of judgement and discretion and must work much more independently.

The community environment may also pose considerable challenges as concerns nursing's commitment to ensure that needed, quality care is provided to clients. The seriousness of these challenges will depend on the extent to which the shift from institutional to community-based care is supported by a sufficient reallocation of resources. Economics, and in particular the expectation that money will be saved by lesser reliance on institutions, is a major factor driving the shift to the community. If some considerable portion of savings incurred as a result of deinstitutional are not redirected to developing infrastructures for care in the community, the shift to the community will amount to abandonment.

Nurses in the community may find themselves working in cooperation with client family members, volunteers, and other less highly skilled caregivers. Nurses recognize that lesser skilled personnel can do many caring jobs and appreciate how valuable and important the work of family members and volunteers can be. However, they also know that caring attitudes and good intentions alone may not be enough for effective, quality care. Given budget constraints, there is reason for concern that volunteers and under-qualified personnel may be delegated tasks beyond their competence, and family members may be burdened with care responsibilities beyond their abilities. This could have serious implications with regard to the quality and safety of care.

Issues of integrity will arise for nurses in the community to the extent that supporting resources, and in particular human resources, are insufficient to ensure the kind of safe and quality care to which nurses are professionally devoted. These issues will be all the more pronounced the greater the responsibility the nurse has for the care of the client — including the supervision or coordination of lesser qualified or even under-qualified caregivers.

Integrity and Moral Distress

In reality, there may be weighty considerations that inhibit the nurse from acting in accordance with professional values. Mappes (1986) states the matter succinctly: "It is well and good to say what nurses should do. It is quite another thing, given the forces at work in the everyday world in which nurses work, to expect nurses to do what they ought to do" (p. 131). The inhibiting "forces" to which she refers include such things as economic pressures, sexism, and power imbalances.

This tension between ethics and reality is a recurrent theme in the literature on nursing ethics. Flaherty (1985), for example, voices the ethical ideal and norm that "nurses are obliged by ethics and by law to question directives and policies about which they have concern" (p. 102). She acknowledges, however, that pressing realities may make it difficult to practise in accordance with this obligation:

> Nurses often find themselves in situations in which they have limited authority, and when they attempt to exercise their broad ethical and legal responsibilities to and for patients, they feel powerless, excluded and dependent if there is a lack of nurse/physician/administrator collaboration and cooperation. (p. 110)

Unfortunately, such a lack of "collaboration and cooperation" is not altogether rare in health care.

Along similar lines, Yarling and McElmurry (1986) speak of a gap between what nurses are taught about how they *should* act and how in reality they are *expected* to act. They describe "a profound moral dissonance between nursing education and nursing practice," which in their view "extends to the core of professional identity and leaves nurses essentially morally *unintegrated* [italics added] professionals who are not self-determining, moral agents" (p. 67).

These observations describe a common predicament. In each case, the ethical problem has to do not so much with deciding what is morally right, but rather with doing it in a constrained environment unconducive to the realization of professional values. The fact is that, despite being supported by professional values, and even to some extent because of them, nurses sometimes find themselves in situations in which it is difficult or costly to do what they know to be right.

Being in such a predicament creates stress, or more precisely what Jameton (1984) refers to as "moral distress." This arises, he says, "when one knows the right thing to do, but institutional constraints make it nearly impossible to pursue the right course of action" (p. 6). In such situations, it is difficult to realize or uphold the values and principles to which one is promised. It is difficult to maintain integrity.

Moral distress is a very serious problem in nursing.[9] One area in which moral distress is particularly troublesome is care of the critically or dying. Rodney (1994) reports that "given the situational constraints they experience in their practice," nurses "often experience moral distress when they care for patients undergoing life-prolonging treatment (p. 41). These contraints "go beyond the purview of bioethics (patient-centred problems) into professional and institutional problems such as communication conflicts, questionable competence, and excessive workloads" (p. 41). Moreover, the problems identified are likely to be compounded by "an overall problem of resource allocation" (p. 42). Given current trends in resource allocation, it seems reasonable to suppose that moral distress will be an even greater concern for nurses in the forseeable future.

Commenting on the kind of predicament in which nurses often find themselves, Theis (1986) asks:

> What do they do about it? Some become burned out and quit because they cannot take the stress. Some stop thinking about what they are doing and become callous and indifferent. Others act as advocates for patients and are successful in having their concerns listened to and addressed by supportive employers and understanding physicians. (p. 1223)

The problem is that some employers are not very "supportive," and some physicians will be less "understanding" than others.

Nurses in such situations will have to cope as best they can to maintain their integrity, but the problem also needs to be addressed in broader and more general terms. One of the challenges facing the nursing profession is to work toward attitudinal and structural changes that will make the practice environment more conducive to ethical nursing. Mappes (1986) states the challenge clearly: "Nurses have a moral responsibility to act on behalf of the patient, but in order to expect them to carry out that responsibility, changes must be made in the workplace" (p. 132).

Integrity, Conflict, and Cooperation

Given the realities that cause moral distress, one can understand Yarling and McElmurry's (1986) claim that "professional nurses are conceived in moral contradiction and born in compromise" (p. 67). Often, ideals are contradicted by realities; ethical promise is driven toward unholy compromise. "The fundamental moral predicament of nurses," Yarling and McElmurry charge, "is that often they are not free to be moral because they are deprived of their free exercise of moral agency" (p. 65).

Certainly these authors are correct in identifying the lack of autonomy as a problem, especially for nurses working in hospitals and other sometimes authoritarian environments. And just as certainly, Curtin (1993) is correct in saying that "institutional policies should provide some moral space for nurses" (p. 19). As important as it is, however, the goal of increased autonomy for nursing needs to be interpreted in conjunction with other important values, and especially with cooperation and collaboration (Curtin, 1982a). Bishop and Scudder (1987) have criticized Yarling and McElmurry for being too one-sided in promoting nursing autonomy. They point out that "nurses generally promote the patient's well-being by working together with other health care professionals" (p. 40). Moreover, "an excessive concern for autonomy can put health care workers in conflict with each other" (p. 40).

It is important to be principled and willing to stand for one's principles, but it is also important to work together with others. Integrity should not be confused with sanctimony or self-righteousness; steadfastness should not be confused with dogmatic rigidity, uncooperativeness, and closed-mindedness.

The reality is that the individual moral agent lives in community with others. In the health care context, this community, in theory at least, is defined by the shared goal of serving the client. Unreasonable and inflexible adherence to principle is counterproductive to this goal.

A moral life is not a monologue. Thoughtful dialogue and discussion can go a long way toward warding off or resolving conflict. There is a connection between *promise* and *compromise* (promising *with* others).[10] The difficulty is in deciding at what point adherence to promise is unreasonable, and at what point compromise becomes breach of promise. In some instances the line between being cooperative and being co-opted may be very fine indeed. Nevertheless, a line can and should be drawn.

Case 1: Conscience and Assignment Refusal

As employees of institutions, nurses do not have as much freedom as do physicians, who have a different institutional status and accordingly much greater freedom in accepting and rejecting assignments.

Nurses might wish or even feel obliged to refuse assignments for one or more of several reasons.[11] Concern for personal health and safety is one such reason. For example, nurses who are occupationally exposed to infectious diseases may lack confidence in existing infection control measures to the point of being concerned for their own safety.

Such nurse-centred reasons for assignment refusal can be distinguished from client-centred reasons, which tend to be based either on beneficence or respect for autonomy. In some instances, nurse-centred and client-centred reasons may overlap. Nurses who are overworked may wish to refuse further assignments both in their own interests *and* those of their clients.[12] Lack of competence may raise more purely client-centred concerns. For example, a nurse asked to relieve in an intensive care unit but lacking adequate preparation may have an obligation to refuse the assignment out of concern for client good.[13]

Both nurse-centred and client-centred reasons for assignment refusal may be bound up with concerns having to do with professional integrity. A nurse may be asked to do something counter to the express values of the profession, such as cover up the fact that a mistake has been made in a client's treatment. Concern for professional integrity may arise more directly when an assignment is thought to be inconsistent with the dignity of a professional nurse, or not a proper nursing activity at all.

Finally, the nurse may feel obliged to refuse an assignment that, while not inconsistent with personal safety or professional practice, is contrary to conscience. In this regard, abortion can raise some very difficult issues, as the following case shows:[14]

Anita Resario has worked in the obstetrics and gynaecology unit of a small community hospital for the past six years. She enjoys her job, and gets along well with other staff members.

Anita recently became very concerned when she learned that, owing to increased demand in the community, her hospital would begin doing abortions. She is staunchly opposed to abortion, and indeed has been active in a local pro-life group. Anita has made it clear to her supervisor that under no circumstances will she assist in abortions. Her initial decision to accept the job at the hospital was partly based on the consideration that the hospital did not do abortions. Indeed, she refused a more lucrative offer from another hospital solely because it performed abortions.

In response, her supervisor explained that, although the logistics of offering this new service have yet to be worked out, as long as Nurse Resario remained in the unit she would probably have no choice. The supervisor expressed sympathy, but told her that if she feels strongly about the matter, she should start looking for another job.

Since discussing the matter with her supervisor, Nurse Resario has been agonizing over whether she should resign or continue in her job.

Commentary

In any work setting, nurses and their employers should seek to establish a good working relationship based on mutual respect and concern for each other's values and interests. Both parties should define the scope of the rights, responsibilities, and expectations of each party during the pre-employment stage. In addition, an agreement to maintain open lines of communication between the parties is essential to a productive working relationship.

Preparedness before the fact is usually a good prophylaxis against the type of difficulty Nurse Resario now faces. If at the time of hiring a nurse states as a condition of employment that she or he will not assist in abortions, the employer who accepts the condition will be bound by the agreement. In unforeseeable situations in which the nurse is requested to provide care inconsistent with personal values, some form of negotiation may remedy the problem. Even so, in an emergency situation involving imminent jeopardy to the client, the nurse's obligation to the client would arguably take precedence.

Unfortunately, due to unforseen circumstances beyond Nurse Resario's control, the rules of the game have changed since she came to work at the hospital. Through no fault of her own, she has been thrown into a difficult choice. Her job and her integrity hang in the balance.

An ideal solution to this problem would be one that allowed her to keep both her job and her integrity, but there does not appear to be much hope of this. Although her supervisor has not ruled out the possibility that, perhaps through careful personnel scheduling, Nurse Resario might be exempted from assisting in abortions, she has indicated that this is unlikely. To determine how unlikely this is, we would have to know more about such things as the climate of labour relations in the hospital, her pre-employment agreement, and the logistical realities with which her supervisor would have to contend. In a small hospital, with a small number of staff, such an exemption may understandably prove to be administratively impossible, especially if other nurses asked for the same exemption. Certainly, the hospital is obliged to do everything it can to accommodate Nurse Resario, but not at the expense of its duty to the good of its clients.

Should an exemption option be ruled out, as seems likely, Nurse Resario might consider staying on in the unit with the resolve to refuse to participate in abortions if and when called upon to do so. This option has several things going against it.

In the first place, unless her employment contract included specific provisions to the contrary, the hospital would be within its rights to interpret such refusal as insubordination. Nurse Resario has been given advance notice of what will be expected of her. Refusal would probably lead to dismissal, and it may be better to resign now than to be dismissed later.

In the second place, and more importantly, by staying on Nurse Resario would have assumed a duty to clients using the service. If her refusal to participate in abortions endangered clients, it would amount to a kind of abandonment for which she could be held morally and legally accountable. She may be opposed to abortion, but it *is* legally available, and participation in abortions falls within the scope of legitimate nursing practice. Certainly she is within her rights to oppose abortion, and even to lobby the hospital to change its policy, but the clients who will use the service have a right to quality care.

In analyzing the option of staying on and refusing to assist in abortions, it is important to realize that this bears on what might happen in the future. At the present time, Nurse Resario is under no obligation to participate in abortions, or to choose now to do so in the future. Her profession respects her rights of conscience on the matter. To refuse now would not be in violation of any duty to clients because she has not yet entered into a relationship with these clients, and they would have no right to demand or expect her care.

Thus Nurse Resario does have a choice in the matter, but the time to exercise that choice is now, and not in some future situation in which she would be counted on and needed. In the future, she will have assumed other obligations that will limit her choice. The problem, of course, is that neither of the options she has to choose between are appealing. If, as seems to be the case, staying on means that she will be required to assist in abortions, the choice may be between her integrity and her job. Should she stay on or resign?

In weighing these options, two main considerations will have to be balanced. On the one side, Nurse Resario will have to weigh how strongly she feels against participating in abortions. If she is convinced that abortion is morally wrong, it may be impossible for her to maintain her integrity and assist in abortions. To do so might require her to compromise or even sacrifice her principles. On the other side, she will have to weigh how important the job is to her. What would she be giving up by resigning? She likes her job, but what job satisfaction will she have when participating in abortions is added to her job description? What other job opportunities are available, and how do they compare? Given that the hospital has forced her into this problem in the first place, it may very well recognize an obligation to arrange a transfer to another unit in the hospital. How attractive would that be to Nurse

Resario? Would it mean less pay, or a less desirable shift, or a clinical posting outside of her interest and expertise? What if no other jobs are available?

The reality in today's job market is that Nurse Rosario would have a very hard time finding another job. In recent years, the job market has changed from very high demand to high supply. Although the number of nurses has remained more or less constant, the number of jobs has declined. The greater the likelihood that Nurse Rosario would not be able to find alternative employment, the more pressured she will be to do whatever is necessary to maintain her present job. For all their worth, one cannot buy groceries with principles.

In considering the option of staying on — and the very fact that she is struggling with the decision indicates that this is a live option for her — considerations other than those of personal integrity also come into play. Staying on would mean entering professional relationships with and assuming duties to women having abortions. Having an abortion can be very traumatic. Some clients will be made vulnerable by mixed emotions, or by a measure of guilt. Would Nurse Resario be able to set her feelings aside as required of a professional and give these women unprejudiced care? Might her moral objection to abortion somehow translate into moral repugnance for the clients with whom she would be dealing? Would she be able to act in accordance with beneficence in such a situation?

Whatever one's views on abortion, one can sympathize with Nurse Resario. She has been forced into a decision that is very agonizing for her. The case raises questions that go beyond the decision at hand. How well did the hospital handle the situation? Should legal provisions be implemented whereby nurses put in situations like Nurse Resario's can "opt out" of participating in abortions, with the hospital assuming responsibility for accommodating them?[15]

Perhaps changes can and should be made that would prevent such situations in the future, but this will not help Nurse Resario now. She must make her choice in what is a less than perfect world. The very fact of abortion, as understood from her perspective, will already have made this painfully clear to her.

Case 2: Disagreement within the Health Team

Health care today, especially in hospitals, may involve numerous practitioners with diverse backgrounds and experiences. These individuals
will bring different perspectives to bear on the care of the client. Ideally,
perspectives will be complementary, but in some instances two or more
may be in conflict.

Nurses may disagree with other practitioners about a client's plan of
care for a number of reasons. The disagreement may stem directly from
value differences, such as the relative weight that should be assigned to
respecting autonomy as against beneficence. Alternatively, practitioners may be guided by the same value, yet disagree about how best to
realize it, as when opinions differ about what will best benefit the
client. Mappes (1986, p. 129) lists several factors that may inform disagreement between practitioners, such as differences in training, experience, and contact with or knowledge about the client.

Reasonable people should be able to deal with such conflicts in a
process of free and open discussion.[16] However, not everyone will be
reasonable, and some forums for discussion will be less free and open
than others. Things like personality differences and social and political
realities are to some degree always a factor in human interactions.

Conflict resolution can be more difficult when the practitioners in
disagreement come from different professions, and therefore share less
common ground to begin with. It is especially difficult when there are
inequalities or power imbalances between the parties involved.
Unfortunately, nurses often find themselves in precisely such a situation.

Whatever the dynamics, situations of conflict within the health care
team raise numerous issues for nurses, as the following case illustrates:

*Following a serious suicide attempt, Maria Sanchez, a forty year
old woman, was admitted to an acute care psychiatric setting. She
required physical care for the first week of hospitalization, but
gradually responded and began to attend therapy sessions. At the
end of the third week, she asked for and received a weekend pass*

to visit her family — her brother and his wife. The weekend went well and she returned to her fourth and final week of hospitalization.

The health team on this unit meets for an hour every morning, and at their Monday morning meeting everyone agreed that the client had made remarkable progress. After comparing notes, it was decided to discharge Ms. Sanchez into the care of her family on Friday, with weekly follow-up visits to her therapist.

The next day, Nurse Johnson overheard Ms. Sanchez telling another client, "I'll be gone from here for good on Friday. First chance I get, I'm going to take pills again, but this time I'll do it right." Nurse Johnson reported this to the charge nurse and documented it in the record.

When the team met again the next day, Nurse Johnson reported what she had overheard and said that she thought the decision to discharge Ms. Sanchez should be revoked. Others on the team, however, did not share her concern. Indeed the psychiatrist said that he knew the client well, and that she was probably boasting. "Don't worry, I'll be seeing her every week," he assured Nurse Johnson. "I just met with her half an hour ago, and she certainly isn't depressed now."

Nurse Johnson has worked in psychiatric nursing for twenty years, and has known more than one suicidal client who has gone on to commit suicide shortly after discharge. The psychiatrist, on the other hand, has only been practising for a year. A number of nursing staff have commented that they find him arrogant. Nurse Johnson believes that he is inexperienced. She feels strongly that Ms. Sanchez should not be discharged, but is uncertain how to proceed.

Commentary

Nurse Johnson believes that the health team has decided on a course of action that is likely to be tragically inconsistent with the good of the client. She is professionally bound to put her commitment to the client foremost in her deliberations. However, she is unsure how best to realize her commitment, and how far she should go in advocating for the client's best interests. At the limit, her integrity as a professional may be at stake.

A number of variables, many of them unknown to us, bear heavily on the issue at hand. How certain is Nurse Johnson about the risk of suicide? What are the social dynamics of the team? What mechanisms and resources are available in the institution for dealing with such problems?

In situations of conflict or disagreement, it is generally a good rule to begin by discussing the issue with the parties with whom one disagrees. Nurse Johnson had an obvious opportunity to do this during the initial meeting of the team. The fact that the issue was not resolved to her satisfaction at the initial meeting itself raises important questions. Why were the psychiatrist and the other members of the team not more concerned about the danger to the client, especially in light of her recent history? Does the psychiatrist know something that Nurse Johnson does not know, something which might lead her to change her mind about what should be done? Might others have been in agreement with her, but for one reason or another afraid or unwilling to state their opinion? How clearly and forcefully did Nurse Johnson present her point of view?

Fortunately, two days remain before the discharge. Nurse Johnson still has time to do some further thinking about the issue. She will also have an opportunity to raise the issue again with the team. Before doing so, however, she should clarify a number of questions in her own mind.

In the first place, she needs to question her assessment that Ms. Sanchez will attempt suicide once again upon discharge. The more certain she is of the danger, the greater is her moral obligation to intervene on Ms. Sanchez's behalf. If she failed to intervene, and Ms. Sanchez did subsequently commit suicide, Nurse Johnson would bear some responsibility for the tragic outcome. Unfortunately, the signs by which to predict the likelihood of suicide can be very unreliable. Taken at face value, Ms. Sanchez's statement is certainly alarming, but what was the context in which it was made? Perhaps she knew she was being overheard. Perhaps she wanted to be overheard. Maybe she was issuing an indirect plea for help. Maybe, as the psychiatrist seems to think, she was boasting.

Nurse Johnson needs also to clarify the values in the name of which she feels obligated to intervene on behalf of Ms. Sanchez. From the information given, beneficence appears to be the value inclining her toward intervention. Has she weighed this against respect for Ms. Sanchez's autonomy? Ms. Sanchez wishes to be discharged, and it would be paternalistic to refuse her this. Would such paternalism be justified? What are the requirements of the law and of the institution's policy? Is there evidence of mental incompetence? Is an overheard remark sufficient grounds for keeping Ms. Sanchez against her will? Until now, Ms. Sanchez has been permitted to go home on weekends, and no incident has occurred. If she is determined to kill herself, could she not do it as well on a weekend pass as on a permanent discharge? Would Nurse Johnson also deny her weekend passes?

Additional questions need also to be raised having to do with such things as details about Ms. Sanchez's family life and her psychiatric history. Nurse Johnson should seek the input of others on these questions, and the place to do so is at the next team meeting. If she clarifies her point of view and expresses it clearly and confidently, she should stand a good chance of persuading others. At the same time, she ought to be open to the possibility of being persuaded by others. The outcome of a free and open discussion is not a foregone conclusion. The chance of a good outcome is greatest if she approaches the situation in a spirit of cooperation rather than confrontation, regarding it as an opportunity for learning and new growth, both for herself and for the team as a whole.

Short of persuading others to reverse the earlier decision, it may be that some compromise solution can be worked out. Would it be enough if the psychiatrist agreed to a reassessment and to confront Ms. Sanchez directly about the overheard remark? What if steps could be taken to ensure that Ms. Sanchez will not have access to lethal doses of medication? What if the team agreed to solicit the opinion and support of family members?

If, having given her best effort, Nurse Johnson remains dissatisfied with the outcome of the meeting, subsequent options become increasingly even more disruptive. Upping the ante, but still keeping the issue within the team, she might resort to more forceful forms of persuasion. For example, she might threaten that if indeed the client does commit suicide upon release, she will see to it that the team is held accountable.

Failing to obtain a satisfactory solution with the team, through whatever form of persuasion, a further step would be to go outside the team. How she might proceed here would depend in part on the institutional policies and mechanisms in place. Does the hospital have a patient advocate or an ethicist? Who in the administrative structure of the hospital is responsible for the health team?

Each further step taken would escalate the issue to a new level and would entail more serious consequences. Threatening the team is likely to be more disruptive than gentler forms of persuasion. Going outside the team would carry more serious risks of alienating the others, and might even be construed as "whistle-blowing." Her working relationships could be severely damaged. Especially if she stood alone, she might fare badly in the fallout from the issue.

Each escalating step would also be indicative of a failure to achieve resolution at a previous level. At every step up, it would be incumbent upon Nurse Johnson to question whether she played a part in the failure. If she has good reasons for holding her position, why can she not convince others? Are the dynamics of the team so poor that good reasons count for nothing? The apparent unwillingness of the psychiatrist to give due consideration to the opinions of a nurse with twenty years experience seems somewhat bizarre, and requires some explanation. Is Nurse Johnson really the only one on the team who truly has the good of the client at heart? Alternatively, might she herself be unreasonable and rigid in her position? A hero sometimes must stand alone, but so too does the villain or the fool.

With good will and thoughtful discussion, the issue should not go beyond the first step: A happy resolution should be within reach at the next meeting of the health team. Failing that, however, how far would Nurse Johnson be obligated to go in advocating on behalf of Ms.

Sanchez? The answer to this question will depend on a careful weighing of considerations such as have been raised above. It may be that, as events unfold, what she decides is morally required of her will entail personal risks. Concern for self would certainly be an understandable and legitimate consideration, but what integrity would she be left with if she assigned it a higher priority than her professionally mandated commitment to the good of the client? In the worst case scenario, what words would she have left for Ms. Sanchez's grieving family?

Case 3: Colleague Incompetence and Client Good

The trust of the public is essential to a profession. A profession earns this trust by publicly professing certain standards and values for its members, and accepting responsibility for ensuring that they are upheld. This responsibility encompasses not only technical standards, but ethical ones as well, such as are professed in a code of ethics.

The behaviour of a professional reflects, for good or for ill, on her or his profession as a whole. Professionals who fail to live up to the standards of their profession may endanger not only the public, but also the reputation of their profession. If sufficiently serious and frequent, such failures could undermine the confidence of the public in the profession and call its integrity into question.

A profession has certain powers by which it can make good on its promise to the public. The power to grant and revoke licenses/registrations to practise is foremost among these. In granting a licence/registration, a profession is indirectly assuring the public that it has confidence in its members' ability and willingness to practise in conformity with professed standards and values. The applicant in turn wins this confidence by such things as meeting specified educational requirements and passing certain other tests. Professions also have disciplinary powers which, in extreme cases, enable them to revoke the licence/registration of members who through their actions lose the confidence of the profession. In turn, the knowledge that such disciplinary powers will be exercised as required adds an additional incentive for members to conduct themselves in a professional manner. Even so, a profession must rely to a great extent upon the integrity of individual members as reason enough for them to uphold professional standards and values.

Professions also rely on a sort of "peer review" to ensure that their standards and values are upheld. Most professions have provisions to the effect that, in addition to being responsible for their own conduct, members are also to some extent responsible for the conduct of colleagues. For example, the *Code for Nurses with Interpretive Statements* of the American Nurses' Association ([1976] 1985) requires the nurse to participate "in the profession's effort to protect the public from misinformation and misrepresentation and to maintain the integrity of nursing" (Statement 10). Even more specifically, it states that "the nurse acts to safeguard the client and the public when health care and safety are affected by incompetent, unethical, or illegal practice by any person" (Statement 3).

If called upon to discharge these obligations, collegiality or even friendship may be at stake. In principle the obligation to the public good is primary, but the bonds of loyalty to colleagues and friends are very strong.[17] Moreover, the personal costs of what may seem to some as betrayal can be very high. The *Code of Ethics for Nursing* of the Canadian Nurses Association (1991) almost understates the point: "The nurse who attempts to protect clients threatened by incompetent or unethical conduct may be placed in a difficult position" (Value VIII, 3). The following case, which is not uncommon, illustrates just how "difficult" it may be to deal with the incompetent conduct of a nursing colleague. At stake is the integrity of the profession, but also the professional integrity of the nurse who is aware of incompetence.

When checking medication tickets against the physician's orders, Nurse Weber discovered and subsequently verified that the team-leader on the day shift had incorrectly transcribed a client's morphine dose as 15mg q4h instead of 5mg q4h. This means that the client has now received two doses at this higher level. Nurse Weber, having assessed the client, determined that, except for some drowsiness, he has suffered no ill effects from this error.

Nurse Weber knows that the day team-leader has recently separated from her husband, and is under considerable stress. Furthermore, this is not an isolated incident. In the last three months she has had three incident reports of medication errors, none of which resulted in serious injury. It is known that the head nurse is observing the team-leader's practice very carefully.

Nurse Weber feels that she must do something, and is debating whether she should simply raise the matter with the team-leader, or go to the head nurse, in which case a formal incident report would certainly be filed. The team-leader is very popular with the other staff, and until recently has been widely regarded as one of the most capable nurses in the unit. In addition to being concerned for the team-leader, Nurse Weber is concerned for herself. She fears that if she reports the error her colleagues will be angry with her, especially as it did not result in any injury to the client. A nursing colleague who reported one of the other incidents left the hospital soon afterwards because she found the ensuing climate of collegiality "too chilly."

Commentary

The judgement that a colleague is or has been acting incompetently is a serious matter, and should be made only after a careful review of the facts of the matter. Sometimes the evidence for this judgement will be ambiguous or otherwise indecisive. Everyone from time to time makes mistakes, but such mistakes are not necessarily indicative of a general incompetence to carry out one's duties. Moreover, errors are more likely to occur under some systems and routines than under others. In some instances, the system or routine may be so seriously flawed that people working within it can hardly be blamed for errors they make.

The facts of this case, however, are unambiguous enough to raise serious doubts about the team-leader's present competence to carry out the responsibilities with which she is charged. The medication error involves morphine, a central nervous system depressant. The client has received two doses of three times the prescribed amount of this powerful drug. Fortunately, little or no harm has been done to the client, but nevertheless this is a serious error. Moreover, this is not an isolated incident that might be explained away as something that can happen to anyone. It fits into what is emerging as a pattern of error. There is reason to expect that whatever factors led to this and to the previous ones might also result in future errors. The next error may have more tragic consequences.

In deciding on a morally justifiable response in this situation, Nurse Weber will have to weigh several considerations. In the first place, she is professionally obligated to intervene if she has reason to doubt the competence of a colleague. Directly, this obligation is owed to present and future clients who may be endangered by incompetence. Indirectly, it is owed to the profession, whose integrity may be put in question by substandard practice. Secondly, Nurse Weber will have to weigh loyalty to and concern for her colleague, and even for the good of the unit in which she is working. Finally, she will to have weigh considerations related to how her own interests may be affected by whatever course of action she chooses. The policy of the hospital regarding the reporting of medication errors will be especially relevant in this regard.

In the matter of ordering these considerations, the position of her profession is clear. Professional codes of ethics in nursing invariably place the rights and safety of the client above the protection of a colleague. For example, if she consulted the *Code of Ethics for Nursing* (CNA, 1991), she would be advised that "the first consideration of the nurse who suspects incompetence or unethical conduct must be the welfare of present clients or potential harm to future clients" (Value VIII, 1).

This ordering of considerations alone may not be enough to decide between the two options Nurse Weber has identified; namely, confining the matter to herself and the team-leader alone or reporting the error to the head nurse. Either option *may* be compatible with the primary obligation to client good. If equal in this respect, the choice between them would depend on how each fared as assessed in light of other considerations.

If keeping the matter between herself and the team-leader, in addition to satisfying the primary obligation to client good, was also best as concerns the good of her colleague, unit, and herself, this would incline the decision toward this option. Having stated that the primary responsibility of the nurse in such situations is to client good, the passage cited above from the *Code of Ethics for Nursing* (CNA, 1991) goes on to say: "Relationships in the health care team should not be disrupted unnecessarily. If a situation can be resolved without peril to present or future clients by direct discussion with the colleague suspected of providing incompetent or unethical care, that should be done" (Value VIII, 1b).

There may be reason to debate whether keeping the matter private (if indeed this is even possible) would indeed be best for the team-leader, but it seems reasonable to think that it might be. What is much less certain, and much more crucial to the decision, is whether in this manner the problem could be "resolved without peril to present or future clients." This will depend on what Nurse Weber and the team-leader can work out between them.

Suppose, for example, that Nurse Weber could "persuade" the team-leader to take a leave of absence or sick leave, during which time she would go for counselling. Her present incompetence, after all, appears to be the result of a correctable problem. Aside from these recent incidents, she is known to be a good nurse. If she works on her problem, she might very well continue to be so in the future. Nurse Weber's primary concern is to safeguard present and future clients. If this can be achieved without disrupting relationships and jeopardizing her colleague, so much the better.

The problem is that, whatever agreement Nurse Weber and the team-leader privately work out, there may remain some uncertainty as to how effectively it will safeguard client good. The option of reporting the incident to the head nurse, for whatever else counts against it, may result in steps being taken that will more certainly safeguard client good. The less certain Nurse Weber is that keeping the matter private will indeed safeguard client good, the more compelling is her obligation to report the incident to the head nurse. For example, an assurance from the team-leader that she will be more careful in the future would not be very reassuring at all. If this were the best agreement Nurse Weber could get, the option of going to the head nurse becomes more compelling.

If a satisfactory solution cannot be worked out privately (and deciding whether a solution is "satisfactory" will itself be difficult), Nurse Weber will have to weigh other considerations against her primary obligation to the client. One set of considerations follows from concern for the good of her colleague. What will happen to the team-leader if the incident is reported? Could she lose her job? On the other hand, would it really serve the team-leader's good not to report her? So far she has been fortunate, and no injury has resulted from her mistakes. The next time, she may not be so fortunate, and the consequences of her error, for others and herself, may be much more serious.

Certainly it would make the option of going to the head nurse more attractive if Nurse Weber had reason to believe that the team-leader would be treated with compassion. Arguably, she needs help, and not discipline. Is there an employee assistance program in place? What kind of support will she receive from her superiors? Will she be dealt with in a kind and compassionate way?

Another set of considerations follows from Nurse Weber's concern for her own good. It is understandable that she is concerned about the personal consequences that might follow from reporting the incident. We are told that she fears that her colleagues will be angry. However, if Nurse Weber is convinced that reporting the incident is morally obligatory, and indeed specifically mandated by professional norms, she should be able to gain the understanding, if not approval, of her nursing colleagues. After all, they too have promised to place concern for client good above all else.

Nevertheless, it is possible that the level of professionalism among her colleagues is very low. Nurse Weber may decide that the chances of winning their support are not very good. In this event, the pressure not to report may be considerable. What kind of support could Nurse Weber expect from the head nurse and others in the institution? Alternatively, if, as is likely, the hospital has a policy that requires reporting medication errors in all cases, what consequences might follow if it was learned that she did not report this incident?

Sometimes the challenge of ethics consists less in *deciding* what is right than in *doing* what is right in an unsupportive environment. If the issue comes to this, Nurse Weber's integrity will be on the line in choosing between what is morally right and what is personally safe. The pressure to conform to the less than professional standards of her colleagues may be considerable. Nevertheless, integrity or authenticity, as Nelson (1982) says, involves "adhering to a personal value system and having the courage to resist peer pressure for mediocre practice should such pressure exist" (p. 3).

How the main issue in this case should be decided may depend as well on how another marginal issue gets decided: Is there an obligation to inform the client about the medication error? Informing him would quite probably be incompatible with the option of keeping the matter private between colleagues.

Three main values come into play in relation to this marginal issue. The case for not informing might best be made in terms of beneficence, which encompasses the desire to promote the good of the client and to avoid doing harm. What good would it do the client to know? It may not do any good at all, and in fact may do harm if it undermines his confidence in the nursing staff, which is essential to supportive caregiving.

On the other side, the case for informing could be made either in terms of the duty to respect autonomy or the duty to be truthful with clients. With regard to the former, it could be argued that, regardless of the predicted effect of this information *vis-à-vis* the good of the client, he is entitled to know what happened insofar as this bears on his control over his plan of care, and could conceivably influence his future decision-making. For all we know, this may be one in a series of errors which have been made in this person's treatment, and he may be considering a law suit.

Considered from the point of view of the duty to tell the truth, the relevant point is that a deliberate decision not to tell would amount to withholding or concealing information, and would border on deception. Could this be justified? The *Code of Ethics for Nursing* of the Canadian Nurses Association (1991), under the section dealing with incompetence, states forcefully that "it is unethical for a nurse to participate in efforts to deceive or mislead clients about the cause of alleged harm or injury resulting from unethical or incompetent care" (Value VIII, 1e). In the present situation, however, it appears that there has been no injury. How does this bear on the obligation to be truthful? What would be an appropriate response if the client raised questions about his drowsiness?

In the end, Nurse Weber may have to make her choice in a situation where some of the variables that bear on the choice remain uncertain. Furthermore, it may turn out that whichever course of action she chooses will have negative consequences for her or others. In any event, it will be important for her to be able to justify her choice to others if called upon to do so.

Conclusion

In some ways, life would be easier if we were not moral agents. Nurses might simply adapt themselves to the realities of the workplace and conform their activity to whatever was expected of them or whatever they were told to do. Some nurses do just that. This is not a moral option. Nurses are moral agents in their professional role, and as such are responsible and accountable for conducting themselves in accordance with personal and professional values and principles.

The challenge of integrity is to realize and uphold these values and principles, even and especially in situations where countervailing forces pull in an opposite direction. As Mappes (1986, p. 129) emphasizes, "the nurse's moral obligation is no less real" when she or he is constrained or pressured by difficult realities.

Integrity requires the nurse to address fundamentally the value of her or his values. When personal risks are associated with standing up for what is right, this may take courage. However, the courage to take a stand is foolhardy if one has not first explored and exhausted all options that might allow one to stand with, rather than against, others.

Notes

1   The elucidation that follows borrows from but goes beyond Mitchell's (1982) helpful analysis of the concept of integrity.

2   Moral autonomy, which is the sense of autonomy mainly at issue in this chapter, is similar in meaning to autonomy as moral reflection, which was discussed in the chapter on beneficence.

3   There continues to be some debate about whether nursing today is a *bona fide* profession (Hammond, 1990). The question, of course, depends on how one defines a profession. One feature that is common in many definitions is professing a set of professional values or a code of ethics (Conway, 1983; Greenwood, 1983; Flaherty, 1985). At least in this much, contemporary nursing qualifies as a profession. For an excellent discussion of professionalism and nursing, see the chapter "Professionalism" in Jameton (1984, pp. 18-35).

4   For an account of this struggle from an ethical point of view, see the chapter "Nursing's Struggle for Autonomy" in Jameton (1984, pp. 36-57). Crowder (1974) also has a good discussion of the history of nursing ethics *vis-à-vis* various codes of ethics.

5   Davis (1983) has a thought-provoking discussion of the challenges facing nurses who work in hospital settings.

6   Curtin (1982c) adds an important qualification to this point:

> If the differences between the patient and the professional are irreconcilable, the professional must withdraw from the care of the patient and refer him or her to someone whose value system is in accord with the patient's. (p. 91)

7   Scherer (1987) reports the following story involving a nurse:

> One evening, a family member was screaming at me because there was some trash in his mother's room. I was pretty frantic that evening because of the staffing situation, and this person screamed at me because of the garbage. I couldn't believe it. I'm not asking for non-professionals to do *my* job, I'm asking for non-professionals to do *their* job so I can do my job." (p. 1289)

8   For a thought-provoking discussion of the nurse-physician relation-
     ship, see MacIntyre (1983).

9   Some of the literature and studies on moral distress are reviewed in
     Wilkinson (1988) and Rodney & Starzomski (1993). See also Rodney
     (1988, 1989).

10   For a discussion of "integrity-preserving compromise," see Benjamin
     and Curtis (1986, pp. 105-108).

11   Whether these reasons are morally justifiable is another question,
     which would have to be decided with reference to the particulars of
     the case (refusals having to do with discrimination are of course inde-
     fensible regardless of circumstances). Even so, being justified is no
     guarantee that one will not suffer negative consequences from the
     decision. See Cushing (1988b) for advice on how to proceed in situa-
     tions of assignment refusal.

12   Cushing (1988a) discusses the issues surrounding rejecting an assign-
     ment due to being overworked.

13   Of course, the availability of other more suitable nurses and whether
     or not the situation was of an emergency nature would be important
     considerations.

14   Curtin (1982b) gives an insightful discussion of conscientious refusal
     to participate in abortions with reference to a somewhat different
     case.

15   Dowling-Smout (1988) gives some useful background on the "opting-
     out" issue with reference to a case in Ontario that received consider-
     able media coverage.

16   Flaherty (1985) writes:

     Physicians, nurses, and administrators who demonstrate what
     they profess — that is, participatory membership on a health care
     team — practice as *colleagues* [italics added], with respect for
     each other's expertise and contributions, consideration of each
     other's points of view, and genuine collaboration in the common
     goal of the promotion of functional competence in the recipients
     of health care. (p. 111)

Certainly she is right in stating the *ideal*, but the *reality* in which nurses work sometimes falls far short of this ideal.

17 Kotyk, McKnight, and Wortzman (1988) discuss this with reference to alcohol and drug addiction among nurses. In this regard, they note that there is sometimes a "conspiracy of silence" among nurses in these matters: "Nurses tend to fear that confronting another nurse with a problem will only bring further problems such as loss of employment and licence" (p. 19).

References

American Nurses' Association. ([1976] 1985). *Code for nurses with interpretive statements*. Kansas City: Author.

Benjamin, M., & Curtis, J. (1986). *Ethics in nursing* (2nd ed.). New York: Oxford University Press.

Bishop, A.H., & Scudder, J.R. Jr. (1987). Nursing ethics in an age of controversy. *Advances in Nursing Science, 9* (3), 34-43.

Canadian Nurses Association. (1991). *Code of ethics for nursing*. Ottawa: Author.

Carnerie, F. (1989). Patient advocacy. *The Canadian Nurse, 85* (11), 20.

Conway, M.E. (1983). Prescription for professionalization. In N.L. Chaska (Ed.), *The nursing profession: A time to speak* (pp. 29-37). New York: McGraw-Hill.

Crowder, E. (1974). Manners, morals, and nurses: An historical overview of nursing ethics. *Texas Reports on Biology and Medicine, 32* (1), 173-180.

Curtin, L.L. (1982a). Autonomy, accountability and nursing practice. *Advances in Nursing Science, 4* (1), 7-14.

Curtin, L.L. (1982b). Case study V: Abortion, privacy, and conscience [with commentary by M.J. Flaherty]. In L.L. Curtin & M.J. Flaherty (Eds.), *Nursing ethics: Theories and pragmatics* (pp. 239-254). Bowie, MD: Robert J. Brady.

Curtin, L.L. (1982c). The nurse-patient relationship: Foundations, purposes, responsibilities, and rights. In L.L. Curtin & M.J. Flaherty (Eds.), *Nursing ethics: Theories and pragmatics* (pp. 79-96). Bowie, MD: Robert J. Brady.

Curtin, L.L. (1993). Creating moral space for nurses. *Nursing Management*, 24 (3), 18-19.

Cushing, M. (1988a). Accepting or rejecting an assignment part 1: Are you abandoning your patients? *American Journal of Nursing, 88* (11), 1470-1476.

Cushing, M. (1988b). Refusing an unreasonable assignment part 2: strategies for problem solving. *American Journal of Nursing, 88* (12), 1635-1637.

Davis, A.J. (1983). Authority, autonomy, ethical decision-making, and collective bargaining in hospitals. In C.P. Murphy & J. Hunter (Eds.), *Ethical problems in the nurse-patient relationship* (pp. 63-76). Boston: Allyn & Bacon.

Dowling-Smout, C.D. (1988). Should a nurse be required to assist at abortions. *The Nursing Report: A Canadian Nursing Management Supplement, 9*, 39-42.

Flaherty, M.J. (1985). Ethical issues. In M. Stewart, J. Innes, S. Searl, & C. Smillie (Eds.), *Community health nursing in Canada* (pp. 97-113). Toronto: Gage.

Greenwood, E. (1983). Attributes of a profession. In B. Baumrin & B. Freedman (Eds.), *Moral responsibility and the professions* (pp. 20-32). New York: Haven Publications.

Hammond, M. (1990). Is nursing a semi-profession? *The Canadian Nurse, 86* (2), 20-23.

International Council of Nurses. ([1973] 1982). *Code for nurses: Ethical concepts applied to nursing.* Geneva: Author.

Jameton, A.L. (1984). *Nursing practice: The ethical issues.* Englewood Cliffs, NJ: Prentice-Hall.

Johnstone, M.J. (1988). Law, professional ethics and the problem of conflict with personal values. *International Journal of Nursing Studies, 25* (2), 147-157.

Kotyk, V., McKnight, K., & Wortzman, A. (1988). Manitoba's response: Nurses at risk. *The Canadian Nurse, 84* (4), 18-21.

MacIntyre, A. (1983). To whom is the nurse responsible? In C.P. Murphy & J. Hunter (Eds.), *Ethical problems in the nurse-patient relationship* (pp. 79-83). Boston: Allyn & Bacon.

Mappes, E.J.K. (1986). Ethical dilemmas for nurses: Physicians' orders versus patients' rights. In T.A. Mappes & J.S. Zembaty (Eds.), *Biomedical ethics* (2nd ed., pp. 127-134). New York: McGraw-Hill.

Mitchell, C. (1982). Integrity in interprofessional relationships. In G.J. Agich (Ed.), *Responsibility in health care* (pp. 163-184). Boston: D. Reidel.

Nelson, M.J. (1982). Authenticity: Fabric of ethical nursing practice. *Advances in Nursing Science, 4* (1), 1-6.

Robb, I.H. (1900). *Nursing ethics: For hospital and private use.* Cleveland: Koeckert.

Rodney, P. (1988) Moral distress in critical care nursing. *Canadian Critical Care Nursing Journal, 5* (2), 9-11.

Rodney, P. (1989). Towards ethical decision-making in nursing practice. *Canadian Journal of Nursing Administration, 2* (2), 11-13.

Rodney, P. (1994). A nursing perspective on life-prolonging treatment. *Journal of Palliative Care Medicine, 10* (2), 40-44.

Rodney, P., & Starzomski, R. (1993). Constraints on the moral agency of nurses. *Canadian Nurse, 89* (9), 23-26.

Scherer, P. (1987). When every day is Saturday: The shortage. *American Journal of Nursing, 87* (10), 1284-1290.

Storch, J.L. (1988). Ethics in nursing practice. In A.J. Baumgart & J. Larsen (Eds.), *Nursing faces the future: Development and change* (pp. 211-221). St. Louis: C.V. Mosby.

Theis, E.C. (1986). Ethical issues: A nursing perspective. *The New England Journal of Medicine, 315* (9), 1222-1224.

Thompson J.E., & Thompson, H.O. (1988). Living with ethical decisions with which you disagree. *MCN: American Journal of Child Maternal Nursing, 13* (4), 245-248, 250.

Tunna, K., & Conner, M. (1993). You are your ethics. *The Canadian Nurse, 89* (5), 25-26.

Wilkinson, J.M. (1988). Moral distress in nursing practice: Experience and effect. *Nursing Forum, 23* (1), 16-29.

Yarling, R.R., & McElmurry, B.J. (1986). The moral foundation of nursing. *Advances in Nursing Science, 8* (2), 63-73.

STUDY QUESTIONS: INTEGRITY

Case 1: Conscience and Assignment Refusal

1. Give arguments for and against the proposal that legislative provisions should be made to allow nurses to "opt out" of participating in abortions without fear of reprisal.

2. Some nurses have claimed a right to refuse to care for people with Acquired Immunodeficiency Syndrome (AIDS). How would such a "right" (if indeed it is a right) be different than the right to refuse to participate in abortions?

3. From the standpoint of a nurse opposed to abortion, is there a morally relevant difference between assisting in abortion and giving post-operative care?

4. "A professional is expected to put personal values aside in caring for clients." State whether and why you agree or disagree with this statement.

Case 2: Disagreement within the Health Team

1. How might Ms. Sanchez's family play a part in resolving this issue?

2. Create a scenario in which you, assuming the role of another nurse on the team, are convinced that Nurse Johnson is being rigid and unreasonable.

3. We are told that Nurse Johnson thinks the psychiatrist is "arrogant." How might personality assessments of this sort come into play in the dynamics of a health team? Should they?

4. The view that "the majority should prevail" is very prevalent in our society. On what grounds can Nurse Johnson, a minority of one, assert herself against the will of the majority opinion of the health team?

Case 3: Colleague Incompetence and Client Good

1. What is the difference between professional *incompetence* and professional *misconduct*?

2. Discuss the statement: "Whatever our intentions, our ways of dealing with incompetent practitioners tend to be more punitive than compassionate."

3. What difference would it make if this were only the first instance of a medication error, and not the fourth?

4. Beneficence is normally associated with concern for the good of the client. Does one owe a duty of beneficence to one's colleagues as well?

Appendix A

Code for Nurses: Ethical Concepts Applied to Nursing

International Council of Nurses (1973)

- The fundamental responsibility of the nurse is fourfold: to promote health, to prevent illness, to restore health and alleviate suffering.

- The need for nursing is universal. Inherent in nursing is respect for life, dignity and rights of man. It is unrestricted by considerations of nationality, race, creed, colour, age, sex, politics or social status.

- Nurses render health services to the individual, the family and the community and coordinate their services with those of related groups.

Nurses and people

- The nurse's primary responsibility is to those people who require nursing care.

- The nurse, in providing care, promotes an environment in which the values, customs, and spiritual beliefs of the individual are respected.

- The nurse holds in confidence personal information and uses judgement in sharing this information.

Nurses and practice

- The nurse carries personal responsibility for nursing practice and for maintaining competence by continual learning.

- The nurse maintains the highest standards of nursing care possible within the reality of a specific situation.

- The nurse uses judgement in relation to individual competence when accepting and delegating responsibilities.

- The nurse when acting in a professional capacity should at all times maintain standards of personal conduct which reflect credit upon the profession.

Nurses and society

- The nurse shares with other citizens the responsibility for initiating and supporting action to meet the health and social needs of the public.

Nurses and co-workers

- The nurse sustains a cooperative relationship with co-workers in nursing and other fields.

- The nurse takes appropriate action to safeguard the individual when his care is endangered by a co-worker or any other person.

Nurses and the profession

- The nurse plays the major role in determining and implementing desirable standards of nursing practice and nursing education.

- The nurse is active in developing a core of professional knowledge.

- The nurse, acting through the professional organization, participates in establishing and maintaining equitable social and economic working conditions in nursing.

APPENDIX B

CODE OF ETHICS FOR NURSING

Canadian Nurses Association

Preamble

Nursing practice can be defined generally as a "dynamic, caring, helping relationship in which the nurse assists the client to achieve and maintain optimal health."[1] Nurses in clinical practice, education, administration and research share the common goal of maintaining competent care and improving nursing practice. "Nurses direct their energies toward the promotion, maintenance and restoration of health, the prevention of illness, the alleviation of suffering and the ensuring of a peaceful death when life can no longer be sustained."[2]

The nurse, by entering the profession, is committed to moral norms of conduct and assumes a professional commitment to health and the well-being of clients. As citizens, nurses continue to be bound by the moral and legal norms shared by all other participants in society. As individuals, nurses have a right to choose to live by their own values (their personal ethics) as long as those values do not compromise care of their clients.

This Code deals with the ethics rather than the laws governing nursing practice. Laws and ethics of health care necessarily overlap considerably, since both share the concern that the conduct of health care professionals reflects respect for the well-being, dignity and liberty of patients. An ideal system of law would be compatible with ethics, in that adherence to the law ought never require the violation of ethics.

---

1. Canadian Nurses Association. *A Definition of Nursing Practice, Standards for Nursing Practice*. Ottawa: CNA, 1987. p.iii.
2. Ibid, p.ii.

Still, the two domains, law and ethics, remain distinct, and this Code, while prepared with awareness of the law, is addressed solely to ethical obligations.

The adoption of this Code represents a conscious undertaking on the part of the Canadian Nurses Association and its members to be responsible for upholding the following statements (values, obligations, and limitations). This Code expresses and seeks to clarify the obligations of nurses to use their knowledge and skills for the benefit of others, to minimize harm, to respect client autonomy and to provide fair and just care for their clients. For those entering the profession, this Code identifies the basic moral commitments of nursing and may serve as a source for education and reflection. For those within the profession, the Code also serves as a basis for self-evaluation and for peer review. For those outside the profession, this Code may serve to establish expectations for the ethical conduct of nurses.

Ethical Problems

Situations often arise that present ethical problems for nurses in their practice. These situations tend to fall into three categories:

(a) *Ethical violations* involve the neglect of moral obligation; for example, a nurse who neglects to provide competent care to a client because of personal inconvenience has ethically failed the client.

(b) *Ethical dilemmas* arise where ethical reasons both for and against a particular course of action are present and one option must be selected. For example, a client who is likely to refuse some appropriate form of health care presents the nurse with an ethical dilemma. In this case, substantial moral reasons may be offered on behalf of several opposing options.

(c) *Ethical distress* occurs when nurses experience the imposition of practices that provoke feelings of guilt, concern or distaste.

Such feelings may occur when nurses are ethically obliged to provide particular types of care despite their personal disagreement or discomfort with the course of treatment prescribed. For example, a nurse may think that continuing to tube feed an irreversibly unresponsive person is contrary to that client's well-being, but nonetheless is required to do so because that view is not shared by other caregivers.

This Code provides clear direction for avoiding ethical violations. When a course of action is mandated by the Code, and there exists no opposing ethical principle, ethical conduct requires that course of action.

This Code cannot serve the same function for all ethical dilemmas or for ethical distress. There is room within the profession of nursing for conscientious disagreement among nurses. The resolution of any dilemma often depends upon the specific circumstances of the case in question, and no particular resolution may be definitive of good nursing practice. Resolution may also depend upon the relative weight of the opposing principles, a matter about which reasonable people may disagree.

The Code cannot relieve ethical distress but it may serve as a guide for nurses to weigh and consider their responsibilities in the particular situation. Inevitably, nurses must reconcile their actions with their consciences in caring for clients.

The Code tries to provide guidance for those nurses who face ethical problems. Proper consideration of the Code should lead to better decision-making when ethical problems are encountered.

It should be noted that many problems or situations seen as ethical in nature are problems of miscommunication, failure of trust or management dilemmas in disguise. There is, therefore, a distinct need to clarify whether the problem is an ethical one or one of another sort.

Elements of the Code

This Code contains different elements designed to help the nurse in its interpretation. The values and obligations are presented by topic and not in order of importance. There is intentional variation in the normative terminology used in the Code (the nurse *should* or *must*) to indicate differences in the moral force of the statements; the term *should* indicates a moral preference, while *must* indicates an obligation. A number of distinctions between ethics and morals may be found in the literature. Since no distinction has been uniformly adopted by writers on ethics, these terms are used interchangeably in this Code.

- *Values* express broad ideals of nursing. They establish correct directions for nursing. In the absence of a conflict of ethics, the fact that a particular action promotes a *value* of nursing may be decisive in some specific instances. Nursing behaviour can always be appraised in terms of values: How closely did the behaviour approach the value? How widely did it deviate from the value? The values expressed in this Code must be adhered to by all nurses in their practice. Because they are so broad, however, values may not give specific guidance in difficult instances.

- *Obligations* are moral norms that have their basis in nursing values. However, obligations provide more specific direction for conduct than do values; obligations spell out what a value requires under particular circumstances.

- *Limitations* describe exceptional circumstances in which a value or obligation cannot be applied. Limitations have been included separately to emphasize that, in the ordinary run of events, the values and obligations will be decisive.

It is also important to emphasize that even when a value or obligation must be limited, it nonetheless carries moral weight. For example, a nurse who is compelled to testify in a court of law on confidential matters is still subject to the values and obligations of confidentiality. While the requirement to testify is a justified limitation upon confidentiality, in other respects confidentiality must be observed. The nurse must only reveal that confidential information that is pertinent to the case at hand, and such revelation must take place within the appropriate context. The general obligation to preserve the client's confidences remains despite particular limiting circumstances.

Rights and Responsibilities

Clients possess both legal and moral rights. These serve as one foundation for the responsibilities of nurses. However, for several reasons this Code emphasizes the obligations of nurses, rather than the rights of clients. Because the rights of clients do not depend upon professional acceptance of those rights, it would be presumptuous for a profession to claim to define the rights of clients. Emphasizing the rights of clients may also seem unduly legalistic and restrictive, ignoring the fact that sometimes ethics require nurses to go beyond the letter of the law. (For one example, see Value II, Obligation 3.) Finally, because it is sometimes beyond the power of a nurse to *secure* the rights of a client — an achievement that requires the cooperative and scrupulous efforts of all members of the health care team — it is better for a professional code of nursing to emphasize the responsibilities of nurses rather than to detail the entitlements of clients.

Nurses, too, possess legal and moral rights, as persons and as professionals. It is beyond the scope of this Code to address the personal rights of nurses. However, to the extent that conditions of employment have an impact on the establishment of ethical nursing, this Code must deal with that issue.

The satisfaction of some ethical responsibilities requires action taken by the nursing profession as a whole. The fourth section of the Code contains values and obligations concerned with those collective responsibilities of nursing; this section is particularly addressed to professional associations. Ethical reflection must be ongoing and its facilitation is a continuing responsibility of the Canadian Nurses Association.

The body of the Code is divided into sections corresponding to the sources of nursing obligations:

- **Clients**
- **Nursing Roles and Relationships**
- **Nursing Ethics and Society**
- **The Nursing Profession**

Clients

Value I: Respect for Needs and Values of Clients

Value

A nurse treats clients with respect for their individual needs and values.

Obligations

1. The client's perceived best interests must be a prime concern of the nurse.

2. Factors such as the client's race, religion or absence thereof, ethnic origin, social or marital status, sex or sexual orientation, age, or health status must not be permitted to compromise the nurse's commitment to that client's care.

3. The expectations and normal life patterns of clients are acknowledged. Individualized programs of nursing care are designed to accommodate the psychological, social, cultural and spiritual needs of clients, as well as their biological needs.

4. The nurse does more than respond to the requests of clients; the nurse accepts an affirmative obligation within the context of health care to aid clients in their expression of needs and values, including their right to live at risk.

5. Recognizing the client's membership in a family and a community, the nurse, with the client's consent, should attempt to facilitate the participation of significant others in the care of the client.

Value II: Respect for Client Choice

Value

Based upon respect for clients and regard for their right to control their own care, nursing care reflects respect for the right of choice held by clients.

Obligations

1. The competent client's consent is an essential precondition to the provision of health care. Nurses bear the primary responsibility to inform clients about the nursing care available to them.

2. Consent may be signified in many different ways. Verbal permission and knowledgeable cooperation are the usual forms by which clients consent to nursing care. In each case, however, a valid consent represents the free choice of the competent client to undergo that care.

3. Consent, properly understood, is the process by which a client becomes an active participant in care. All clients should be aided in becoming active participants in their care to the maximum extent that circumstances permit. Professional ethics

may require of the nurse actions that exceed the legal requirements of consent. For example, although a child may be legally incompetent to consent, nurses should nevertheless attempt to inform and involve the child.

4. Force, coercion and manipulative tactics must not be employed in the obtaining of consent.

5. Illness or other factors may compromise the client's capacity for self-direction. Nurses have a continuing obligation to value autonomy in such clients; for example, by creatively providing clients with opportunities for choices within their capabilities, the nurse helps them to maintain or regain some degree of autonomy.

6. Whenever information is provided to a client, this must be done in a truthful, understandable and sensitive way. The nurse must proceed with an awareness of the individual client's needs, interests and values.

7. Nurses have a responsibility to assess the understanding of clients about their care and to provide information and explanation when in possession of the knowledge required to respond accurately. When the client's questions require information beyond that known to the nurse, the client must be informed of that fact and assisted to obtain the information from a health care practitioner who is in possession of the required facts.

Value III: Confidentiality

Value

The nurse holds confidential all information about a client learned in the health care setting.

Obligations

1. The rights of persons to control the amount of personal information revealed applies with special force in the health care setting. It is, broadly speaking, up to clients to determine who shall be told of their condition, and in what detail.

2. In describing professional confidentiality to a client, its boundaries should be revealed:

    a) Competent care requires that other members of a team of health personnel have access to or be provided with the relevant details of a client's condition.

    b) In addition, discussions of the client's care may be required for the purpose of teaching or quality assurance. In this case, special care must be taken to protect the client's anonymity.

    Whenever possible, the client should be informed of these necessities at the onset of care.

3. An affirmative duty exists to institute and maintain practices that protect client confidentiality for example, by limiting access to records or by choosing the most secure method of communicating client information.

4. Nurses have a responsibility to intervene if other participants in the health care delivery system fail to respect the confidentiality of client information.

Limitations

The nurse is not morally obligated to maintain confidentiality when the failure to disclose information will place the client or third parties in danger. Generally, legal requirements or privileges to disclose are morally justified by these same criteria. In facing such a situation, the first concern of the nurse must be the safety of the client or the third party.

Even when the nurse is confronted with the necessity to disclose, confidentiality should be preserved to the maximum possible extent. Both the amount of information disclosed and the number of people to whom disclosure is made should be restricted to the minimum necessary to prevent the feared harm.

Value IV: Dignity of Clients

Value

The nurse is guided by consideration for the dignity of clients.

Obligations

1. Nursing care must be done with consideration for the personal modesty of clients.

2. A nurse's conduct at all times should acknowledge the client as a person. For example, discussion of care in the presence of the client should actively involve or include that client.

3. Nurses have a responsibility to intervene when other participants in the health delivery system fail to respect any aspect of client dignity.

4. As ways of dealing with death and the dying process change, nursing is challenged to find new ways to preserve human values, autonomy and dignity. In assisting the dying client, measures must be taken to afford the client as much comfort, dignity and freedom from anxiety and pain as possible. Special consideration must be given to the need of the client's family or significant others to cope with their loss.

Value V: Competent Nursing Care

Value

The nurse provides competent care to clients.

Obligations

1. Nurses should engage in continuing education and in the upgrading of knowledge and skills relevant to their area of practice, that is, clinical practice, education, research or administration.

2. In seeking or accepting employment, nurses must accurately state their areas of competence as well as limitations.

3. Nurses assigned to work outside an area of present competence must seek to do what, under the circumstances, is in the best interests of their clients. The nurse manager on duty, or others, must be informed of the situation at the earliest possible moment so that protective measures can be instituted. As a temporary measure, the safety and welfare of clients may be better served by the best efforts of the nurse under the circumstances than by no nursing care at all. Nurse managers are obligated to support nurses who are placed in such difficult situations and to make every effort to remedy the problem.

4. When called upon outside an employment setting to provide emergency care, nurses fulfil their obligations by providing the best care that circumstances, experience and education permit.

Limitations

A nurse is not ethically obliged to provide requested care when compliance would involve a violation of her or his moral beliefs. When that request falls within recognized forms of health care, however, the client must be referred to a health care practitioner who is willing to provide the service. Nurses who have or are likely to encounter such situations are morally obligated to seek to arrange conditions of employment so that the care of clients will not be jeopardized.

Nursing Roles and Relationships

Value VI: Nursing Practice, Education, Research and Administration

Value

The nurse maintains trust in nurses and nursing.

Obligations

1. Nurses accepting professional employment must ascertain to the best of their ability that conditions will permit the provision of care consistent with the values and obligations of the Code. Prospective employers should be informed of the provisions of the Code so that realistic and ethical expectations may be established at the beginning of the nurse‚ employer relationship.

2. Nurse managers, educators and peers are morally obligated to provide timely and accurate feedback to nurses, nurse man-

agers, students of nursing and nurse educators. Objective performance appraisal is essential to the growth of nurses and is required by a concern for present and future clients.

3. Nurse managers bear special ethical responsibilities that flow from a concern for present and future clients. The nurse manager must seek to ensure that the competencies of personnel are used efficiently. Working within available resources, the nurse manager must seek to ensure the welfare of clients. When competent care is threatened due to inadequate resources or for some other reason, the nurse manager must act to minimize the present danger and to prevent future harm.

4. Student-teacher and student-client encounters are essential elements of nursing education. These encounters must be conducted in accordance with ethical nursing practices. The nurse educator is obligated to treat students of nursing with respect and honesty and to provide fair guidance in developing nursing competence. The nurse educator should ensure that students of nursing are acquainted with and comply with the provisions of the Code. Student-client encounters must be conducted with client consent and require special attention to the dignity of the client.

5. Research is necessary to the development of the profession of nursing. Nurses should be acquainted with advances in research, so that established results may be incorporated into clinical practice, education and administration. The individual nurse's competencies may also be used to promote, to engage in or to assist health care research designed to enhance the health and welfare of clients.

The conduct of research must conform to ethical practice. The self-direction of clients takes on added importance in this context. Further direction is provided in the Canadian Nurses Association publication *Ethical Guidelines for Nursing Research Involving Human Subjects.*[1]

Value VII: Cooperation in Health Care

Value

The nurse recognizes the contribution and expertise of colleagues from nursing and other disciplines as essential to excellent health care.

Obligations

1. The nurse functions as a member of the health care team.

2. The nurse should participate in the assessment, planning, implementation and evaluation of comprehensive programs of care for individual clients and client groups. The scope of a nurse's responsibility should be based upon education and experience, as well as legal considerations of licensure or registration.

3. The nurse accepts responsibility to work with colleagues and other health care professionals, with nursing interest groups and through professional nurses' associations to secure excellent care for clients.

---

1. Canadian Nurses Association. *Ethical Guidelines for Nursing Research Involving Human Subjects.* Ottawa: CNA, 1983. [Editor's Note: this document has since been updated. See CNA 1994]

Value VIII: Protecting Clients from Incompetence

Value

The nurse takes steps to ensure that the client receives competent and ethical care.

Obligations

1. The first consideration of the nurse who suspects incompetence or unethical conduct must be the welfare of present clients or potential harm to future clients. Subject to that principle, the following must be considered:

    a) The nurse is obliged to ascertain the facts of the situation before deciding upon the appropriate course of action.

    b) Relationships in the health care team should not be disrupted unnecessarily. If a situation can be resolved without peril to present or future clients by direct discussion with the colleague suspected of providing incompetent or unethical care, that discussion should be done.

    c) Institutional mechanisms for reporting incidents or risks of incompetent or unethical care must be followed.

    d) The nurse must report any reportable offence stipulated in provincial or territorial professional nursing legislation.

    e) It is unethical for a nurse to participate in efforts to deceive or mislead clients about the cause of alleged harm or injury resulting from unethical or incompetent conduct.

2. Guidance on activities that may be delegated by nurses to assistants and other health care workers is found in legislation and policy statements. When functions are delegated, the nurse should be satisfied about the competence of those who will be fulfilling these functions. The nurse has a duty to provide continuing supervision in such a cases

3. The nurse who attempts to protect clients or colleagues threatened by incompetent or unethical conduct may be placed in a difficult position. Colleagues and professional associations are morally obliged to support nurses who fulfil their ethical obligations under the Code.

Value IX: Conditions of Employment

Value

Conditions of employment should contribute in a positive way to client care and the professional satisfaction of nurses.

Obligations

1. Nurses accepting professional employment must ascertain, to the best of their ability, that employment conditions will permit provision of care consistent with the values and obligations of the Code.

2. Nurse managers must seek to ensure that the agencies where they are employed comply with all pertinent provincial or territorial legislation.

3. Nurse managers must seek to ensure the welfare of clients and nurses. When competent care is threatened due to inadequate resources or for some other reason, the nurse manager should act to minimize the present danger and to prevent future harm.

4. Nurse managers must seek to foster environments and conditions of employment that promote excellent care for clients and a good worklife for nurses.

5. Structures should exist in the work environment that provide nurses with means of recourse if conditions that promote a good worklife are absent.

Value X: Job Action

Value

Job action by nurses is directed toward securing conditions of employment that enable safe and appropriate care for clients and contribute to the professional satisfaction of nurses.

Obligations

1. In the final analysis, the improvement of conditions of nursing employment is often to the advantage of clients. Over the short term, however, there is a danger that action directed toward this goal could work to the detriment of clients. In view of their ethical responsibility to current as well as future clients, nurses must respect the following principles:

   a) The safety of clients is the *first* concern in planning and implementing any job action.

   b) Individuals and groups of nurses participating in job actions share the ethical commitment to the safety of clients. However, their responsibilities may lead them to express this commitment in different but equally appropriate ways.

   c) Clients whose safety requires ongoing or emergency nursing care are entitled to have those needs satisfied throughout the duration of any job action. Individuals and groups of nurses participating in job actions have a duty through coordination and communication to take steps to ensure the safety of clients.

d) Members of the public are entitled to know of the steps taken to ensure the safety of clients.

Nursing Ethics and Society

Value XI: Advocacy of the Interests of Clients, the Community and Society

Value

The nurse advocates the interests of clients.

Obligations

1. Advocating the interests of individual clients and groups of clients includes helping them to gain access to good health care. For example, by providing information to clients privately or publicly, the nurse enables them to satisfy their rights to health care.

2. When speaking in a public forum or in court, the nurse owes the public the same duties of accurate and relevant information as are owed to clients within the employment setting.

Value XII: Representing Nursing Values and Ethics

Value

The nurse represents the values and ethics of nursing before colleagues and others.

Obligations

1. Nurses serving on committees concerned with health care or research should see their role as including the vigorous representation of nursing's professional ethics.

2. Many public issues include health as a major component. Involvement in public activities may give the nurse the opportunity to further the objectives of nursing as well as to fulfil the duties of a citizen.

The Nursing Profession

Value XIII: Responsibilities of Professional Nurses' Associations

Value

Professional nurses' organizations are responsible for clarifying, securing and sustaining ethical nursing conduct. The fulfilment of these tasks requires that professional nurses' organizations remain responsive to the rights, needs and legitimate interests of clients and nurses.

Obligations

1. Sustained communication and cooperation between the

Canadian Nurses Association, provincial or territorial associations and other organizations of nurses are essential steps toward securing ethical nursing conduct.

2.   Activities of professional nurses' associations must at all times reflect a prime concern for excellent client care.

3.   Professional nurses' associations should represent nursing interests and perspectives before non- nursing bodies, including legislatures, employers, the professional organizations of other health disciplines and the public communication media.

4.   Professional nurses' associations should provide and encourage organizational structures that facilitate ethical nursing conduct.

> a) Education in the ethical aspects of nursing should be available to nurses throughout their careers. Nurses' associations should actively support or develop structures to enhance sensitivity to, and application of, norms of ethical nursing conduct. Associations should also promote the development and dissemination of knowledge about ethical decision-making through nursing research.
>
> b) Changing circumstances call for ongoing review of this Code. Supplementation of the Code may be necessary to address special situations. Professional associations should consider the ethics of nursing on a regular and continuing basis and be prepared to provide assistance to those concerned with its implementation.

Appendix C

Code for Nurses

with Interpretive Statements

(Abridged)

American Nurses' Association (1985)

Preamble

A code of ethics makes explicit the primary goals and values of the profession. When individuals become nurses, they make a moral commitment to uphold the values and special moral obligations expressed in their code. The Code for Nurses is based on a belief about the nature of individuals, nursing, health, and society. Nursing encompasses the protection, promotion, and restoration of health; the prevention of illness; and the alleviation of suffering in the care of clients, including individuals, families, groups, and communities. In the context of these functions, nursing is defined as the diagnosis and treatment of human responses to actual or potential health problems.

Since clients themselves are the primary decision makers in matters concerning their own health, treatment, and well-being, the goal of nursing actions is to support and enhance the client's responsibility and self-determination to the greatest extent possible. In this context, health is not necessarily an end in itself, but rather a means to a life that is meaningful from the client's perspective.

When making clinical judgments, nurses base their decisions on consideration of consequences and of universal moral principles, both of which prescribe and justify nursing actions. The most fundamental of these principles is respect for persons. Other principles stemming from this basic principle are autonomy (self-determination), beneficence (doing good), nonmaleficence (avoiding harm), veracity (truth-telling), confidentiality (respecting privileged information), fidelity (keeping promises), and justice (treating people fairly).

In brief, then, the statements of the code and their interpretation provide guidance for conduct and relationships in carrying out nursing responsibilities consistent with the ethical obligations of the profession and with high quality in nursing care.

Introduction

A code of ethics indicates a profession's acceptance of the responsibility and trust with which it has been invested by society. Under the terms of the implicit contract between society and the nursing profession, society grants the profession considerable autonomy and authority to function in the conduct of its affairs. The development of a code of ethics is an essential activity of a profession and provides one means for the exercise of professional self-regulation.

Upon entering the profession, each nurse inherits a measure of both the responsibility and the trust that have accrued to nursing over the years, as well as the corresponding obligation to adhere to the profession's code of conduct and relationships for ethical practice. The *Code for Nurses with Interpretative Statements* is thus more a collective expression of nursing conscience and philosophy than a set of external rules imposed upon an individual practitioner of nursing. Personal and professional integrity can be assured only if an individual is committed to the profession's code of conduct.

A code of ethical conduct offers general principles to guide and evaluate nursing actions. It does not assure the virtues required for professional practice within the character of each nurse. In particular situations, the justification of behavior as ethical must satisfy not only the individual nurse acting as a moral agent but also the standards for professional peer review.

The Code for Nurses was adopted by the American Nurses'

Association in 1950 and has been revised periodically. It serves to inform both the nurse and society of the profession's expectations and requirements in ethical matters. The code and the interpretive statements together provide a framework within which nurses can make ethical decisions and discharge their responsibilities to the public, to other members of the health team, and to the profession.

Although a particular situation by its nature may determine the use of specific moral principles, the basic philosophical values, directives, and suggestions provided here are widely applicable to situations encountered in clinical practice. The Code for Nurses is not open to negotiation in employment settings, nor is it permissible for individuals or groups of nurses to adapt or change the language of this code.

The requirements of the code may often exceed those of the law. Violations of the law may subject the nurse to civil or criminal liability. The state nurses' associations, in fulfilling the profession's duty to society, may discipline their members for violations of the code. Loss of the respect and confidence of society and of one's colleagues is a serious sanction resulting from violation of the code. In addition, every nurse has a personal obligation to uphold and adhere to the code and to ensure that nursing colleagues do likewise....

Code for Nurses

1. *The nurse provides services with respect for human dignity and the uniqueness of the client, unrestricted by considerations of social or economic status, personal attributes, or the nature of health problems.*

2. *The nurse safeguards the client's right to privacy by judiciously protecting information of a confidential nature.*

3. *The nurse acts to safeguard the client and the public when health care and safety are affected by the incompetent, unethical, or illegal practice of any person.*

4.   The nurse assumes responsibility and accountability for individual nursing judgments and actions.

5.   The nurse maintains competence in nursing.

6.   The nurse exercises informed judgment and uses individual competence and qualifications as criteria in seeking consultation, accepting responsibilities, and delegating nursing activities to others.

7.   The nurse participates in activities that contribute to the ongoing development of the profession's body of knowledge.

8.   The nurse participates in the profession's efforts to implement and improve standards of nursing.

9.   The nurse participates in the profession's effort to establish and maintain conditions of employment conducive to high quality nursing care.

10.   The nurse participates in the profession's effort to protect the public from misinformation and misrepresentation and to maintain the integrity of nursing.

11.   The nurse collaborates with members of the health professions and other citizens in promoting community and national efforts to meet the health needs of the public.

Code For Nurses With Interpretive Statements

1. The nurse provides services with respect for human dignity and the uniqueness of the client, unrestricted by considerations of social or economic status, personal attributes, or the nature of health problems.

1.1 Respect for Human Dignity

The fundamental principle of nursing practice is respect for the inherent dignity and worth of every client. Nurses are morally obligated to respect human existence and the individuality of all persons who are the recipients of nursing actions. Nurses therefore must take all reasonable means to protect and preserve human life when there is hope of recovery or reasonable hope of benefit from life-prolonging treatment.

Truth telling and the process of reaching informed choice underlie the exercise of self-determination, which is basic to respect for persons. Clients should be as fully involved as possible in the planning and implementation of their own health care. Clients have the moral right to determine what will be done with their own person; to be given accurate information, and all the information necessary for making informed judgments; to be assisted with weighing the benefits and burdens of options in their treatment; to accept, refuse, or terminate treatment without coercion; and to be given necessary emotional support. Each nurse has an obligation to be knowledgeable about the moral and legal rights of all clients and to protect and support those rights. In situations in which the client lacks the capacity to make a decision, a surrogate decision maker should be designated.

Individuals are interdependent members of the community. Taking into account both individual rights and the interdependence of persons in decision making, the nurse recognizes those situations in which individual rights to autonomy in health care may temporarily be overridden to preserve the life of the human community; for example, when a disaster demands triage or when an individual presents a direct danger to others. The many variables involved make it imperative that each case be considered with full awareness of the need to preserve the rights and responsibilities of clients and the demands of justice. The suspension of individual rights must always be considered a deviation to be tolerated as briefly as possible....

1.3 The Nature of Health Problems

The nurse's respect for the worth and dignity of the individual human being applies, irrespective of the nature of the health problem. It is reflected in care given the person who is disabled as well as one without disability, the person with long-term illness as well as one with acute illness, the recovering patient as well as one in the last phase of life. This respect extends to all who require the services of the nurse for the promotion of health, the prevention of illness, the restoration of health, the alleviation of suffering, and the provision of supportive care of the dying. The nurse does not act deliberately to terminate the life of any person.

The nurse's concern for human dignity and for the provision of high quality nursing care is not limited by personal attitudes or beliefs. If ethically opposed to interventions in a particular case because of the procedures to be used, the nurse is justified in refusing to participate. Such refusal should be made known in advance and in time for other appropriate arrangements to be made for the client's nursing care. If the nurse becomes involved in such a case and the client's life is in jeopardy, the nurse is obliged to provide for the client's safety, to avoid abandonment, and to withdraw only when assured that alternative sources of nursing care are available to the client....

2. The nurse safeguards the client's right to privacy by judiciously protecting information of a confidential nature.

2.1 The Client's Right to Privacy

The right to privacy is an inalienable human right. The client trusts the nurse to hold all information in confidence. This trust could be destroyed and the client's welfare jeopardized by injudicious disclosure of information provided in confidence. The duty of confidentiality, however, is not absolute when innocent parties are in direct jeopardy.

2.2 Protection of Information

The rights, well-being, and safety of the individual client should be the determining factors in arriving at any professional judgment concerning the disposition of confidential information received from the client relevant to his or her treatment. The standards of nursing practice and the nursing responsibility to provide high quality health services require that relevant data be shared with members of the health team. Only information pertinent to a client's treatment and welfare is disclosed, and it is disclosed only to those directly concerned with the client's care....

3. *The nurse acts to safeguard the client and the public when health care and safety are affected by the incompetent, unethical, or illegal practice of any person.*

3.1 Safeguarding the Health and Safety of the Client

The nurse's primary commitment is to the health, welfare, and safety of the client. As an advocate for the client, the nurse must be alert to and take appropriate action regarding any instances of incompetent, unethical, or illegal practice by any member of the health care team or the health care system, or any action on the part of others that places the rights or best interests of the client in jeopardy. To function effectively in this role, nurses must be aware of the employing institution's policies and procedures, nursing standards of practice, the Code for Nurses, and laws governing nursing and health care practice with regard to incompetent, unethical, or illegal practice.

3.2 Acting on Questionable Practice

When the nurse is aware of inappropriate or questionable practice in the provision of health care, concern should be expressed to the person carrying out the questionable practice and attention called to the possible detrimental effect upon the client's welfare. When factors in the health care delivery system threaten the welfare of the client, similar action should be directed to the responsible administrative person. If indicated, the practice should then be reported to the appropriate authority within the institution, agency, or larger system.

There should be an established process for the reporting and handling of incompetent, unethical, or illegal practice within the employment setting so that such reporting can go through official channels without causing fear of reprisal. The nurse should be knowledgeable about the process and be prepared to use it if necessary. When questions are raised about the practices of individual practitioners or of health care systems, written documentation of the observed practices or behaviors must be available to the appropriate authorities. State nurses' associations should be prepared to provide assistance and support in the development and evaluation of such processes and in reporting procedures.

When incompetent, unethical, or illegal practice on the part of anyone concerned with the client's care is not corrected within the employment setting and continues to jeopardize the client's welfare and safety, the problem should be reported to other appropriate authorities such as practice committees of the pertinent professional organizations or the legally constituted bodies concerned with licensing of specific categories of health workers or professional practitioners. Some situations may warrant the concern and involvement of all such groups. Accurate reporting and documentation undergird all actions....

4. The nurse assumes responsibility and accountability for individual nursing judgments and actions.

4.1 Acceptance of Responsibility and Accountability

The recipients of professional nursing services are entitled to high quality nursing care. Individual professional licensure is the protective mechanism legislated by the public to ensure the basic and minimum competencies of the professional nurse. Beyond that, society has accorded to the nursing profession the right to regulate its own practice. The regulation and control of nursing practice by nurses demand that individual practitioners of professional nursing must bear primary responsibility for the nursing care clients receive and must be individually accountable for their own practice....

4.3 Accountability for Nursing Judgment and Action

Accountability refers to being answerable to someone for something one has done. It means providing an explanation or rationale to oneself, to clients, to peers, to the nursing profession, and to society. In order to be accountable, nurses act under a code of ethical conduct that is grounded in the moral principles of fidelity and respect for the dignity, worth, and self-determination of clients.

The nursing profession continues to develop ways to clarify nursing's accountability to society. The contract between the profession and society is made explicit through such mechanisms as (a) the Code for Nurses, (b) the standards of nursing practice, (c) the development of nursing theory derived from nursing research in order to guide nursing actions, (d) educational requirements for practice, (e) certification, and (f) mechanisms for evaluating the effectiveness of the nurse's performance of nursing responsibilities.

Nurses are accountable for judgments made and actions taken in the course of nursing practice. Neither physicians' orders nor the employing agency's policies relieve the nurse of accountability for actions taken and judgments made.

5. *The nurse maintains competence in nursing.*

5.1 Personal Responsibility for Competence

The profession of nursing is obligated to provide adequate and competent nursing care. Therefore it is the personal responsibility of each nurse to maintain competency in practice. For the client's optimum well-being and for the nurse's own professional development, the care of the client reflects and incorporates new techniques and knowledge in health care as these develop, especially as they relate to the nurse's particular field of practice. The nurse must be aware of the need for continued professional learning and must assume personal responsibility for currency of knowledge and skills....

6. The nurse exercises informed judgment and uses individual competence and qualifications as criteria in seeking consultation, accepting responsibilities, and delegating nursing activities to others.

6.1 Changing Functions

Nurses are faced with decisions in the context of the increased complexity of health care, changing patterns in the delivery of health services, and the development of evolving nursing practice in response to the health needs of clients. As the scope of nursing practice changes, the nurse must exercise judgment in accepting responsibilities, seeking consultation, and assigning responsibilities to others who carry out nursing care.

6.2 Accepting Responsibilities

The nurse must not engage in practices prohibited by law or delegate to others activities prohibited by practice acts of other health care personnel or by other laws. Nurses determine the scope of their practice in light of their education, knowledge, competency, and extent of experience. If the nurse concludes that he or she lacks competence or is inadequately prepared to carry out a specific function, the nurse has the responsibility to refuse that work and to seek alternative sources of care based on concern for the client's welfare. In that refusal, both the client and the nurse are protected. Inasmuch as the nurse is responsible for the continuous care of patients in health care settings, the nurse is frequently called upon to carry out components of care delegated by other health professionals as part of the client's treatment regimen. The nurse should not accept these interdependent functions if they are so extensive as to prevent the nurse from fulfilling the responsibility to provide appropriate nursing care to clients....

7. The nurse participates in activities that contribute to the ongoing development of the profession's body of knowledge.

7.1 The Nurse and Development of Knowledge

Every profession must engage in scholarly inquiry to identify, verify, and continually enlarge the body of knowledge that forms the foundation for its practice. A unique body of verified knowledge provides both framework and direction for the profession in all of its activities and for the practitioner in the provision of nursing care. The accrual of scientific and humanistic knowledge promotes the advancement of practice and the well-being of the profession's clients. Ongoing scholarly activity such as research and the development of theory is indispensable to the full discharge of a profession's obligations to society. Each nurse has a role in this area of professional activity, whether as an investigator in furthering knowledge, as a participant in research, or as a user of theoretical and empirical knowledge....

8. The nurse participates in the profession's efforts to implement and improve standards of nursing.

8.1 Responsibility to the Public for Standards

Nursing is responsible and accountable for admitting to the profession only those individuals who have demonstrated the knowledge, skills, and commitment considered essential to professional practice. Nurse educators have a major responsibility for ensuring that these competencies and a demonstrated commitment to professional practice have been achieved before the entry of an individual into the practice of professional nursing.

Established standards and guidelines for nursing practice provide guidance for the delivery of professional nursing care and are a means for evaluating care received by the public. The nurse has a personal responsibility and commitment to clients for implementation and maintenance of optimal standards of nursing practice....

9. The nurse participates in the profession's efforts to establish and maintain conditions of employment conducive to high quality nursing care.

9.1 Responsibility for Conditions of Employment

The nurse must be concerned with conditions of employment that (a) enable the nurse to practise in accordance with the standards of nursing practice and (b) provide a care environment that meets the standards of nursing service. The provision of high quality nursing care is the responsibility of both the individual nurse and the nursing profession. Professional autonomy and self-regulation in the control of conditions of practice are necessary for implementing nursing standards....

10. The nurse participates in the profession's effort to protect the public from misinformation and misrepresentation and to maintain the integrity of nursing....

10.2 Maintaining the Integrity of Nursing

The use of the title *registered nurse* is granted by state governments for the protection of the public. Use of that title carries with it the responsibility to act in the public interest. The nurse may use the title R.N. and symbols of academic degrees or other earned or honorary professional symbols of recognition in all ways that are legal and appropriate. The title and other symbols of the profession should not be used, however, for benefits unrelated to nursing practice or the profession, or used by those who may seek to exploit them for other purposes.

Nurses should refrain from casting a vote in any deliberations involving health care services or facilities where the nurse has business or other interests that could be construed as a conflict of interest.

11. The nurse collaborates with members of the health professions and other citizens in promoting community and national efforts to meet the health needs of the public....

11.2 Responsibility to the Public

The nursing profession is committed to promoting the welfare and safety of all people. The goals and values of nursing are essential to effective delivery of health services. For the benefit of the individual client and the public at large, nursing's goals and commitments need adequate representation. Nurses should ensure this representation by active participation in decision making in institutional and political arenas to assure a just distribution of health care and nursing resources....

APPENDIX D

THE ETHICAL FRAMEWORK FOR NURSING IN ONTARIO

College of Nurses of Ontario (1995)

I. ASSUMPTIONS

Consideration of ethical issues is an essential component of providing care within the therapeutic nurse-client relationship. As stated in the *Nursing Act, 1991,* this relationship enables the client to attain, maintain or regain optimal function by promoting the client's health, and assessing, providing care for and treating the client's health conditions. This is achieved by supportive, preventative, therapeutic, palliative and rehabilitative means. The relationship with the client may be a direct practice role or indirect, by means of management, education, and research roles. Nurses maintain competence relevant to their area of practice.

The therapeutic relationship changes as a result of the interactions between the nurse and the client, and varies with the nurse's and client's personal and cultural values and beliefs. Inherent in the therapeutic relationship is caring, which includes trust, respect, intimacy, and the appropriate use of power.

Caring is defined in the literature in a number of different ways.... Caring can be considered the behaviours, actions, and attributes of nurses. Caring nurses listen to and are empathetic with the clients' points of views. Generally, caring requires a recognition of clients as unique individuals whose goals nurses facilitate.

All nurses have their own personal values which must not interfere with clients' right to receive care. Clients' values, however, are of primary consideration when planning care.

The client may be an individual, family, group, or community.

Clients are capable of making decisions about their health care and consent is required before nursing care can be provided. Some clients may be only partly competent to make decisions. Other clients may be incompetent. When clients are incompetent, nurses need to ensure that a therapeutic relationship is maintained within the limits possible for those clients and with the substitute decision-makers. When individual clients are incompetent to make decisions, substitute decision-makers are always consulted.

Health care, including nursing care, is usually provided within the context of a multidisciplinary health team. The health team is an inter-disciplinary group of individuals who are either directly or indirectly involved in a client's care. Depending on the practice environment, the composition of the team will vary. The team includes the client and family or substitute decision-maker.

When providing care, nurses consider the setting in which care is given. Each setting has an impact on the ability to provide ethical care. Appropriate professional preparation, suitable conditions for nursing practice, respect for nurses as responsible decision-makers, and recognition of professional expertise are required in the environment in which ethical care is given.

Understanding and communicating beliefs and values helps nurses prevent ethical conflicts and also helps nurses work them through when they occur. There are many ways of working through and understanding ethical situations and one example is included in the third part of this section.

These guidelines describe ethical values most relevant to the nursing profession in Ontario and are intended to provide nurses with information about CNO's expectations of ethical conduct. The guidelines are one consideration when committees of CNO assess the practice of a nurse. They need to be considered carefully when making decisions about ethical care.

The guidelines are not intended to provide a comprehensive course in nursing ethics. Nurses are encouraged to make use of the selected annotated bibliography to increase their knowledge about ethics [Editor's Note: This bibliography has not been reprinted here.]. Nurses are also encouraged to attend conferences and to become involved in ethics committees and rounds in their facilities in order to continue learning about ethics.

II. ETHICAL VALUES

CNO has identified the values of client wellbeing, client choice, privacy and confidentiality, sanctity of life, maintaining commitments, truthfulness, and fairness as most relevant to providing nursing care in Ontario. The values are defined for the purpose of this document and are not discussed in order of priority, although it is recognized that client wellbeing and client choice are primary values.

When two or more ethical values apply to a situation, but these values support mutually inconsistent courses of action, an ethical conflict exists. Nurses may experience ethical uncertainty when unsure of what values apply to a situation or even what the moral problem is. They may also experience ethical distress when they know the "right" thing to do but various constraints make doing the "right" thing difficult (Jameton, 1984, p.6).

Not all nurses experience the same situation in the same way and some situations which cause conflict, uncertainty, or distress for some nurses may be straightforward for others. By discussing and understanding values and reviewing case situations, nurses can prepare themselves for ethical practice. Working through ethical conflicts is an ongoing part of care and nurses can use the framework of the nursing process to assist in resolving conflicts. A resolution of the conflict, that everyone is happy with, is not always possible. At these times, the best possible outcome is identified in consultation with the client, and the heath team works to achieve that outcome. As with other aspects of care, documenting the discussions and decisions is necessary.

In each of the following sections, the value is explained and one or two illustrations, which are based on real situations, are used to assist in understanding how that specific value can conflict with other values. Nurses can use the illustrations to generate discussions and questions, and to think about situations. These illustrations may not pose a problem for all nurses because of the different value systems of different nurses. It is important, however, to understand why it may be a problem for some caregivers. . . .

Each section also includes specific behavioural directives which describe expected behaviours from Registered Nurses (RNs) and Registered Practical Nurse (RPNs). The directives are not prioritized and are not designed to work through the illustrations or to give an answer, but rather provide general expectations. If nurses decided not to follow the directives, a good rationale for their action would be necessary. It must be emphasized that while these directives provide some guidance, nurses need to use judgement at all times in deciding a course of action.

A. Client Wellbeing

Client wellbeing, in this document, is both promoting someone's good or welfare and preventing or removing harm. At times it is difficult to decide what is "good" or optimal in a particular situation. Whose view of "good" do nurses choose? What outcome will be the best for all those concerned? Determining the best action is not always easy, but it is necessary, as a beginning point, to differentiate between nurses' and clients' views of what is beneficial. Sometimes it is also difficult balancing the potential benefits with the potential harm. Nurses must use clients' views as a starting point.

The following situations illustrate ethical conflicts related to client wellbeing.

1. Nurses perform procedures on children, such as debridement, which may cause severe pain.

2. A nurse has explained the benefits of taking medication to one of her clients and firmly believes that the medication is in the client's best interest. The client understands the nurse's explanation but refuses to take the medication. The client states that the side effects of the medication cancel out any benefits.

Behavioural Directives:

Nurses demonstrate a regard for client wellbeing by

1. Listening and understanding clients' values, opinions, needs and ethnocultural and racial beliefs;

2. Helping clients find the best possible solution, given clients' personal values, beliefs, and different decision-making styles;

3. Using their knowledge and skill to promote clients' best interest, in an empathic manner;

4. Promoting and preserving the self-esteem and self-confidence of clients;

5. Seeking assistance when ethical conflicts arise (ethics committees, clergy, literature);

6. Trying to improve the level of health care in the community by working with individuals, groups, other health professionals, employers, or government to advocate for needed health policy and health resources;

7. Respecting informed, voluntary decisions.

B. Client Choice

Client choice, in this document, means self-determination and includes the right to the information necessary to make choices and to consent to or refuse care. There are limits to client choice. Clients do not have the right to endanger the safety of others or the right to health care which would be medically futile. Client choice is also influenced by the resources available in a particular situation.

Clients know the context in which they live and their own beliefs and values. As a result, when they have the necessary information, they can decide what is best for themselves. Clients who are not competent in all areas may still be capable of sound choice in some areas of their lives and need to be allowed an opportunity to make decisions in those areas. In Ontario, both legislation* and common law requires that the wishes of clients or substitute decision-makers be respected.

There may be situations when clients request nurses to perform an act which is illegal or which may cause serious harm. In these situations, nurses refuse to follow the clients' wishes and depending on the circumstances, discuss the matter with others on the health team.

Consideration of clients' wishes may be difficult when clients' beliefs and values differ from those of nurses. Nurses have their own personal values and may experience an ethical conflict when they disagree with clients' decisions. Nurses may believe that, as health professionals, they know what is best for clients.

When a client's wish conflicts with a nurse's personal values, and the nurse believes that she or he cannot provide care, the nurse needs to arrange for another care giver and withdraw from the situation. If no other care giver can be arranged, the nurse must provide the immediate care required. If no other solution can be found, the nurse may have to leave a particular place of employment in order to adhere to her or his moral values.

The following situation illustrates an ethical conflict related to client choice.

A competent 85-year-old gentleman in a long-term care facility has been taking walks along a busy highway every day. He has always said that he could not bear to live without his walks. Recently the nurses have noticed that his gait has become unsteady and they are concerned about his safety along the busy road. They are afraid that he may fall into traffic.

---

*   Other CNO documents, for example, the Statement on Cardio-Pulmonary Resuscitation, discuss the consent legislation in greater detail.

Behavioural Directives:

Nurses demonstrate regard for client choice by

1. Exploring clients' rationale before acceding to their wishes (Can other options be found which agree with clients' wishes and with nurses' knowledge and judgement?);

2. Respecting clients even when clients' wishes are not the same as nurses';

3. Following clients' wishes within the obligations of the law and the standards of practice;

4. Providing information to promote informed consent;

5. Advocating for clients to access information before consenting or refusing care, treatment, and participation in research;

6. Helping to identify substitute decision-makers if clients are not competent to make choices regarding health care.

C. Privacy and Confidentiality

Privacy is limiting access to a person, the person's body, conversations, bodily functions, and objects immediately associated with the person unless access is necessary to give care. People have different beliefs and values about privacy so that the important aspects of privacy need to be identified by individual clients. Nurses need to provide care which maintains the dignity and privacy of clients.

Confidentiality is a means by which personal information is kept private. All information relating to the physical, psychological, and social health of clients is confidential. Any information collected during the course of providing nursing services is confidential. Clients may consent to sharing information with others.

Clients have the right to confidentiality and nurses make an implicit promise to maintain confidentiality. Relevant information is shared with other members of the health team who are also obligated to maintain confidentiality. Nurses need to explain to clients that information will be shared with others on the health team.

At times, nurses learn information which, if not revealed, will result in serious harm to the client or others. Nurses need to consult with the health team and, if appropriate, report the information to the person or institution concerned. The client or substituted decision-maker must be told of the need to report the information and given the opportunity to take action herself or himself. Some legislation also requires that nurses reveal confidential information to others, for example, the *Child and Family Services Act*.

The following situation illustrates an ethical conflict related to confidentiality.

The plant manager, who is the occupational health nurse's supervisor, has asked to see one of the workers' health records. The nurse refuses to release the health record to the manager. The manager becomes angry and says she will discipline the nurse for not taking direction from a supervisor.

Behavioural Directives:

Nurses demonstrate regard for privacy and confidentiality by

1. Keeping all personal and health information confidential within the obligations of the law and standards of practice;

2. Informing clients or substitute decision-makers that other health care team members will have access to any information obtained while caring for clients;

3. Refraining from collecting information which is unnecessary to provide health care;

4. Protecting clients' physical and emotional privacy.

D. Sanctity of Life

Sanctity of life, in this document, means that human life is precious, needs to be respected, protected, and treated with consideration.... Sanctity of life also includes consideration of the quality of life. It is difficult sometimes to identify what is human life and what society wants, values, and protects in relation to human life. It is even more difficult for health professionals, including nurses, to identify their own beliefs in relation to human life.

Health professionals have made every reasonable effort to preserve human life. Technology now allows life to be preserved almost indefinitely. Many health professionals and clients believe that some treatments which preserve life at all costs are unacceptable when the quality of life is questionable.

When a client's wish conflicts with a nurse's personal values, and the nurse believes that she or he cannot provide health care, the nurse needs to arrange for another care giver and withdraw from the situation. If no other care giver can be arranged, the nurse must provide the immediate care required. If no other situation can be found, the nurse may have to leave a particular place of employment in order to adhere to her or his moral values.

The following situation illustrates an ethical conflict related to sanctity of life.

A client's daughter, who is the substitute decision-maker, has decided, after much soul-searching, that her confused mother, who is critically ill with pneumonia, should no longer be treated with antibiotics. The mother has gangrene in both feet and will likely need an amputation when the pneumonia is cured. The daughter believes that, were her mother aware, she would intensely object to any further treatment and would not want to live in her present state. The nursing staff are very upset about this decision: to them, the antibiotics are not extraordinary treatment. The client, although confused, has always seemed to enjoy life....

Behavioural Directives:

Nurses demonstrate regard for sanctity of life by

1. Identifying, when possible, clients' values when sanctity of life and quality of life values may conflict;

2. Respecting clients' values and following their directives within the obligations of the law and standards of practice;

3. Following substitute decision-makers' directives if clients are incompetent to make decisions about their care within the obligations of the law and standards of practice;

4. Advocating for palliative measures when active treatment is withheld;

5. Providing peaceful and dignified palliative care.

E. Maintaining Commitments

Nurses have an obligation to maintain commitments that they acquire as regulated health professionals. Maintaining commitments, in this document, means keeping promises, being honest, and meeting implicit or explicit obligations towards their clients, themselves, their employers, and the profession of nursing.

1. Maintaining commitments to clients

Nurses, as self-regulated professionals, implicitly promise to provide safe, effective, and ethical care. Because of their commitment to clients, nurses try to act in the best interest of clients, according to clients' wishes and standards of practice. Nurses are obliged to refrain from abandoning, abusing, or neglecting clients, and to provide empathic and knowledgeable care. The commitment to clients also includes a commitment to family members, some of whose needs may conflict with those of clients.

The following situation illustrates an ethical conflict related to maintaining commitments to clients.

A client wants to die at home in peace and comfort. The family knows that the presence of the client at home will create intolerable stress for other family members. The nurse is being pressured by other members of the health team to talk the family into taking the client home.

Behavioural Directives:

Nurses demonstrate a regard for maintaining commitments to clients by

1. Putting the needs and wishes of the clients first;

2. Identifying when clients' needs and wishes conflict with those of families or others, and encouraging further discussion about clients' needs;

3. Identifying needed resources and support to enable clients to follow their wishes;

4. Identifying when their own values and beliefs conflict with the

ability to keep implicit and explicit promises and taking appropriate action;

5. Providing knowledgeable and client-centred nursing care;

2. Maintaining commitments to oneself

As people learn and grow they develop their own moral values and beliefs. Nurses need to recognize and function within their own value system and be true to themselves. Nurses' values sometimes differ from those of other health professionals, employers, and clients which may cause ethical conflict. Nurse must provide ethical care while at the same time remaining committed to their own values.

When the conflict involves a client and the nurse believes that she or he cannot provide care, the nurse needs to arrange for another care giver and withdraw from the situation. If no other care giver can be arranged, the nurse must provide the immediate care required. If no other solution can be found, the nurse may have to leave a particular place of employment in order to adhere to her or his moral values.

The following situation illustrates an ethical conflict related to maintaining commitments to oneself.

The family of a client who has been in a coma for some time has requested that the feeding tube be withdrawn and the client be allowed to die. One nurse is very upset about the prospect of caring for a client when she is not allowed to provide nourishment. She believes that providing nourishment is fundamental to caring.

Behavioural Directives:

Nurses demonstrate a regard for maintaining commitments to themselves by

1. Clarifying their own values in client situations;

2. Identifying situations when a conflict of their own values interferes with the care of clients;

3. Exploring alternative options for treatment and seeking consultation when values conflict;

4. Determining and communicating their own values pertinent to the position before accepting employment;

5. Recognizing the impact of their own health on the care being given.

3. Maintaining commitments to the profession of nursing

Nurses have a commitment to help regulate nursing to protect the public interest. Nurses also have a commitment to the profession of nursing. It is in the interest of the public that the profession continue to develop and change with the changes in health care and society. As members of the profession, nurses have an obligation to promote these changes.

Being a member of the profession brings with it the respect and trust of the public. To continue to deserve this respect, nurses have a duty to participate in and promote the growth of the profession, and to conduct themselves in a manner which is becoming to the profession.

Nurses need to care for one another and respect their colleagues. They need to work collaboratively with other nurses, trust in the expertise of one another, and refer to others when they do not have the necessary knowledge and expertise themselves.

The safety and well-being of clients, however, takes precedence over respect for colleagues. Nurses, therefore, take action when colleagues put clients at risk.

The following situations illustrate ethical conflicts relating to maintaining commitments to the profession of nursing.

1. A nurse knows that the wrong medication has been prescribed for and administered to a client. There was no bad effect on the client and the proper treatment has been resumed. The physician and the nurse involved in the incident are excellent practitioners and are very upset by the error. No one has informed the client of this mistake believing that informing may have professional implications for the nurse and the physician and may erode the client's trust in the health care team.

2. A nurse has a friend at work who is under significant personal stress. The friend has indicated that she is thankful for the support and help that she is receiving from her colleagues. The nurse, however, has begun to notice that her friend's practice has become much less competent. The friend is failing to do appropriate assessments of her clients. The nurse has noted that her friend's judgement has become impaired and that the friend is becoming increasingly disorganized. The friend is also short-tempered with other staff and abrupt to clients. No serious mistakes have been made as yet, but the nurse realizes that action needs to be taken. She does not, however, wish to add to her friend's problems by reporting the friend to the nurse manager.

Behavioural Directives:

Nurses demonstrate regard for maintaining commitments to the profession of nursing by

1. Contributing to positive team functioning and supporting colleagues;

2. Discussing ethical conflicts and concerns with the health team so as to work through them;

3. Intervening in situations where the safety and well-being of clients is compromised;

4. Reporting to the appropriate authority any health professional who abuses her or his clients physically, verbally, emotionally, sexually, or financially;

5. Being aware of the expertise of nursing and other health professionals, and referring clients to them when clients would benefit from that expertise;

6. Furthering the goals of the profession without interfering with the needs of clients;

7. Conducting oneself in a way which promotes respect for the profession;

8. Identifying and explaining the value of nursing in the care of clients;

9. Contributing to continuous improvement initiatives;

10. Cooperating with regulatory functions;

11. Following standards and guidelines of the profession;

12. Identifying issues for CNO that are relevant for safe, effective, and ethical care;

13. Assisting CNO in developing position statements, standards, and guidelines.

4. Maintaining commitments to employers

Nurses have an implicit commitment that when accepting employment they will be honest in their dealings with the employer and respect the employer's philosophy and policies.

Employers also have an implicit commitment to their employees. This commitment requires employers who hire nurses to provide an environment that allows nurses to function within acceptable standards of practice. Nurses who function in management positions need to provide a safe environment as well as sufficient resources to give the required care.

The following situation illustrates an ethical conflict related to maintaining commitments to employers.

A number of nurses have been very unhappy with staffing in their facility. They believe that clients are receiving unsafe care. They have spoken with management about their concerns but have been told that the changes implemented are in the best interest of client care. Someone has suggested they talk to their MPP about the care, but others are concerned that doing so would harm their employer's reputation.

Behavioural Directives:

Nurses demonstrate regard for maintaining commitments to their employers by

1. Making the employer aware of concerns within the facility;

2. Putting the needs of clients first but considering the philosophy and the policies of employers;

3. Exploring solutions within the organization which will meet the needs of clients and also those of employers;

4. Advocating for input into policies relating to client care.

5. Determining and communicating their own values pertinent to the position before accepting employment.

Nurses managers demonstrate their commitment to employees by

6. Determining and communicating values to perspective employees;

7. Providing needed resources so that safe, effective, and ethical nursing care can be given;

8. Providing support and encouragement to employees.

F. Truthfulness

Truthfulness in this document means speaking or acting without intending to deceive. Truthfulness also refers to providing enough information so that clients are informed. Omissions are as untruthful as false information. As health care has changed, so have the restrictions on disclosure in dealing with clients. It was formerly believed by many health professionals that clients could be harmed by knowing details of their illness.

Most health professionals now believe that clients have the right to, and will benefit from, full disclosure. Honesty builds trust which is essential to the therapeutic relationship between nurses and clients.

Clients from different cultures, however, may view truthfulness differently than the health team. Situations may arise where full disclosure is difficult and where conflicts develop between different members of the health team. Conflicts may also occur between the health team, the family, and the client, as each brings their own particular values to the situation.

The following situations illustrate ethical conflicts related to truthfulness.

1. A family member does not want the client informed about her or his condition. The client, however, is asking the nurse questions and wants to know more.

2. The client indicates directly or indirectly that she or he does not wish to hear the truth. The nurse is obligated to be truthful yet the client has the right to decide the care she or he receives.

Behavioural Directives:

Nurses demonstrate a regard for truthfulness by

1. Discussing clients' direct questions about their diagnosis with the health team and advocating for clients' right to receive the information;

2. Assessing clients' readiness for information;

3. Answering clients' direct questions if they (nurses) have the information* or seeking out the answer for clients;

---

*   Currently the Regulated Health Professions Act authorizes only physicians to communicate a diagnosis to a client in circumstances in which it is reasonably foreseeable that the individual will rely on the diagnosis. This controlled act is being discussed in terms of how pervasive it is.

4. Using professional judgement and consulting with the health team if further information is relevant to clients, but is not asked for because they do not know the information exists;

5. Explaining to clients their right to information;

6. Assisting clients to understand information when ethnocultural and racial, or literacy concerns apply;

7. Assessing the whole situation when clients indicate they do not want to know something;

8. Accepting families' point of view when they do not want clients to be told about their health condition.

G. Fairness

Fairness, in this document, means making equitable decisions related to the allocation of resources to provide care. All Canadians have the right to health care. Health care resources, however, are limited and at the same time there are more options available. This makes decisions about who receives care and what kind of care more difficult.

Decisions for entitlement to care could be made in a number of ways. Nurses could consider that all clients should have equal attention, regardless of needs. Nurses might also make decisions based on prioritizing individual clients' needs according to the critical nature of that need. Nurses could also look at who will benefit most from the care they can give. Which criteria are used to make the decisions will depend on the context and what nurses' specific role is in the situation. Nurses need to be aware of the rationale they have used to make the decision in the particular situation. In some situations, no decision will adequately address all the concerns.

The following situation illustrates an ethical conflict related to fairness.

Clients on a busy obstetrical unit are currently being discharged shortly after delivery of their baby. The nursing staff have been advising the mothers to contact them by phone if there are any difficulties. Staff have intervened by telephone in a number of potentially dangerous situations. Unfortunately, the hospital budget calls for reduced staffing on the unit. Staff have been asked to reduce the time spent in responding to the telephone calls.

Behavioural Directives:

Nurses demonstrate regard for fairness by

1. Being clear about how their own values relate to the demands of fairness;

2. Discussing resource allocation issues with nursing administration and the health team so that all can be involved in resolving a problem;

3. Advocating for input into policies and procedures about the use of resources;

4. Working with other health professionals to ensure that social changes do not adversely affect health care or endanger clients' health;

5. Demonstrating a willingness to explore alternative ways of providing care which continue to value clients' wellbeing.

III. Working Through Ethical Situations In Nursing Practice

Because of the nature of ethics, it is sometimes difficult to identify the issues exactly. Complex, moral, and value-laden situations are not easily understood and dealt with. Working through ethical situations begins with understanding the values of all concerned. Nearly every ethical situation involves other members of the health team and these people need to be part of the discussion in attempting to resolve the issues and developing an acceptable plan of care. An ethics resource person in the agency such as an ethicist, clergy, or an ethics committee will be of assistance....

There are many ways of working through and understanding ethical situations and one example is included in this section. . . .

The nursing process provides one viable approach for examining situations involving ethical values, due to its familiarity to nurses. These situations may be ethical uncertainty, ethical distress, or ethical conflicts.

A. Assessment/Description of the Situation

- Nurses need to pay close attention to all aspects of the situation, taking clients' beliefs, values, wishes, and ethnocultural and racial background into account.

- Nurses need to examine not only their own beliefs, values and knowledge, ... but also those of others on the health team. Nurses also need to consider policies and procedures, professional codes of ethics, and relevant legislation. Values, identified in the previous section of this document, need to be considered as well.

- A discussion needs to be held with all involved. When thoughtful consideration has been given to all these factors, the conflict of values of all concerned is clarified or the issues involved are identified.

- Identify a broad range of options and their consequences. Options which at first do not seem feasible need to be considered as that will provide for better analysis and decision-making. Aspects of non-feasible options can be chosen. For example, staff believe that client care is compromised because of short staffing. One option is to hire more staff, but fiscal restraint makes it impossible. Perhaps organizing the work differently so that nurses could concentrate on nursing care would alleviate the workload.

B. Plan/Approach

- Develop a plan of action considering the factors from the assessment, options, and consequences. Sometimes doing nothing will be the best course of action. This should be a conscious decision, since doing nothing will still affect the outcome and is not a means of avoiding a decision.

- Decide which of the courses of action is best. Sometimes a completely "good" outcome is impossible; the best possible outcome may be the one which is "least bad." (In the previous example it may be that reorganizing the work allows nurses to give safe care, although the nurses may still believe there is a threat to quality care.)

C. Implementation/Action

- Carry out the actions agreed upon. Sensitivity, good communication, and good interpersonal skills are necessary. All who are affected by the situation need to be kept informed.

- Consult with anyone who disagrees and consider their position. Perhaps a further assessment of the situation needs to take place and the dissenting person needs to be involved in the planning. If a person is involved in the decision-making process but disagrees with the plan, she or he has an obligation to support the outcome and not sabotage the process.

- Provide for the support of family and care givers as implementation may be very stressful.

D. Evaluation/Outcome

- Identify if the result was unsatisfactory.

- Involve those who were part of the initial assessment and planning, including the client.

- Reassess and replan if many are concerned with the outcome. For example, a client refuses treatment that the health team recommends. The health team has done everything possible to inform the client of the consequences of this refusal. Further assessment might uncover enthocultural and racial beliefs which make it impossible for the client to agree to the treatment. In light of this information, the health team has either to recommend another treatment or to accept the client's decision.

- Consider policies and guidelines for subsequent situations and decisions, and revise them as necessary.

Many ethical situations occur when there is not enough time to consider the issues properly.

Evaluation will help sensitize participants to ethical thinking and improve their ability to work through ethical situations.

Conclusion

These guidelines give direction to nurses when they find themselves involved in ethical situations. The guidelines will not address every situation that arises and nurses will need to use their own judgement based on the particulars of the situation. Continuing education about ethical issues and conflicts helps nurses and other health professionals understand and resolve new ethical situations. Reading and discussing the guidelines is a beginning step in the process. . . .

[Reprinted with permission from the College of Nurses of Ontario. (1995). *Ethical guidelines for professional behaviour* (pp. 6-17). Toronto: Author.]

APPENDIX E

CODE OF ETHICS

The Canadian Medical Association (1990)

Principles of Ethical Behaviour for all physicians, including those who may not be engaged directly in clinical practice.

I

Consider first the well-being of the patient.

II

Honour your profession and its traditions.

III

Recognize your limitations and the special skills of others in the prevention and treatment of disease.

IV

Protect the patient's secrets.

V

Teach and be taught.

VI

Remember that integrity and professional ability should be your best advertisement.

VII

Be responsible in setting a value on your services.

GUIDE TO THE ETHICAL BEHAVIOUR

OF PHYSICIANS

A physician should be aware of the standards established by tradition and act within the general principles which have governed professional conduct.

The Oath of Hippocrates represented the desire of the members of that day to establish for themselves standards of conduct in living and in the practice of their art. Since then the principles established have been retained as our basic guidelines for ethical living with the profession of medicine.

The International Code of Ethics and the Declaration of Geneva (1948), developed and approved by the World Medical Association, have modernized the ancient codes. They have been endorsed by each member organization, including The Canadian Medical Association, as a general guide having worldwide application.

The Canadian Medical Association accepts the responsibility of delineating the standard of ethical behaviour expected of Canadian physicians.

An interpretation of these principles is developed in the following pages, as a guide for individual physicians and provincial authorities.

Responsibilities to the Patient

An Ethical Physician:

Standard of care

1. will practise the art and science of medicine to the best of his/her ability;

2. will continue self education to improve his/her standards of medical care;

Respect for patient

3. will practise in a fashion that is above reproach and will take neither physical, emotional nor financial advantage of the patient;

Patient's rights

4. will recognize his/her limitations and, when indicated, recommend to the patient that additional opinions and services be obtained;

5. will recognize that a patient has the right to accept or reject any physician and any medical care recommended. The patient having chosen a physician has the right to request of that physician opinions from other physicians of the patient's choice;

6. will keep in confidence information derived from a patient or from a colleague regarding a patient, and divulge it only with the permission of the patient except when otherwise required by law;

7. when acting on behalf of a third party will assure ensure that the patient understands the physician's legal responsibility to the third party before proceeding with the examination;

8. will recommend only diagnostic procedures that are believed necessary to assist in the care of the patient, and therapy that is believed necessary for the well-being of the patient. The physician will recognize a responsibility in advising the patient of the findings and recommendations and will exchange such information with the patient as is necessary for the patient to reach a decision;

9. will, on a patient's request, supply the information that is required to enable the patient to receive any benefits to which the patient may be entitled;

10. will be considerate of the anxiety of the patient's next-of-kin and cooperate with them in the patient's interest;

Choice of patient

11. will recognize the responsibility of the physician to render medical service to any person regardless of colour, religion or political belief;

12. shall, except in an emergency, have the right to refuse to accept a patient;

13. will render all possible assistance to any patient, where an urgent need for medical care exists;

14. will, when the patient is unable to give consent and an agent of the patient is unavailable to give consent, render such therapy as the physiscian believes to be in the patient's interest;

Continuity of care

15. will, if absent, ensure the availability of medical care to his/her patients if possible; will, once having accepted professional responsibility for an acutely ill patient, continue to provide services until they are no longer required, or until arrangements have been made for the services of another suitable physician; may, in any other situation, withdraw from the responsibility for the care of any patient provided that the patient is given adequate notice of that intention;

Personal morality

16. will inform the patient when personal morality or religious conscience prevent the recommendation of some form of therapy;

Clinical research

17. will ensure that, before initiating any clinical research involving humans, such research is appraised scientifically and ethically and approved by a responsible committee and is sufficiently planned and supervised that the individuals are unlikely to suffer any harm. The physician will ascertain that previous research and the purpose of the experiment justify this additional method of investigation. Before proceeding, the physician will obtain the consent of all involved

persons or their agents, and proceed only after explaining the purpose of the clinical investigation and any possible health hazard that can be reasonably forseen;

The dying patient

18. will allow death to occur with dignity and comfort when death of the body appears to be inevitable;

19. may support the body when clinical death of the brain has occurred, but need not prolong life by unusual or heroic means;

Transplantation

20. may, when death of the brain has occurred, support cellular life in the body when some parts of the body might be used to prolong the life or improve the health of others;

21. will recognize a responsibility to a donor of organs to be transplanted and will give to the donor or the donor's relatives full disclosure of the intent and purpose of the procedure; in the case of a living donor, the physician will also explain the risks of the procedure;

22. will refrain from determining the time of death of the donor patient if there is a possibility of being involved as a participant in the transplant procedure or when his/her association with the proposed recipient might improperly influence professional judgement;

23. may treat the transplant recipient subsequent to the transplant procedure in spite of having determined the time of death of the donor;

Fees to patients

24. will consider, in determining professional fees, both the nature of the service provided and the ability of the patient to pay, and will be prepared to discuss the fee with the patient.

Responsibilities to the Profession

An Ethical Physician:

Personal conduct

25. will recognize that the profession demands integrity from each physician and dedication to its search for truth and its service to mankind;

26. will recognize that self discipline of the profession is a privilege and that each physician has a continuing responsibility to merit the retention of this privilege;

27. will behave in a way beyond reproach and will report to the appropriate professional body any conduct by a colleague which might be generally considered as being unbecoming to the profession;

28. will behave in such a manner as to merit the respect of the public for members of the medical profession;

29. will avoid impugning the reputation of any colleague;

Contracts

30. will, when aligned in practice with other physicians, insist that the standards enunciated in this Code of Ethics and the Guide to the Ethical Behaviour of Physicians be maintained;

31. will only enter into a contract regarding professional services which allows fees derived from physicians' services to be controlled by the physician rendering the services;

32. will enter into a contract with an organization only if it will allow maintainance of professional integrity;

33. will only offer to a colleague a contract which has terms and conditions equitable to both parties;

Reporting medical research

34. will first communicate to colleagues, through recognized scientific channels, the results of any medical research, in order that those colleagues may establish an opinion of its merits before they are presented to the public;

Addressing the public

35. will recognize a responsibility to give the generally held opinions of the profession when interpreting scientific knowledge to the public; when presenting an opinion which is contrary to the generally held opinion of the profession, the physician will so indicate and will avoid any attempt to enhance his/her own professional reputation;

Advertising

36. will build a professional reputation based on ability and integrity, and will only advertise professional services or make professional announcements as regulated by legislation or as permitted by the provincial medical licensing authority;

37. will avoid advocacy of any product when identified as a member of the medical profession;

38. will avoid the use of secret remedies;

Consultation

39. will request the opinion of an appropriate colleague acceptable to the patient when diagnosis or treatment is difficult or obscure, or when the patient requests it. Having requested the opinion of a colleague, the physician will make available all relevant information and indicate clearly whether the consultant is to assume the continuing care of the patient during this illness;

40. will, when consulted by a colleague, report in detail all pertinent findings and recommendations to the attending physician and may outline an opinion to the patient. The consultant will continue with the care of the patient only at the specific request of the attending physician and with the consent of the patient;

Patient care

41. will cooperate with those individuals who, in the opinion of the physician, may assist in the care of that patient;

42. will make available to another physician, upon the request of the patient, a report of pertinent findings and treatment of that patient;

43. will provide medical services to a colleague and dependent family without fee, unless specifically requested to render an account;

44. will limit self-treatment or treatment of family members to minor or emergency services only; such treatments should be without fee;

Financial arrangements

45. will avoid any personal profit motive in ordering drugs, appliances or diagnostic procedures from any facility in which the physician has a financial interest;

46. will refuse to accept any commission or payment, direct or indirect, for any service rendered to a patient by other persons excepting direct employees and professional colleagues with whom there is a formal partnership or similar agreement.

Responsibilities to Society

Physicians who act under the principles of this Guide to Ethical Behaviour for Physicians will find that they have fulfilled many of their responsibilities to society.

An Ethical Physician

47. will strive to improve the standards of medical services in the community; will accept a share of the profession's responsibility to society in matters relating to the health and safety of the public, health education, and legislation affecting the well-being of the community.

48. will recognize the responsibility as a witness to assist the court in arriving at a just decision;

49. will, in the interest of providing good and adequate medical care, support the opportunity of other physicians to obtain hospital privileges according to individual personal and professional qualifications.

"The complete physician is not a man apart and cannot content himself with the practice of medicine alone, but should make his contribution, as does any good citizen, towards the well-being and betterment of the community in which he lives."

APPENDIX F

Ethical/Stakeholder Analysis (Respect)

Ethicists have formalized the process of ethical analysis in various decision-procedures or guides. Often, these are organized sequentially in terms of steps in the decision-making process.

The ethical analysis and decision-procedure offered below (acronym: RESPECT) incorporates the main features identified in most such procedures. The points are listed sequentially, but responsible decision-making need not follow this sequence literally.

This analytic tool is oriented around the idea of stakeholders. A stakeholder is someone who will be effected by a given decision and who in virtue of this effect is entitled to have his or her interests and values considered and respected in the decision-making process. A stakeholder is also someone to whom one owes an account for one's decision.

1. RECOGNIZE MORAL DIMENSION OF TASK OR PROBLEM

2. ENUMERATE GUIDING AND EVALUATIVE PRINCIPLES

3. SPECIFY STAKEHOLDERS AND THEIR GUIDING PRINCIPLES

4. PLOT VARIOUS ACTION ALTERNATIVES

5. EVALUATE ALTERNATIVES IN LIGHT OF PRINCIPLES & STAKEHOLDERS

6. CONSULT & INVOLVE STAKEHOLDERS AS APPROPRIATE

7. TELL STAKEHOLDERS THE REASONS FOR THE DECISION

It is important to understand that this is not a formula that can be mechanically applied to output "right" answers to moral questions. Rather, it is a process to be followed to ensure that all considerations relevant to a given moral issue or decision are carefully identified and weighed. Working through such a process will help ensure that the decision one reaches will be morally justifiable and defensible and that one will therefore be able to give proper account for it. The checkmarks beside each point can be viewed as reminders of the sorts of things one should consider and review in advance of making a moral decision or a decision with a signficant moral component.

About The Authors

Jean Dalziel (R.N., M.A.) has taught in both diploma and degree programs in nursing. At the time of writing, she was Director, Nursing Practice, College of Nurses of Ontario. In this capacity, she was actively involved in the preparation of the *Guidelines for Ethical Behaviour in Nursing* (CNO, 1988) and the *Standards of Nursing Practice for Registered Nurses and Registered Nursing Assistants* (CNO, 1990). She is currently engaged in private consulting in nursing.

Ann Ford (R.N., M.Sc.N) is a retired nursing professor. She is a member of the Governing Board of St. Vincent de Paul Hospital in Brockville and Chair of the Hospital's Ethics Committee. Her publications include a booklet on the history of the College of Nurses of Ontario as well as articles on nursing roles, in-service education, and home care.

Gail Donner (R.N., Ph.D.) is an Associate Professor in the Faculty of Nursing, University of Toronto.

Irene Krahn (B.N., M.Sc.N.) is Director of Occupational Health and Accident Prevention with Extendicare Health Servies Incorporated, Markham, Ontario. She has been active in researching and developing occupational health and programs in health care facilities.

Sandra Mitchell (C.N.P., M.Sc.N., A.O.C.N) works as a Nurse Practitioner in Oncology at the Roswell Cancer Institute in Buffalo, New York.

Trudy Molke (R.N., B.Sc.N) is a Nursing Practice Advisor at the College of Nurses of Ontario. She has strong interests in ethics and mental health nursing and has published on various topics in the *Communiqué* of the College of Nurses of Ontario.

Anne Moorhouse (R.N., Ph.D.) is Assistant Professor, Faculty of Nursing, and a member of the Joint Centre for Bioethics, University of Toronto.

Michael Yeo (Ph.D.) is an Ethicist in the Research Directorate of the Canadian Medical Association. He has published on a variety of topics, including resource allocation, ethics and regionalization, and ethics and nursing theory.